SOLUTIONS MANUAL

Options, Futures, and Other Derivatives

Eighth Edition

John C. Hull

Maple Financial Group Professor of Derivatives
and Risk Management
Joseph L. Rotman School of Management
University of Toronto

Pearson Prentice Hall, Upper Saddle River, NJ 07458

Acquisitions Editor: Tessa O'Brien
Editorial Project Manager: Amy Foley
Associate Production Project Manager: Alison Eusden
Senior Manufacturing Buyer: Carol Melville

Prentice Hall
is an imprint of

www.pearsonhighered.com

1 2 3 4 5 6 EB 15 14 13 12 11

ISBN-13: 978-0-13-216496-2
ISBN-10: 0-13-216496-5

Contents

Preface   v

Chapter 1   Introduction   1
Chapter 2   Mechanics of Futures Markets   10
Chapter 3   Hedging Strategies Using Futures   16
Chapter 4   Interest Rates   22
Chapter 5   Determination of Forward and Futures Prices   30
Chapter 6   Interest Rate Futures   38
Chapter 7   Swaps   45
Chapter 8   Securitization and the Credit Crisis of 2007   54
Chapter 9   Mechanics of Options Markets   57
Chapter 10   Properties of Stock Options   65
Chapter 11   Trading Strategies Involving Options   72
Chapter 12   Binomial Trees   79
Chapter 13   Wiener Processes and Ito's Lemma   87
Chapter 14   The Black-Scholes-Merton Model   94
Chapter 15   Employee Stock Options   107
Chapter 16   Options on Stock Indices and Currencies   110
Chapter 17   Options on Futures   119
Chapter 18   Greek Letters   127
Chapter 19   Volatility Smiles   139
Chapter 20   Basic Numerical Procedures   146
Chapter 21   Value at Risk   162
Chapter 22   Estimating Volatilities and Correlations   167
Chapter 23   Credit Risk   173
Chapter 24   Credit Derivatives   183
Chapter 25   Exotic Options   190
Chapter 26   More on Models and Numerical Procedures   198
Chapter 27   Martingales and Measures   209
Chapter 28   Interest Rate Derivatives: The Standard Market Models   216
Chapter 29   Convexity, Timing and Quanto Adjustments   223
Chapter 30   Interest Rate Derivatives: Models of the Short Rate   229
Chapter 31   Interest Rate Derivatives: HJM and LMM   239
Chapter 32   Swaps Revisited   244
Chapter 33   Energy and Commodity Derivatives   247
Chapter 34   Real Options   250

Preface

This book contains solutions to the questions and problems that appear at the ends of chapters in my book *Options, Futures, and Other Derivatives*, 8th edition. The questions and problems have been designed to help readers study on their own and test their understanding of the material. They range from quick checks on whether a key point is understood to much more challenging applications of analytical techniques. Some problems prove or extend results presented in the book.

To maximize the benefits from this book readers are urged to sketch out their own solutions to the problems before consulting mine.

I welcome comments on either *Options, Futures, and Other Derivatives*, 8th edition or this book. My e-mail address is

hull@rotman.utoronto.ca

John C. Hull
Maple Financial Professor of Derivatives and Risk Management
Joseph L. Rotman School of Management
University of Toronto

CHAPTER 1
Introduction

Problem 1.1
What is the difference between a long forward position and a short forward position?

When a trader enters into a long forward contract, she is agreeing to *buy* the underlying asset for a certain price at a certain time in the future. When a trader enters into a short forward contract, she is agreeing to *sell* the underlying asset for a certain price at a certain time in the future.

Problem 1.2.
Explain carefully the difference between hedging, speculation, and arbitrage.

A trader is *hedging* when she has an exposure to the price of an asset and takes a position in a derivative to offset the exposure. In a *speculation* the trader has no exposure to offset. She is betting on the future movements in the price of the asset. *Arbitrage* involves taking a position in two or more different markets to lock in a profit.

Problem 1.3.
What is the difference between entering into a long forward contract when the forward price is $50 and taking a long position in a call option with a strike price of $50?

In the first case the trader is obligated to buy the asset for $50. (The trader does not have a choice.) In the second case the trader has an option to buy the asset for $50. (The trader does not have to exercise the option.)

Problem 1.4.
Explain carefully the difference between selling a call option and buying a put option.

Selling a call option involves giving someone else the right to buy an asset from you. It gives you a payoff of
$$-\max(S_T - K, 0) = \min(K - S_T, 0)$$
Buying a put option involves buying an option from someone else. It gives a payoff of
$$\max(K - S_T, 0)$$
In both cases the potential payoff is $K - S_T$. When you write a call option, the payoff is negative or zero. (This is because the counterparty chooses whether to exercise.) When you buy a put option, the payoff is zero or positive. (This is because you choose whether to exercise.)

Problem 1.5.
An investor enters into a short forward contract to sell 100,000 British pounds for US dollars at an exchange rate of 1.4000 US dollars per pound. How much does the investor gain or lose if the exchange rate at the end of the contract is (a) 1.3900 and (b) 1.4200?

   (a) The investor is obligated to sell pounds for 1.4000 when they are worth 1.3900. The gain is (1.4000-1.3900) ×100,000 = $1,000.

1

(b) The investor is obligated to sell pounds for 1.4000 when they are worth 1.4200. The loss is (1.4200-1.4000)×100,000 = $2,000

Problem 1.6.
A trader enters into a short cotton futures contract when the futures price is 50 cents per pound. The contract is for the delivery of 50,000 pounds. How much does the trader gain or lose if the cotton price at the end of the contract is (a) 48.20 cents per pound; (b) 51.30 cents per pound?

(a) The trader sells for 50 cents per pound something that is worth 48.20 cents per pound. Gain $= (\$0.5000 - \$0.4820) \times 50,000 = \$900$.

(b) The trader sells for 50 cents per pound something that is worth 51.30 cents per pound. Loss $= (\$0.5130 - \$0.5000) \times 50,000 = \$650$.

Problem 1.7.
Suppose that you write a put contract with a strike price of $40 and an expiration date in three months. The current stock price is $41 and the contract is on 100 shares. What have you committed yourself to? How much could you gain or lose?

You have sold a put option. You have agreed to buy 100 shares for $40 per share if the party on the other side of the contract chooses to exercise the right to sell for this price. The option will be exercised only when the price of stock is below $40. Suppose, for example, that the option is exercised when the price is $30. You have to buy at $40 shares that are worth $30; you lose $10 per share, or $1,000 in total. If the option is exercised when the price is $20, you lose $20 per share, or $2,000 in total. The worst that can happen is that the price of the stock declines to almost zero during the three-month period. This highly unlikely event would cost you $4,000. In return for the possible future losses, you receive the price of the option from the purchaser.

Problem 1.8.
What is the difference between the over-the-counter market and the exchange-traded market? What are the bid and offer quotes of a market maker in the over-the-counter market?

The over-the-counter market is a telephone- and computer-linked network of financial institutions, fund managers, and corporate treasurers where two participants can enter into any mutually acceptable contract. An exchange-traded market is a market organized by an exchange where traders either meet physically or communicate electronically and the contracts that can be traded have been defined by the exchange. When a market maker quotes a bid and an offer, the bid is the price at which the market maker is prepared to buy and the offer is the price at which the market maker is prepared to sell.

Problem 1.9.
You would like to speculate on a rise in the price of a certain stock. The current stock price is $29, and a three-month call with a strike of $30 costs $2.90. You have $5,800 to invest. Identify two alternative strategies, one involving an investment in the stock and the other involving investment in the option. What are the potential gains and losses from each?

One strategy would be to buy 200 shares. Another would be to buy 2,000 options. If the share

2

price does well the second strategy will give rise to greater gains. For example, if the share price goes up to $40 you gain $[2,000 \times (\$40 - \$30)] - \$5,800 = \$14,200$ from the second strategy and only $200 \times (\$40 - \$29) = \$2,200$ from the first strategy. However, if the share price does badly, the second strategy gives greater losses. For example, if the share price goes down to $25, the first strategy leads to a loss of $200 \times (\$29 - \$25) = \$800,$ whereas the second strategy leads to a loss of the whole $5,800 investment. This example shows that options contain built in leverage.

Problem 1.10.
Suppose you own 5,000 shares that are worth $25 each. How can put options be used to provide you with insurance against a decline in the value of your holding over the next four months?

You could buy 50 put option contracts (each on 100 shares) with a strike price of $25 and an expiration date in four months. If at the end of four months the stock price proves to be less than $25, you can exercise the options and sell the shares for $25 each.

Problem 1.11.
When first issued, a stock provides funds for a company. Is the same true of an exchange-traded stock option? Discuss.

An exchange-traded stock option provides no funds for the company. It is a security sold by one investor to another. The company is not involved. By contrast, a stock when it is first issued is sold by the company to investors and does provide funds for the company.

Problem 1.12.
Explain why a futures contract can be used for either speculation or hedging.

If an investor has an exposure to the price of an asset, he or she can hedge with futures contracts. If the investor will gain when the price decreases and lose when the price increases, a long futures position will hedge the risk. If the investor will lose when the price decreases and gain when the price increases, a short futures position will hedge the risk. Thus either a long or a short futures position can be entered into for hedging purposes.
If the investor has no exposure to the price of the underlying asset, entering into a futures contract is speculation. If the investor takes a long position, he or she gains when the asset's price increases and loses when it decreases. If the investor takes a short position, he or she loses when the asset's price increases and gains when it decreases.

Problem 1.13.
Suppose that a March call option to buy a share for $50 costs $2.50 and is held until March. Under what circumstances will the holder of the option make a profit? Under what circumstances will the option be exercised? Draw a diagram showing how the profit on a long position in the option depends on the stock price at the maturity of the option.

The holder of the option will gain if the price of the stock is above $52.50 in March. (This ignores the time value of money.) The option will be exercised if the price of the stock is above $50.00 in March. The profit as a function of the stock price is shown in Figure S1.1.

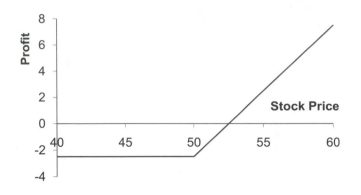

Figure S1.1 Profit from long position in Problem 1.13

Problem 1.14.
Suppose that a June put option to sell a share for $60 costs $4 and is held until June. Under what circumstances will the seller of the option (i.e., the party with a short position) make a profit? Under what circumstances will the option be exercised? Draw a diagram showing how the profit from a short position in the option depends on the stock price at the maturity of the option.

The seller of the option will lose money if the price of the stock is below $56.00 in June. (This ignores the time value of money.) The option will be exercised if the price of the stock is below $60.00 in June. The profit as a function of the stock price is shown in Figure S1.2.

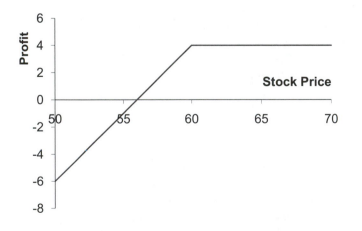

Figure S1.2 Profit from short position in Problem 1.14

Problem 1.15.

It is May and a trader writes a September call option with a strike price of $20. The stock price is $18, and the option price is $2. Describe the investor's cash flows if the option is held until September and the stock price is $25 at this time.

The trader has an inflow of $2 in May and an outflow of $5 in September. The $2 is the cash received from the sale of the option. The $5 is the result of the option being exercised. The investor has to buy the stock for $25 in September and sell it to the purchaser of the option for $20.

Problem 1.16.
A trader writes a December put option with a strike price of $30. The price of the option is $4. Under what circumstances does the trader make a gain?

The trader makes a gain if the price of the stock is above $26 at the time of exercise. (This ignores the time value of money.)

Problem 1.17.
A company knows that it is due to receive a certain amount of a foreign currency in four months. What type of option contract is appropriate for hedging?

A long position in a four-month put option can provide insurance against the exchange rate falling below the strike price. It ensures that the foreign currency can be sold for at least the strike price.

Problem 1.18.
A US company expects to have to pay 1 million Canadian dollars in six months. Explain how the exchange rate risk can be hedged using (a) a forward contract; (b) an option.

The company could enter into a long forward contract to buy 1 million Canadian dollars in six months. This would have the effect of locking in an exchange rate equal to the current forward exchange rate. Alternatively the company could buy a call option giving it the right (but not the obligation) to purchase 1 million Canadian dollars at a certain exchange rate in six months. This would provide insurance against a strong Canadian dollar in six months while still allowing the company to benefit from a weak Canadian dollar at that time.

Problem 1.19.
A trader enters into a short forward contract on 100 million yen. The forward exchange rate is $0.0080 per yen. How much does the trader gain or lose if the exchange rate at the end of the contract is (a) $0.0074 per yen; (b) $0.0091 per yen?

a) The trader sells 100 million yen for $0.0080 per yen when the exchange rate is $0.0074 per yen. The gain is 100×0.0006 millions of dollars or $60,000.
b) The trader sells 100 million yen for $0.0080 per yen when the exchange rate is $0.0091 per yen. The loss is 100×0.0011 millions of dollars or $110,000.

Problem 1.20.
The Chicago Board of Trade offers a futures contract on long-term Treasury bonds. Characterize the investors likely to use this contract.

Most investors will use the contract because they want to do one of the following:

a) Hedge an exposure to long-term interest rates.
b) Speculate on the future direction of long-term interest rates.
c) Arbitrage between the spot and futures markets for Treasury bonds.

This contract is discussed in Chapter 6.

Problem 1.21.
"Options and futures are zero-sum games." What do you think is meant by this statement?

The statement means that the gain (loss) to the party with the short position is equal to the loss (gain) to the party with the long position. In aggregate, the net gain to all parties is zero.

Problem 1.22.
Describe the profit from the following portfolio: a long forward contract on an asset and a long European put option on the asset with the same maturity as the forward contract and a strike price that is equal to the forward price of the asset at the time the portfolio is set up.

The terminal value of the long forward contract is:
$$S_T - F_0$$
where S_T is the price of the asset at maturity and F_0 is the delivery price, which is the same as the forward price of the asset at the time the portfolio is set up). The terminal value of the put option is:
$$\max(F_0 - S_T, 0)$$
The terminal value of the portfolio is therefore
$$S_T - F_0 + \max(F_0 - S_T, 0)$$
$$= \max(0, S_T - F_0]$$

This is the same as the terminal value of a European call option with the same maturity as the forward contract and a strike price equal to F_0. This result is illustrated in the Figure S1.3.

The profit equals the terminal value of the call option less the amount paid for the put option. (It does not cost anything to enter into the forward contract.

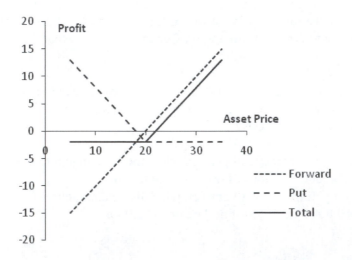

Figure S1.3 Profit from portfolio in Problem 1.22

Problem 1.23.

In the 1980s, Bankers Trust developed index currency option notes (ICONs). These are bonds in which the amount received by the holder at maturity varies with a foreign exchange rate. One example was its trade with the Long Term Credit Bank of Japan. The ICON specified that if the yen–U.S. dollar exchange rate, S_T, is greater than 169 yen per dollar at maturity (in 1995), the holder of the bond receives \$1,000. If it is less than 169 yen per dollar, the amount received by the holder of the bond is

$$1,000 - \max\left[0,\, 1,000\left(\frac{169}{S_T} - 1\right)\right]$$

When the exchange rate is below 84.5, nothing is received by the holder at maturity. Show that this ICON is a combination of a regular bond and two options.

Suppose that the yen exchange rate (yen per dollar) at maturity of the ICON is S_T. The payoff from the ICON is

$$
\begin{array}{lll}
1,000 & \text{if} & S_T > 169 \\[2mm]
1,000 - 1,000\left(\dfrac{169}{S_T} - 1\right) & \text{if} & 84.5 \le S_T \le 169 \\[2mm]
0 & \text{if} & S_T < 84.5
\end{array}
$$

When $84.5 \le S_T \le 169$ the payoff can be written

$$2,000 - \frac{169,000}{S_T}$$

The payoff from an ICON is the payoff from:
   (a) A regular bond
   (b) A short position in call options to buy 169,000 yen with an exercise price of 1/169
   (c) A long position in call options to buy 169,000 yen with an exercise price of 1/84.5
This is demonstrated by the following table, which shows the terminal value of the various components of the position

	Bond	Short Calls	Long Calls	Whole position
$S_T > 169$	1000	0	0	1000
$84.5 \le S_T \le 169$	1000	$-169,000\left(\frac{1}{S_T} - \frac{1}{169}\right)$	0	$2000 - \frac{169,000}{S_T}$
$S_T < 84.5$	1000	$-169,000\left(\frac{1}{S_T} - \frac{1}{169}\right)$	$169,000\left(\frac{1}{S_T} - \frac{1}{84.5}\right)$	0

Problem 1.24.
On July 1, 2011, a company enters into a forward contract to buy 10 million Japanese yen on January 1, 2012. On September 1, 2011, it enters into a forward contract to sell 10 million Japanese yen on January 1, 2012. Describe the payoff from this strategy.

Suppose that the forward price for the contract entered into on July 1, 2011 is F_1 and that the forward price for the contract entered into on September 1, 2011 is F_2 with both F_1 and F_2

being measured as dollars per yen. If the value of one Japanese yen (measured in US dollars) is S_T on January 1, 2012, then the value of the first contract (in millions of dollars) at that time is

$$10(S_T - F_1)$$

while the value of the second contract (per yen sold) at that time is:

$$10(F_2 - S_T)$$

The total payoff from the two contracts is therefore

$$10(S_T - F_1) + 10(F_2 - S_T) = 10(F_2 - F_1)$$

Thus if the forward price for delivery on January 1, 2012 increased between July 1, 2011 and September 1, 2011 the company will make a profit. (Note that the yen/USD exchange rate is usually expressed as the number of yen per USD not as the number of USD per yen)

Problem 1.25.
Suppose that USD-sterling spot and forward exchange rates are as follows:

Spot	1.4580
90-day forward	1.4556
180-day forward	1.4518

What opportunities are open to an arbitrageur in the following situations?
   (a)   *A 180-day European call option to buy £1 for $1.42 costs 2 cents.*
   (b)   *A 90-day European put option to sell £1 for $1.49 costs 2 cents.*

(a) The arbitrageur buys a 180-day call option and takes a short position in a 180-day forward contract. If S_T is the terminal spot rate, the profit from the call option is

$\max(S_T - 1.42, 0) - 0.02$

The profit from the short forward contract is

   $1.4518 - S_T$

The profit from the strategy is therefore

$\max(S_T - 1.42, 0) - 0.02 + 1.4518 - S_T$
or
$\max(S_T - 1.42, 0) + 1.4318 - S_T$

This is
$1.4318 - S_T$ when $S_T < 1.42$
0.118 when $S_T > 1.42$

This shows that the profit is always positive. The time value of money has been ignored in these calculations. However, when it is taken into account the strategy is still likely to be profitable in all circumstances. (We would require an extremely high interest rate for $0.0118 interest to be required on an outlay of $0.02 over a 180-day period.)

(b) The trader buys 90-day put options and takes a long position in a 90 day forward contract. If S_T is the terminal spot rate, the profit from the put option is

   $\max(1.49 - S_T, 0) - 0.02$

The profit from the long forward contract is

$S_T - 1.4556$

The profit from this strategy is therefore
$$\max(1.49 - S_T, 0) - 0.02 + S_T - 1.4556$$
or
$$\max(1.49 - S_T, 0) + S_T - 1.4756$$
This is

$S_T - 1.4756$ when $S_T > 1.49$

0.0144 when $S_T < 1.49$

The profit is therefore always positive. Again, the time value of money has been ignored but is unlikely to affect the overall profitability of the strategy. (We would require interest rates to be extremely high for $0.0144 interest to be required on an outlay of $0.02 over a 90-day period.)

CHAPTER 2
Mechanics of Futures Markets

Problem 2.1.
Distinguish between the terms open interest and trading volume.

The *open interest* of a futures contract at a particular time is the total number of long positions outstanding. (Equivalently, it is the total number of short positions outstanding.) The *trading volume* during a certain period of time is the number of contracts traded during this period.

Problem 2.2.
What is the difference between a local and a futures commission merchant?

A futures *commission merchant* trades on behalf of a client and charges a commission. A *local* trades on his or her own behalf.

Problem 2.3.
Suppose that you enter into a short futures contract to sell July silver for $17.20 per ounce. The size of the contract is 5,000 ounces. The initial margin is $4,000, and the maintenance margin is $3,000. What change in the futures price will lead to a margin call? What happens if you do not meet the margin call?

There will be a margin call when $1,000 has been lost from the margin account. This will occur when the price of silver increases by 1,000/5,000 = $0.20. The price of silver must therefore rise to $17.40 per ounce for there to be a margin call. If the margin call is not met, your broker closes out your position.

Problem 2.4.
Suppose that in September 2012 a company takes a long position in a contract on May 2013 crude oil futures. It closes out its position in March 2013. The futures price (per barrel) is $68.30 when it enters into the contract, $70.50 when it closes out its position, and $69.10 at the end of December 2012. One contract is for the delivery of 1,000 barrels. What is the company's total profit? When is it realized? How is it taxed if it is (a) a hedger and (b) a speculator? Assume that the company has a December 31 year-end.

The total profit is ($70.50 − $68.30) × 1,000 = $2,200. Of this $(69.10 - \$68.30) \times 1,000$ or $800 is realized on a day-by-day basis between September 2012 and December 31, 2012. A further $(\$70.50 - \$69.10) \times 1,000 = \$1,400$ is realized on a day-by-day basis between January 1, 2013, and March 2013. A hedger would be taxed on the whole profit of $2,200 in 2013. A speculator would be taxed on $800 in 2012 and $1,400 in 2013.

Problem 2.5.
What does a stop order to sell at $2 mean? When might it be used? What does a limit order to sell at $2 mean? When might it be used?

A *stop order* to sell at $2 is an order to sell at the best available price once a price of $2 or less is reached. It could be used to limit the losses from an existing long position. A *limit order* to sell at $2 is an order to sell at a price of $2 or more. It could be used to instruct a broker that a short position should be taken, providing it can be done at a price more favorable than $2.

Problem 2.6.
What is the difference between the operation of the margin accounts administered by a clearing house and those administered by a broker?

The margin account administered by the clearing house is marked to market daily, and the clearing house member is required to bring the account back up to the prescribed level daily. The margin account administered by the broker is also marked to market daily. However, the account does not have to be brought up to the initial margin level on a daily basis. It has to be brought up to the initial margin level when the balance in the account falls below the maintenance margin level. The maintenance margin is usually about 75% of the initial margin.

Problem 2.7.
What differences exist in the way prices are quoted in the foreign exchange futures market, the foreign exchange spot market, and the foreign exchange forward market?

In futures markets, prices are quoted as the number of US dollars per unit of foreign currency. Spot and forward rates are quoted in this way for the British pound, euro, Australian dollar, and New Zealand dollar. For other major currencies, spot and forward rates are quoted as the number of units of foreign currency per US dollar.

Problem 2.8.
The party with a short position in a futures contract sometimes has options as to the precise asset that will be delivered, where delivery will take place, when delivery will take place, and so on. Do these options increase or decrease the futures price? Explain your reasoning.

These options make the contract less attractive to the party with the long position and more attractive to the party with the short position. They therefore tend to reduce the futures price.

Problem 2.9.
What are the most important aspects of the design of a new futures contract?

The most important aspects of the design of a new futures contract are the specification of the underlying asset, the size of the contract, the delivery arrangements, and the delivery months.

Problem 2.10.
Explain how margins protect investors against the possibility of default.

A margin is a sum of money deposited by an investor with his or her broker. It acts as a guarantee that the investor can cover any losses on the futures contract. The balance in the margin account is adjusted daily to reflect gains and losses on the futures contract. If losses are above a certain level, the investor is required to deposit a further margin. This system makes it unlikely that the investor will default. A similar system of margins makes it unlikely that the investor's broker will default on the contract it has with the clearing house member and unlikely that the clearing house member will default with the clearing house.

Problem 2.11.
A trader buys two July futures contracts on frozen orange juice. Each contract is for the delivery of 15,000 pounds. The current futures price is 160 cents per pound, the initial margin is $6,000 per contract, and the maintenance margin is $4,500 per contract. What price change would lead to a margin call? Under what circumstances could $2,000 be withdrawn from the margin account?

There is a margin call if more than $1,500 is lost on one contract. This happens if the futures price of frozen orange juice falls by more than 10 cents to below 150 cents per pound. $2,000 can be withdrawn from the margin account if there is a gain on one contract of $1,000. This will happen if the futures price rises by 6.67 cents to 166.67 cents per pound.

Problem 2.12.
Show that, if the futures price of a commodity is greater than the spot price during the delivery period, then there is an arbitrage opportunity. Does an arbitrage opportunity exist if the futures price is less than the spot price? Explain your answer.

If the futures price is greater than the spot price during the delivery period, an arbitrageur buys the asset, shorts a futures contract, and makes delivery for an immediate profit. If the futures price is less than the spot price during the delivery period, there is no similar perfect arbitrage strategy. An arbitrageur can take a long futures position but cannot force immediate delivery of the asset. The decision on when delivery will be made is made by the party with the short position. Nevertheless companies interested in acquiring the asset may find it attractive to enter into a long futures contract and wait for delivery to be made.

Problem 2.13.
Explain the difference between a market-if-touched order and a stop order.

A market-if-touched order is executed at the best available price after a trade occurs at a specified price or at a price more favorable than the specified price. A stop order is executed at the best available price after there is a bid or offer at the specified price or at a price less favorable than the specified price.

Problem 2.14.
Explain what a stop-limit order to sell at 20.30 with a limit of 20.10 means.

A stop-limit order to sell at 20.30 with a limit of 20.10 means that as soon as there is a bid at 20.30 the contract should be sold providing this can be done at 20.10 or a higher price.

Problem 2.15.
At the end of one day a clearing house member is long 100 contracts, and the settlement price is $50,000 per contract. The original margin is $2,000 per contract. On the following day the member becomes responsible for clearing an additional 20 long contracts, entered into at a price of $51,000 per contract. The settlement price at the end of this day is $50,200. How much does the member have to add to its margin account with the exchange clearing house?

The clearing house member is required to provide $20 \times \$2,000 = \$40,000$ as initial margin for the new contracts. There is a gain of $(50,200 - 50,000) \times 100 = \$20,000$ on the existing contracts. There is also a loss of $(51,000 - 50,200) \times 20 = \$16,000$ on the new contracts. The member must therefore add

$$40,000 - 20,000 + 16,000 = \$36,000$$

to the margin account.

Problem 2.16.
On July 1, 2012, a Japanese company enters into a forward contract to buy \$1 million with yen on January 1, 2013. On September 1, 2012, it enters into a forward contract to sell \$1 million on January 1, 2013. Describe the profit or loss the company will make in dollars as a function of the forward exchange rates on July 1, 2012 and September 1, 2012.

Suppose F_1 and F_2 are the forward exchange rates for the contracts entered into July 1, 2012 and September 1, 2012, and S is the spot rate on January 1, 2013. (All exchange rates are measured as yen per dollar). The payoff from the first contract is $(S - F_1)$ million yen and the payoff from the second contract is $(F_2 - S)$ million yen. The total payoff is therefore $(S - F_1) + (F_2 - S) = (F_2 - F_1)$ million yen.

Problem 2.17.
The forward price on the Swiss franc for delivery in 45 days is quoted as 1.1000. The futures price for a contract that will be delivered in 45 days is 0.9000. Explain these two quotes. Which is more favorable for an investor wanting to sell Swiss francs?

The 1.1000 forward quote is the number of Swiss francs per dollar. The 0.9000 futures quote is the number of dollars per Swiss franc. When quoted in the same way as the futures price the forward price is $1/1.1000 = 0.9091$. The Swiss franc is therefore more valuable in the forward market than in the futures market. The forward market is therefore more attractive for an investor wanting to sell Swiss francs.

Problem 2.18.
Suppose you call your broker and issue instructions to sell one July hogs contract. Describe what happens.

Live hog futures are traded on the Chicago Mercantile Exchange. The broker will request some initial margin. The order will be relayed by telephone to your broker's trading desk on the floor of the exchange (or to the trading desk of another broker). It will then be sent by messenger to a commission broker who will execute the trade according to your instructions. Confirmation of the trade eventually reaches you. If there are adverse movements in the futures price your broker may contact you to request additional margin.

Problem 2.19.
"Speculation in futures markets is pure gambling. It is not in the public interest to allow speculators to trade on a futures exchange." Discuss this viewpoint.

Speculators are important market participants because they add liquidity to the market. However, contracts must be useful for hedging as well as speculation. This is because regulators generally only approve contracts when they are likely to be of interest to hedgers as well as speculators.

Problem 2.20.
Live cattle futures trade with June, August, October, December, February, and April maturities. Why do you think that the open interest for the June contract is less than that for

the August contract in Table 2.2?

Normally, the shorter the maturity of a contract is, the higher the open interest. However, traders tend to close out their positions in the month immediately before the maturity month. This means that the open interest for the closest maturity month can be less than that for the next closest maturity month

Problem 2.21.
What do you think would happen if an exchange started trading a contract in which the quality of the underlying asset was incompletely specified?

The contract would not be a success. Parties with short positions would hold their contracts until delivery and then deliver the cheapest form of the asset. This might well be viewed by the party with the long position as garbage! Once news of the quality problem became widely known no one would be prepared to buy the contract. This shows that futures contracts are feasible only when there are rigorous standards within an industry for defining the quality of the asset. Many futures contracts have in practice failed because of the problem of defining quality.

Problem 2.22.
"When a futures contract is traded on the floor of the exchange, it may be the case that the open interest increases by one, stays the same, or decreases by one." Explain this statement.

If both sides of the transaction are entering into a new contract, the open interest increases by one. If both sides of the transaction are closing out existing positions, the open interest decreases by one. If one party is entering into a new contract while the other party is closing out an existing position, the open interest stays the same.

Problem 2.23.
Suppose that on October 24, 2012, a company sells one April 2013 live-cattle futures contracts. It closes out its position on January 21, 2013. The futures price (per pound) is 91.20 cents when it enters into the contract, 88.30 cents when it closes out its position, and 88.80 cents at the end of December 2012. One contract is for the delivery of 40,000 pounds of cattle. What is the total profit? How is it taxed if the company is (a) a hedger and (b) a speculator? Assume that the company has a December 31 year end.

The total profit is
$$40,000 \times (0.9120 - 0.8830) = \$1,160$$
If the company is a hedger this is all taxed in 2013. If it is a speculator
$$40,000 \times (0.9120 - 0.8880) = \$960$$
is taxed in 2012 and
$$40,000 \times (0.8880 - 0.8830) = \$200$$
is taxed in 2013.

Problem 2.24.
A cattle farmer expects to have 120,000 pounds of live cattle to sell in three months. The live-cattle futures contract traded by the CME Group is for the delivery of 40,000 pounds of cattle. How can the farmer use the contract for hedging? From the farmer's viewpoint, what are the pros and cons of hedging?

The farmer can short 3 contracts that have 3 months to maturity. If the price of cattle falls, the gain on the futures contract will offset the loss on the sale of the cattle. If the price of cattle rises, the gain on the sale of the cattle will be offset by the loss on the futures contract. Using futures contracts to hedge has the advantage that it can at no cost reduce risk to almost zero. Its disadvantage is that the farmer no longer gains from favorable movements in cattle prices.

Problem 2.25.
It is July 2011. A mining company has just discovered a small deposit of gold. It will take six months to construct the mine. The gold will then be extracted on a more or less continuous basis for one year. Futures contracts on gold are available with delivery months every two months from August 2011 to December 2012. Each contract is for the delivery of 100 ounces. Discuss how the mining company might use futures markets for hedging.

The mining company can estimate its production on a month by month basis. It can then short futures contracts to lock in the price received for the gold. For example, if a total of 3,000 ounces are expected to be produced in September 2011 and October 2011, the price received for this production can be hedged by shorting 30 October 2011 contracts.

CHAPTER 3
Hedging Strategies Using Futures

Problem 3.1.
Under what circumstances are (a) a short hedge and (b) a long hedge appropriate?

A *short hedge* is appropriate when a company owns an asset and expects to sell that asset in the future. It can also be used when the company does not currently own the asset but expects to do so at some time in the future. A *long hedge* is appropriate when a company knows it will have to purchase an asset in the future. It can also be used to offset the risk from an existing short position.

Problem 3.2.
Explain what is meant by basis risk when futures contracts are used for hedging.

Basis risk arises from the hedger's uncertainty as to the difference between the spot price and futures price at the expiration of the hedge.

Problem 3.3.
Explain what is meant by a perfect hedge. Does a perfect hedge always lead to a better outcome than an imperfect hedge? Explain your answer.

A *perfect hedge* is one that completely eliminates the hedger's risk. A perfect hedge does not always lead to a better outcome than an imperfect hedge. It just leads to a more certain outcome.
Consider a company that hedges its exposure to the price of an asset. Suppose the asset's price movements prove to be favorable to the company. A perfect hedge totally neutralizes the company's gain from these favorable price movements. An imperfect hedge, which only partially neutralizes the gains, might well give a better outcome.

Problem 3.4.
Under what circumstances does a minimum-variance hedge portfolio lead to no hedging at all?

A minimum variance hedge leads to no hedging when the coefficient of correlation between the futures price changes and changes in the price of the asset being hedged is zero.

Problem 3.5.
Give three reasons why the treasurer of a company might not hedge the company's exposure to a particular risk.

If the company's competitors are not hedging, the treasurer might feel that the company will experience less risk if it does not hedge. (See Table 3.1.) The shareholders might not want the company to hedge because the risks are hedged within their portfolios. If there is a loss on the hedge and a gain from the company's exposure to the underlying asset, the treasurer might feel that he or she will have difficulty justifying the hedging to other executives within the organization.

Problem 3.6.
Suppose that the standard deviation of quarterly changes in the prices of a commodity is $0.65, the standard deviation of quarterly changes in a futures price on the commodity is $0.81, and the coefficient of correlation between the two changes is 0.8. What is the optimal hedge ratio for a three-month contract? What does it mean?

The optimal hedge ratio is

$$0.8 \times \frac{0.65}{0.81} = 0.642$$

This means that the size of the futures position should be 64.2% of the size of the company's exposure in a three-month hedge.

Problem 3.7.
A company has a $20 million portfolio with a beta of 1.2. It would like to use futures contracts on the S&P 500 to hedge its risk. The index futures is currently standing at 1080, and each contract is for delivery of $250 times the index. What is the hedge that minimizes risk? What should the company do if it wants to reduce the beta of the portfolio to 0.6?

The formula for the number of contracts that should be shorted gives

$$1.2 \times \frac{20,000,000}{1080 \times 250} = 88.9$$

Rounding to the nearest whole number, 89 contracts should be shorted. To reduce the beta to 0.6, half of this position, or a short position in 44 contracts, is required.

Problem 3.8.
In the corn futures contract, the following delivery months are available: March, May, July, September, and December. State the contract that should be used for hedging when the expiration of the hedge is in a) June, b) July, and c) January

A good rule of thumb is to choose a futures contract that has a delivery month as close as possible to, but later than, the month containing the expiration of the hedge. The contracts that should be used are therefore
   (a) July
   (b) September
   (c) March

Problem 3.9.
Does a perfect hedge always succeed in locking in the current spot price of an asset for a future transaction? Explain your answer.

No. Consider, for example, the use of a forward contract to hedge a known cash inflow in a foreign currency. The forward contract locks in the forward exchange rate — which is in general different from the spot exchange rate.

Problem 3.10.
Explain why a short hedger's position improves when the basis strengthens unexpectedly and worsens when the basis weakens unexpectedly.

The basis is the amount by which the spot price exceeds the futures price. A short hedger is long the asset and short futures contracts. The value of his or her position therefore improves as the basis increases. Similarly, it worsens as the basis decreases.

Problem 3.11.
Imagine you are the treasurer of a Japanese company exporting electronic equipment to the United States. Discuss how you would design a foreign exchange hedging strategy and the arguments you would use to sell the strategy to your fellow executives.

The simple answer to this question is that the treasurer should
1. Estimate the company's future cash flows in Japanese yen and U.S. dollars
2. Enter into forward and futures contracts to lock in the exchange rate for the U.S. dollar cash flows.

However, this is not the whole story. As the gold jewelry example in Table 3.1 shows, the company should examine whether the magnitudes of the foreign cash flows depend on the exchange rate. For example, will the company be able to raise the price of its product in U.S. dollars if the yen appreciates? If the company can do so, its foreign exchange exposure may be quite low. The key estimates required are those showing the overall effect on the company's profitability of changes in the exchange rate at various times in the future. Once these estimates have been produced the company can choose between using futures and options to hedge its risk. The results of the analysis should be presented carefully to other executives. It should be explained that a hedge does not ensure that profits will be higher. It means that profit will be more certain. When futures/forwards are used both the downside and upside are eliminated. With options a premium is paid to eliminate only the downside.

Problem 3.12.
Suppose that in Example 3.2 of Section 3.3 the company decides to use a hedge ratio of 0.8. How does the decision affect the way in which the hedge is implemented and the result?

If the hedge ratio is 0.8, the company takes a long position in 16 December oil futures contracts on June 8 when the futures price is $68.00. It closes out its position on November 10. The spot price and futures price at this time are $70.00 and $69.10. The gain on the futures position is
$$(69.10 - 68.00) \times 16,000 = 17,600$$
The effective cost of the oil is therefore
$$20,000 \times 70 - 17,600 = 1,382,400$$
or $69.12 per barrel. (This compares with $68.90 per barrel when the company is fully hedged.)

Problem 3.13.
"If the minimum-variance hedge ratio is calculated as 1.0, the hedge must be perfect." Is this statement true? Explain your answer.

The statement is not true. The minimum variance hedge ratio is
$$\rho \frac{\sigma_S}{\sigma_F}$$
It is 1.0 when $\rho = 0.5$ and $\sigma_S = 2\sigma_F$. Since $\rho < 1.0$ the hedge is clearly not perfect.

Problem 3.14.
"If there is no basis risk, the minimum variance hedge ratio is always 1.0." Is this statement true? Explain your answer.

The statement is true. Using the notation in the text, if the hedge ratio is 1.0, the hedger locks in a price of $F_1 + b_2$. Since both F_1 and b_2 are known this has a variance of zero and must be the best hedge.

Problem 3.15

"For an asset where futures prices are usually less than spot prices, long hedges are likely to be particularly attractive." Explain this statement.

A company that knows it will purchase a commodity in the future is able to lock in a price close to the futures price. This is likely to be particularly attractive when the futures price is less than the spot price.

Problem 3.16.

The standard deviation of monthly changes in the spot price of live cattle is (in cents per pound) 1.2. The standard deviation of monthly changes in the futures price of live cattle for the closest contract is 1.4. The correlation between the futures price changes and the spot price changes is 0.7. It is now October 15. A beef producer is committed to purchasing 200,000 pounds of live cattle on November 15. The producer wants to use the December live-cattle futures contracts to hedge its risk. Each contract is for the delivery of 40,000 pounds of cattle. What strategy should the beef producer follow?

The optimal hedge ratio is

$$0.7 \times \frac{1.2}{1.4} = 0.6$$

The beef producer requires a long position in $200000 \times 0.6 = 120,000$ lbs of cattle. The beef producer should therefore take a long position in 3 December contracts closing out the position on November 15.

Problem 3.17.

A corn farmer argues "I do not use futures contracts for hedging. My real risk is not the price of corn. It is that my whole crop gets wiped out by the weather."Discuss this viewpoint. Should the farmer estimate his or her expected production of corn and hedge to try to lock in a price for expected production?

If weather creates a significant uncertainty about the volume of corn that will be harvested, the farmer should not enter into short forward contracts to hedge the price risk on his or her expected production. The reason is as follows. Suppose that the weather is bad and the farmer's production is lower than expected. Other farmers are likely to have been affected similarly. Corn production overall will be low and as a consequence the price of corn will be relatively high. The farmer's problems arising from the bad harvest will be made worse by losses on the short futures position. This problem emphasizes the importance of looking at the big picture when hedging. The farmer is correct to question whether hedging price risk while ignoring other risks is a good strategy.

Problem 3.18.

On July 1, an investor holds 50,000 shares of a certain stock. The market price is $30 per share. The investor is interested in hedging against movements in the market over the next month and decides to use the September Mini S&P 500 futures contract. The index is *currently 1,500 and one contract is for delivery of $50 times the index. The beta of the stock is 1.3. What strategy should the investor follow? Under what circumstances will it be profitable?*

A short position in

$$1.3 \times \frac{50,000 \times 30}{50 \times 1,500} = 26$$

contracts is required. It will be profitable if the stock outperforms the market in the sense that its return is greater than that predicted by the capital asset pricing model.

Problem 3.19.
Suppose that in Table 3.5 the company decides to use a hedge ratio of 1.5. How does the decision affect the way the hedge is implemented and the result?

If the company uses a hedge ratio of 1.5 in Table 3.5 it would at each stage short 150 contracts. The gain from the futures contracts would be

$$1.50 \times 1.70 = \$2.55$$

per barrel and the company would be $0.85 per barrel better off.

Problem 3.20.
A futures contract is used for hedging. Explain why the daily settlement of the contract can give rise to cash flow problems.

Suppose that you enter into a short futures contract to hedge the sale of an asset in six months. If the price of the asset rises sharply during the six months, the futures price will also rise and you may get margin calls. The margin calls will lead to cash outflows. Eventually the cash outflows will be offset by the extra amount you get when you sell the asset, but there is a mismatch in the timing of the cash outflows and inflows. Your cash outflows occur earlier than your cash inflows. A similar situation could arise if you used a long position in a futures contract to hedge the purchase of an asset at a future time and the asset's price fell sharply. An extreme example of what we are talking about here is provided by Metallgesellschaft (see Business Snapshot 3.2).

Problem 3.21.
An airline executive has argued: "There is no point in our using oil futures. There is just as much chance that the price of oil in the future will be less than the futures price as there is that it will be greater than this price." Discuss the executive's viewpoint.

It may well be true that there is just as much chance that the price of oil in the future will be above the futures price as that it will be below the futures price. This means that the use of a futures contract for speculation would be like betting on whether a coin comes up heads or tails. But it might make sense for the airline to use futures for hedging rather than speculation. The futures contract then has the effect of reducing risks. It can be argued that an airline should not expose its shareholders to risks associated with the future price of oil when there are contracts available to hedge the risks.

Problem 3.22.
Suppose the one-year gold lease rate is 1.5% and the one-year risk-free rate is 5.0%. Both rates are compounded annually. Use the discussion in Business Snapshot 3.1 to calculate the maximum one-year forward price Goldman Sachs should quote for gold when the spot price

is $1,200.

Goldman Sachs can borrow 1 ounce of gold and sell it for $1200. It invests the $1,200 at 5% so that it becomes $1,260 at the end of the year. It must pay the lease rate of 1.5% on $1,200. This is $18 and leaves it with $1,242. It follows that if it agrees to buy the gold for less than $1,242 in one year it will make a profit.

Problem 3.23.
The expected return on the S&P 500 is 12% and the risk-free rate is 5%. What is the expected return on the investment with a beta of (a) 0.2, (b) 0.5, and (c) 1.4?

a) $0.05 + 0.2 \times (0.12 - 0.05) = 0.064$ or 6.4%
b) $0.05 + 0.5 \times (0.12 - 0.05) = 0.085$ or 8.5%
c) $0.05 + 1.4 \times (0.12 - 0.05) = 0.148$ or 14.8%

CHAPTER 4
Interest Rates

Problem 4.1.
A bank quotes you an interest rate of 14% per annum with quarterly compounding. What is the equivalent rate with (a) continuous compounding and (b) annual compounding?

(a) The rate with continuous compounding is

$$4\ln\left(1+\frac{0.14}{4}\right)=0.1376$$

or 13.76% per annum.

(b) The rate with annual compounding is

$$\left(1+\frac{0.14}{4}\right)^{4}-1=0.1475$$

or 14.75% per annum.

Problem 4.2.
What is meant by LIBOR and LIBID. Which is higher?

LIBOR is the London InterBank Offered Rate. It is calculated daily by the British Bankers Association and is the rate a AA-rated bank requires on deposits it places with other banks. LIBID is the London InterBank Bid rate. It is the rate a bank is prepared to pay on deposits from other AA-rated banks. LIBOR is greater than LIBID.

Problem 4.3.
The six-month and one-year zero rates are both 10% per annum. For a bond that has a life of 18 months and pays a coupon of 8% per annum (with semiannual payments and one having just been made), the yield is 10.4% per annum. What is the bond's price? What is the 18-month zero rate? All rates are quoted with semiannual compounding.

Suppose the bond has a face value of $100. Its price is obtained by discounting the cash flows at 10.4%. The price is

$$\frac{4}{1.052}+\frac{4}{1.052^{2}}+\frac{104}{1.052^{3}}=96.74$$

If the 18-month zero rate is R, we must have

$$\frac{4}{1.05}+\frac{4}{1.05^{2}}+\frac{104}{(1+R/2)^{3}}=96.74$$

which gives $R=10.42\%$.

Problem 4.4.
An investor receives $1,100 in one year in return for an investment of $1,000 now. Calculate the percentage return per annum with a) annual compounding, b) semiannual compounding, c) monthly compounding and d) continuous compounding.

(a) With annual compounding the return is

$$\frac{1100}{1000} - 1 = 0.1$$

or 10% per annum.

(b) With semi-annual compounding the return is R where

$$1000\left(1+\frac{R}{2}\right)^2 = 1100$$

i.e.,

$$1+\frac{R}{2} = \sqrt{1.1} = 1.0488$$

so that $R = 0.0976$. The percentage return is therefore 9.76% per annum.

(c) With monthly compounding the return is R where

$$1000\left(1+\frac{R}{12}\right)^{12} = 1100$$

i.e.

$$\left(1+\frac{R}{12}\right) = \sqrt[12]{1.1} = 1.00797$$

so that $R = 0.0957$. The percentage return is therefore 9.57% per annum.

(d) With continuous compounding the return is R where:
$$1000e^R = 1100$$

i.e.,

$$e^R = 1.1$$

so that $R = \ln 1.1 = 0.0953$. The percentage return is therefore 9.53% per annum.

Problem 4.5.

Suppose that zero interest rates with continuous compounding are as follows:

Maturity (months)	Rate (% per annum)
3	8.0
6	8.2
9	8.4
12	8.5
15	8.6
18	8.7

Calculate forward interest rates for the second, third, fourth, fifth, and sixth quarters.

The forward rates with continuous compounding are as follows to

Qtr 2	8.4%
Qtr 3	8.8%
Qtr 4	8.8%
Qtr 5	9.0%
Qtr 6	9.2%

Problem 4.6.

Assuming that zero rates are as in Problem 4.5, what is the value of an FRA that enables the holder to earn 9.5% for a three-month period starting in one year on a principal of $1,000,000? The interest rate is expressed with quarterly compounding.

The forward rate is 9.0% with continuous compounding or 9.102% with quarterly compounding. From equation (4.9), the value of the FRA is therefore

$$[1,000,000 \times 0.25 \times (0.095 - 0.09102)]e^{-0.086 \times 1.25} = 893.56$$

or $893.56.

Problem 4.7.

The term structure of interest rates is upward sloping. Put the following in order of magnitude:

      (a) *The five-year zero rate*
      (b) *The yield on a five-year coupon-bearing bond*
      (c) *The forward rate corresponding to the period between 4.75 and 5 years in the future*

What is the answer to this question when the term structure of interest rates is downward sloping?

When the term structure is upward sloping, $c > a > b$. When it is downward sloping, $b > a > c$.

Problem 4.8.

What does duration tell you about the sensitivity of a bond portfolio to interest rates? What are the limitations of the duration measure?

Duration provides information about the effect of a small parallel shift in the yield curve on the value of a bond portfolio. The percentage decrease in the value of the portfolio equals the duration of the portfolio multiplied by the amount by which interest rates are increased in the small parallel shift. The duration measure has the following limitation. It applies only to parallel shifts in the yield curve that are small.

Problem 4.9.

What rate of interest with continuous compounding is equivalent to 15% per annum with monthly compounding?

The rate of interest is R where:

$$e^R = \left(1 + \frac{0.15}{12}\right)^{12}$$

i.e.,

$$R = 12 \ln\left(1 + \frac{0.15}{12}\right)$$

$$= 0.1491$$

The rate of interest is therefore 14.91% per annum.

Problem 4.10.

A deposit account pays 12% per annum with continuous compounding, but interest is actually paid quarterly. How much interest will be paid each quarter on a $10,000 deposit?

The equivalent rate of interest with quarterly compounding is R where

$$e^{0.12} = \left(1 + \frac{R}{4}\right)^4$$

or

$$R = 4(e^{0.03} - 1) = 0.1218$$

The amount of interest paid each quarter is therefore:

$$10,000 \times \frac{0.1218}{4} = 304.55$$

or $304.55.

Problem 4.11.
Suppose that 6-month, 12-month, 18-month, 24-month, and 30-month zero rates are 4%, 4.2%, 4.4%, 4.6%, and 4.8% per annum with continuous compounding respectively. Estimate the cash price of a bond with a face value of 100 that will mature in 30 months and pays a coupon of 4% per annum semiannually.

The bond pays $2 in 6, 12, 18, and 24 months, and $102 in 30 months. The cash price is
$$2e^{-0.04 \times 0.5} + 2e^{-0.042 \times 1.0} + 2e^{-0.044 \times 1.5} + 2e^{-0.046 \times 2} + 102e^{-0.048 \times 2.5} = 98.04$$

Problem 4.12.
A three-year bond provides a coupon of 8% semiannually and has a cash price of 104. What is the bond's yield?

The bond pays $4 in 6, 12, 18, 24, and 30 months, and $104 in 36 months. The bond yield is the value of y that solves
$$4e^{-0.5y} + 4e^{-1.0y} + 4e^{-1.5y} + 4e^{-2.0y} + 4e^{-2.5y} + 104e^{-3.0y} = 104$$
Using the *Solver* or *Goal Seek* tool in Excel $y = 0.06407$ or 6.407%.

Problem 4.13.
Suppose that the 6-month, 12-month, 18-month, and 24-month zero rates are 5%, 6%, 6.5%, and 7% respectively. What is the two-year par yield?

Using the notation in the text, $m = 2$, $d = e^{-0.07 \times 2} = 0.8694$. Also
$$A = e^{-0.05 \times 0.5} + e^{-0.06 \times 1.0} + e^{-0.065 \times 1.5} + e^{-0.07 \times 2.0} = 3.6935$$
The formula in the text gives the par yield as
$$\frac{(100 - 100 \times 0.8694) \times 2}{3.6935} = 7.072$$
To verify that this is correct we calculate the value of a bond that pays a coupon of 7.072% per year (that is 3.5365 every six months). The value is
$$3.536e^{-0.05 \times 0.5} + 3.5365e^{-0.06 \times 1.0} + 3.536e^{-0.065 \times 1.5} + 103.536e^{-0.07 \times 2.0} = 100$$
verifying that 7.072% is the par yield.

Problem 4.14.
Suppose that zero interest rates with continuous compounding are as follows:

Maturity(years)	Rate (% per annum)
1	2.0
2	3.0
3	3.7
4	4.2
5	4.5

Calculate forward interest rates for the second, third, fourth, and fifth years.

The forward rates with continuous compounding are as follows:
Year 2: 4.0%
Year 3: 5.1%
Year 4: 5.7%
Year 5: 5.7%

Problem 4.15.
Use the rates in Problem 4.14 to value an FRA where you will pay 5% for the third year on $1 million.

The forward rate is 5.1% with continuous compounding or $e^{0.051 \times 1} - 1 = 5.232\%$ with annual compounding. The 3-year interest rate is 3.7% with continuous compounding. From equation (4.10), the value of the FRA is therefore

$$[1,000,000 \times (0.05232 - 0.05) \times 1]e^{-0.037 \times 3} = 2,078.85$$

or $2,078.85.

Problem 4.16.
A 10-year, 8% coupon bond currently sells for $90. A 10-year, 4% coupon bond currently sells for $80. What is the 10-year zero rate? (Hint: Consider taking a long position in two of the 4% coupon bonds and a short position in one of the 8% coupon bonds.)

Taking a long position in two of the 4% coupon bonds and a short position in one of the 8% coupon bonds leads to the following cash flows

$$\text{Year } 0 : 90 - 2 \times 80 = -70$$

$$\text{Year } 10 : 200 - 100 = 100$$

because the coupons cancel out. $100 in 10 years time is equivalent to $70 today. The 10-year rate, R, (continuously compounded) is therefore given by

$$100 = 70e^{10R}$$

The rate is

$$\frac{1}{10} \ln \frac{100}{70} = 0.0357$$

or 3.57% per annum.

Problem 4.17.
Explain carefully why liquidity preference theory is consistent with the observation that the term structure of interest rates tends to be upward sloping more often than it is downward sloping.

If long-term rates were simply a reflection of expected future short-term rates, we would expect the term structure to be downward sloping as often as it is upward sloping. (This is based on the assumption that half of the time investors expect rates to increase and half of the time investors expect rates to decrease). Liquidity preference theory argues that long term rates are high relative to expected future short-term rates. This means that the term structure should be upward sloping more often than it is downward sloping.

Problem 4.18.

"When the zero curve is upward sloping, the zero rate for a particular maturity is greater than the par yield for that maturity. When the zero curve is downward sloping, the reverse is true." Explain why this is so.

The par yield is the yield on a coupon-bearing bond. The zero rate is the yield on a zero-coupon bond. When the yield curve is upward sloping, the yield on an N-year coupon-bearing bond is less than the yield on an N-year zero-coupon bond. This is because the coupons are discounted at a lower rate than the N-year rate and drag the yield down below this rate. Similarly, when the yield curve is downward sloping, the yield on an N-year coupon bearing bond is higher than the yield on an N-year zero-coupon bond.

Problem 4.19.

Why are U.S. Treasury rates significantly lower than other rates that are close to risk free?

There are three reasons (see Business Snapshot 4.1).
1. Treasury bills and Treasury bonds must be purchased by financial institutions to fulfill a variety of regulatory requirements. This increases demand for these Treasury instruments driving the price up and the yield down.
2. The amount of capital a bank is required to hold to support an investment in Treasury bills and bonds is substantially smaller than the capital required to support a similar investment in other very-low-risk instruments.
3. In the United States, Treasury instruments are given a favorable tax treatment compared with most other fixed-income investments because they are not taxed at the state level.

Problem 4.20.

Why does a loan in the repo market involve very little credit risk?

A repo is a contract where an investment dealer who owns securities agrees to sell them to another company now and buy them back later at a slightly higher price. The other company is providing a loan to the investment dealer. This loan involves very little credit risk. If the borrower does not honor the agreement, the lending company simply keeps the securities. If the lending company does not keep to its side of the agreement, the original owner of the securities keeps the cash.

Problem 4.21.

Explain why an FRA is equivalent to the exchange of a floating rate of interest for a fixed rate of interest?

A FRA is an agreement that a certain specified interest rate, R_K, will apply to a certain principal, L, for a certain specified future time period. Suppose that the rate observed in the market for the future time period at the beginning of the time period proves to be R_M. If the FRA is an agreement that R_K will apply when the principal is invested, the holder of the

FRA can borrow the principal at R_M and then invest it at R_K. The net cash flow at the end of the period is then an inflow of $R_K L$ and an outflow of $R_M L$. If the FRA is an agreement that R_K will apply when the principal is borrowed, the holder of the FRA can invest the borrowed principal at R_M. The net cash flow at the end of the period is then an inflow of $R_M L$ and an outflow of $R_K L$. In either case we see that the FRA involves the exchange of a fixed rate of interest on the principal of L for a floating rate of interest on the principal.

Problem 4.22.
A five-year bond with a yield of 11% (continuously compounded) pays an 8% coupon at the end of each year.

    a) *What is the bond's price?*
    b) *What is the bond's duration?*
    c) *Use the duration to calculate the effect on the bond's price of a 0.2% decrease in its yield.*
    d) *Recalculate the bond's price on the basis of a 10.8% per annum yield and verify that the result is in agreement with your answer to (c).*

    a) The bond's price is
$$8e^{-0.11} + 8e^{-0.11\times2} + 8e^{-0.11\times3} + 8e^{-0.11\times4} + 108e^{-0.11\times5} = 86.80$$

    b) The bond's duration is
$$\frac{1}{86.80}\left[8e^{-0.11} + 2\times8e^{-0.11\times2} + 3\times8e^{-0.11\times3} + 4\times8e^{-0.11\times4} + 5\times108e^{-0.11\times5}\right]$$

$$= 4.256 \text{ years}$$

    c) Since, with the notation in the chapter
$$\Delta B = -BD\Delta y$$
the effect on the bond's price of a 0.2% decrease in its yield is
$$86.80\times4.256\times0.002 = 0.74$$
The bond's price should increase from 86.80 to 87.54.

    d) With a 10.8% yield the bond's price is
$$8e^{-0.108} + 8e^{-0.108\times2} + 8e^{-0.108\times3} + 8e^{-0.108\times4} + 108e^{-0.108\times5} = 87.54$$
This is consistent with the answer in (c).

Problem 4.23.
The cash prices of six-month and one-year Treasury bills are 94.0 and 89.0. A 1.5-year bond that will pay coupons of $4 every six months currently sells for $94.84. A two-year bond that will pay coupons of $5 every six months currently sells for $97.12. Calculate the six-month, one-year, 1.5-year, and two-year zero rates.

The 6-month Treasury bill provides a return of $6/94 = 6.383\%$ in six months. This is $2\times6.383 = 12.766\%$ per annum with semiannual compounding or $2\ln(1.06383) = 12.38\%$ per annum with continuous compounding. The 12-month rate is $11/89 = 12.360\%$ with annual compounding or $\ln(1.1236) = 11.65\%$ with continuous compounding. For the $1\frac{1}{2}$ year bond we must have

$$4e^{-0.1238\times0.5} + 4e^{-0.1165\times1} + 104e^{-1.5R} = 94.84$$

where R is the $1\frac{1}{2}$ year zero rate. It follows that

$$3.76 + 3.56 + 104e^{-1.5R} = 94.84$$
$$e^{-1.5R} = 0.8415$$
$$R = 0.115$$

or 11.5%. For the 2-year bond we must have

$$5e^{-0.1238\times0.5} + 5e^{-0.1165\times1} + 5e^{-0.115\times1.5} + 105e^{-2R} = 97.12$$

where R is the 2-year zero rate. It follows that

$$e^{-2R} = 0.7977$$
$$R = 0.113$$

or 11.3%.

Problem 4.24.

"An interest rate swap where six-month LIBOR is exchanged for a fixed rate 5% on a principal of $100 million for five years is a portfolio of nine FRAs." Explain this statement.

Each exchange of payments is an FRA where interest at 5% is exchanged for interest at LIBOR on a principal of $100 million. Interest rate swaps are discussed further in Chapter 7.

CHAPTER 5
Determination of Forward and Futures Prices

Problem 5.1.
Explain what happens when an investor shorts a certain share.

The investor's broker borrows the shares from another client's account and sells them in the usual way. To close out the position, the investor must purchase the shares. The broker then replaces them in the account of the client from whom they were borrowed. The party with the short position must remit to the broker dividends and other income paid on the shares. The broker transfers these funds to the account of the client from whom the shares were borrowed. Occasionally the broker runs out of places from which to borrow the shares. The investor is then short squeezed and has to close out the position immediately.

Problem 5.2.
What is the difference between the forward price and the value of a forward contract?

The forward price of an asset today is the price at which you would agree to buy or sell the asset at a future time. The value of a forward contract is zero when you first enter into it. As time passes the underlying asset price changes and the value of the contract may become positive or negative.

Problem 5.3.
Suppose that you enter into a six-month forward contract on a non-dividend-paying stock when the stock price is $30 and the risk-free interest rate (with continuous compounding) is 12% per annum. What is the forward price?

The forward price is

$$30e^{0.12 \times 0.5} = \$31.86$$

Problem 5.4.
A stock index currently stands at 350. The risk-free interest rate is 8% per annum (with continuous compounding) and the dividend yield on the index is 4% per annum. What should the futures price for a four-month contract be?

The futures price is

$$350e^{(0.08-0.04) \times 0.3333} = \$354.7$$

Problem 5.5.
Explain carefully why the futures price of gold can be calculated from its spot price and other observable variables whereas the futures price of copper cannot.

Gold is an investment asset. If the futures price is too high, investors will find it profitable to increase their holdings of gold and short futures contracts. If the futures price is too low, they will find it profitable to decrease their holdings of gold and go long in the futures market. Copper is a consumption asset. If the futures price is too high, a strategy of buy copper and short futures works. However, because investors do not in general hold the asset, the strategy of sell copper and buy futures is not available to them. There is therefore an upper bound, but no lower bound, to the futures price.

Problem 5.6.
Explain carefully the meaning of the terms convenience yield and cost of carry. What is the relationship between futures price, spot price, convenience yield, and cost of carry?

Convenience yield measures the extent to which there are benefits obtained from ownership of the physical asset that are not obtained by owners of long futures contracts. The *cost of carry* is the interest cost plus storage cost less the income earned. The futures price, F_0, and spot price, S_0, are related by

$$F_0 = S_0 e^{(c-y)T}$$

where c is the cost of carry, y is the convenience yield, and T is the time to maturity of the futures contract.

Problem 5.7.
Explain why a foreign currency can be treated as an asset providing a known yield.

A foreign currency provides a known interest rate, but the interest is received in the foreign currency. The value in the domestic currency of the income provided by the foreign currency is therefore known as a percentage of the value of the foreign currency. This means that the income has the properties of a known yield.

Problem 5.8.
Is the futures price of a stock index greater than or less than the expected future value of the index? Explain your answer.

The futures price of a stock index is always less than the expected future value of the index. This follows from Section 5.14 and the fact that the index has positive systematic risk. For an alternative argument, let μ be the expected return required by investors on the index so that $E(S_T) = S_0 e^{(\mu-q)T}$. Because $\mu > r$ and $F_0 = S_0 e^{(r-q)T}$, it follows that $E(S_T) > F_0$.

Problem 5.9.
A one-year long forward contract on a non-dividend-paying stock is entered into when the stock price is $40 and the risk-free rate of interest is 10% per annum with continuous compounding.
a) *What are the forward price and the initial value of the forward contract?*
b) *Six months later, the price of the stock is $45 and the risk-free interest rate is still 10%. What are the forward price and the value of the forward contract?*

a) The forward price, F_0, is given by equation (5.1) as:

$$F_0 = 40e^{0.1 \times 1} = 44.21$$

or $44.21. The initial value of the forward contract is zero.

b) The delivery price K in the contract is $44.21. The value of the contract, f, after six months is given by equation (5.5) as:

$$f = 45 - 44.21e^{-0.1 \times 0.5}$$

$$= 2.95$$

i.e., it is $2.95. The forward price is:
$$45e^{0.1\times0.5} = 47.31$$

or $47.31.

Problem 5.10.
The risk-free rate of interest is 7% per annum with continuous compounding, and the dividend yield on a stock index is 3.2% per annum. The current value of the index is 150. What is the six-month futures price?

Using equation (5.3) the six month futures price is
$$150e^{(0.07-0.032)\times0.5} = 152.88$$

or $152.88.

Problem 5.11.
Assume that the risk-free interest rate is 9% per annum with continuous compounding and that the dividend yield on a stock index varies throughout the year. In February, May, August, and November, dividends are paid at a rate of 5% per annum. In other months, dividends are paid at a rate of 2% per annum. Suppose that the value of the index on July 31 is 1,300. What is the futures price for a contract deliverable on December 31 of the same year?

The futures contract lasts for five months. The dividend yield is 2% for three of the months and 5% for two of the months. The average dividend yield is therefore
$$\frac{1}{5}(3\times2+2\times5) = 3.2\%$$

The futures price is therefore
$$1300e^{(0.09-0.032)\times0.4167} = 1,331.80$$

or $1331.80.

Problem 5.12.
Suppose that the risk-free interest rate is 10% per annum with continuous compounding and that the dividend yield on a stock index is 4% per annum. The index is standing at 400, and the futures price for a contract deliverable in four months is 405. What arbitrage opportunities does this create?

The theoretical futures price is
$$400e^{(0.10-0.04)\times4/12} = 408.08$$

The actual futures price is only 405. This shows that the index futures price is too low relative to the index. The correct arbitrage strategy is
(a) Buy futures contracts
(b) Short the shares underlying the index.

Problem 5.13.
Estimate the difference between short-term interest rates in Mexico and the United States on May 26, 2010 from the information in Table 5.4.

The settlement prices for the futures contracts are to
Sept: 0.76375

Dec: 0.75625

The December price is about 0.98% below the September price. This suggests that the short-term interest rate in the Mexico exceeded short-term interest rate in the United States by about 0.98% per three months or about 3.92% per year.

Problem 5.14.

The two-month interest rates in Switzerland and the United States are 2% and 5% per annum, respectively, with continuous compounding. The spot price of the Swiss franc is $0.8000. The futures price for a contract deliverable in two months is $0.8100. What arbitrage opportunities does this create?

The theoretical futures price is
$$0.8000e^{(0.05-0.02)\times 2/12} = 0.8040$$
The actual futures price is too high. This suggests that an arbitrageur should buy Swiss francs and short Swiss francs futures.

Problem 5.15.

The spot price of silver is $15 per ounce. The storage costs are $0.24 per ounce per year payable quarterly in advance. Assuming that interest rates are 10% per annum for all maturities, calculate the futures price of silver for delivery in nine months.

The present value of the storage costs for nine months are
$$0.06 + 0.06e^{-0.10\times 0.25} + 0.06e^{-0.10\times 0.5} = 0.176$$
or $0.176. The futures price is from equation (5.11) given by F_0 where
$$F_0 = (15.000 + 0.176)e^{0.1\times 0.75} = 16.36$$
i.e., it is $16.36 per ounce.

Problem 5.16.

Suppose that F_1 and F_2 are two futures contracts on the same commodity with times to maturity, t_1 and t_2, where $t_2 > t_1$. Prove that
$$F_2 \le F_1 e^{r(t_2-t_1)}$$
where r is the interest rate (assumed constant) and there are no storage costs. For the purposes of this problem, assume that a futures contract is the same as a forward contract.

If
$$F_2 > F_1 e^{r(t_2-t_1)}$$
an investor could make a riskless profit by
(a) Taking a long position in a futures contract which matures at time t_1
(b) Taking a short position in a futures contract which matures at time t_2
When the first futures contract matures, the asset is purchased for F_1 using funds borrowed at rate r. It is then held until time t_2 at which point it is exchanged for F_2 under the second contract. The costs of the funds borrowed and accumulated interest at time t_2 is $F_1 e^{r(t_2-t_1)}$. A positive profit of
$$F_2 - F_1 e^{r(t_2-t_1)}$$
is then realized at time t_2. This type of arbitrage opportunity cannot exist for long. Hence:

$$F_2 \leq F_1 e^{r(t_2 - t_1)}$$

Problem 5.17.
When a known future cash outflow in a foreign currency is hedged by a company using a forward contract, there is no foreign exchange risk. When it is hedged using futures contracts, the daily settlement process does leave the company exposed to some risk. Explain the nature of this risk. In particular, consider whether the company is better off using a futures contract or a forward contract when
    a) *The value of the foreign currency falls rapidly during the life of the contract*
    b) *The value of the foreign currency rises rapidly during the life of the contract*
    c) *The value of the foreign currency first rises and then falls back to its initial value*
    d) *The value of the foreign currency first falls and then rises back to its initial value*
Assume that the forward price equals the futures price.

In total the gain or loss under a futures contract is equal to the gain or loss under the corresponding forward contract. However the timing of the cash flows is different. When the time value of money is taken into account a futures contract may prove to be more valuable or less valuable than a forward contract. Of course the company does not know in advance which will work out better. The long forward contract provides a perfect hedge. The long futures contract provides a slightly imperfect hedge.

a) In this case the forward contract would lead to a slightly better outcome. The company will make a loss on its hedge. If the hedge is with a forward contract the whole of the loss will be realized at the end. If it is with a futures contract the loss will be realized day by day throughout the contract. On a present value basis the former is preferable.

b) In this case the futures contract would lead to a slightly better outcome. The company will make a gain on the hedge. If the hedge is with a forward contract the gain will be realized at the end. If it is with a futures contract the gain will be realized day by day throughout the life of the contract. On a present value basis the latter is preferable.

c) In this case the futures contract would lead to a slightly better outcome. This is because it would involve positive cash flows early and negative cash flows later.

d) In this case the forward contract would lead to a slightly better outcome. This is because, in the case of the futures contract, the early cash flows would be negative and the later cash flow would be positive.

Problem 5.18.
It is sometimes argued that a forward exchange rate is an unbiased predictor of future exchange rates. Under what circumstances is this so?

From the discussion in Section 5.14 of the text, the forward exchange rate is an unbiased predictor of the future exchange rate when the exchange rate has no systematic risk. To have no systematic risk the exchange rate must be uncorrelated with the return on the market.

Problem 5.19.
Show that the growth rate in an index futures price equals the excess return of the portfolio underlying the index over the risk-free rate. Assume that the risk-free interest rate and the dividend yield are constant.

Suppose that F_0 is the futures price at time zero for a contract maturing at time T and F_1 is the futures price for the same contract at time t_1. It follows that

$$F_0 = S_0 e^{(r-q)T}$$

$$F_1 = S_1 e^{(r-q)(T-t_1)}$$

where S_0 and S_1 are the spot price at times zero and t_1, r is the risk-free rate, and q is the dividend yield. These equations imply that

$$\frac{F_1}{F_0} = \frac{S_1}{S_0} e^{-(r-q)t_1}$$

Define the excess return of the portfolio underlying the index over the risk-free rate as x. The total return is $r + x$ and the return realized in the form of capital gains is $r + x - q$. It follows that $S_1 = S_0 e^{(r+x-q)t_1}$ and the equation for F_1/F_0 reduces to

$$\frac{F_1}{F_0} = e^{xt_1}$$

which is the required result.

Problem 5.20.

Show that equation (5.3) is true by considering an investment in the asset combined with a short position in a futures contract. Assume that all income from the asset is reinvested in the asset. Use an argument similar to that in footnotes 2 and 4 and explain in detail what an arbitrageur would do if equation (5.3) did not hold.

Suppose we buy N units of the asset and invest the income from the asset in the asset. The income from the asset causes our holding in the asset to grow at a continuously compounded rate q. By time T our holding has grown to Ne^{qT} units of the asset. Analogously to footnotes 2 and 4 of Chapter 5, we therefore buy N units of the asset at time zero at a cost of S_0 per unit and enter into a forward contract to sell Ne^{qT} unit for F_0 per unit at time T. This generates the following cash flows:

Time 0: $-NS_0$

Time 1: $NF_0 e^{qT}$

Because there is no uncertainty about these cash flows, the present value of the time T inflow must equal the time zero outflow when we discount at the risk-free rate. This means that

$$NS_0 = (NF_0 e^{qT})e^{-rT}$$

or

$$F_0 = S_0 e^{(r-q)T}$$

This is equation (5.3).

If $F_0 > S_0 e^{(r-q)T}$, an arbitrageur should borrow money at rate r and buy N units of the asset.

At the same time the arbitrageur should enter into a forward contract to sell Ne^{qT} units of the asset at time T. As income is received, it is reinvested in the asset. At time T the loan is repaid and the arbitrageur makes a profit of $N(F_0 e^{qT} - S_0 e^{rT})$ at time T.

If $F_0 < S_0 e^{(r-q)T}$, an arbitrageur should short N units of the asset investing the proceeds at rate r. At the same time the arbitrageur should enter into a forward contract to buy Ne^{qT} units of the asset at time T. When income is paid on the asset, the arbitrageur owes money on the short position. The investor meets this obligation from the cash proceeds of shorting further units. The result is that the number of units shorted grows at rate q to Ne^{qT}. The cumulative short position is closed out at time T and the arbitrageur makes a profit of $N(S_0 e^{rT} - F_0 e^{qT})$.

Problem 5.21.
Explain carefully what is meant by the expected price of a commodity on a particular future date. Suppose that the futures price of crude oil declines with the maturity of the contract at the rate of 2% per year. Assume that speculators tend to be short crude oil futures and hedgers tended to be long crude oil futures. What does the Keynes and Hicks argument imply about the expected future price of oil?

To understand the meaning of the expected future price of a commodity, suppose that there are N different possible prices at a particular future time: P_1, P_2, ..., P_N. Define q_i as the (subjective) probability the price being P_i (with $q_1 + q_2 + ... + q_N = 1$). The expected future price is

$$\sum_{i=1}^{N} q_i P_i$$

Different people may have different expected future prices for the commodity. The expected future price in the market can be thought of as an average of the opinions of different market participants. Of course, in practice the actual price of the commodity at the future time may prove to be higher or lower than the expected price.
Keynes and Hicks argue that speculators on average make money from commodity futures trading and hedgers on average lose money from commodity futures trading. If speculators tend to have short positions in crude oil futures, the Keynes and Hicks argument implies that futures prices overstate expected future spot prices. If crude oil futures prices decline at 2% per year the Keynes and Hicks argument therefore implies an even faster decline for the expected price of crude oil in this case.

Problem 5.22.
The Value Line Index is designed to reflect changes in the value of a portfolio of over 1,600 equally weighted stocks. Prior to March 9, 1988, the change in the index from one day to the next was calculated as the geometric average of the changes in the prices of the stocks underlying the index. In these circumstances, does equation (5.8) correctly relate the futures price of the index to its cash price? If not, does the equation overstate or understate the futures price?

When the geometric average of the price relatives is used, the changes in the value of the index do not correspond to changes in the value of a portfolio that is traded. Equation (5.8) is therefore no longer correct. The changes in the value of the portfolio are monitored by an index calculated from the arithmetic average of the prices of the stocks in the portfolio. Since the geometric average of a set of numbers is always less than the arithmetic average, equation (5.8) overstates the futures price. It is rumored that at one time (prior to 1988), equation (5.8) did hold for the Value Line Index. A major Wall Street firm was the first to recognize that this represented a trading opportunity. It made a financial killing by buying the stocks underlying the index and shorting the futures.

Problem 5.23.
A U.S. company is interested in using the futures contracts traded by the CME Group to hedge its Australian dollar exposure. Define r as the interest rate (all maturities) on the U.S.

dollar and r_f as the interest rate (all maturities) on the Australian dollar. Assume that r and r_f are constant and that the company uses a contract expiring at time T to hedge an exposure at time $t\,(T > t)$.

(a) Show that the optimal hedge ratio is

$$e^{(r_f - r)(T - t)}$$

(b) Show that, when t is one day, the optimal hedge ratio is almost exactly S_0 / F_0 where S_0 is the current spot price of the currency and F_0 is the current futures price of the currency for the contract maturing at time T.

(c) Show that the company can take account of the daily settlement of futures contracts for a hedge that lasts longer than one day by adjusting the hedge ratio so that it always equals the spot price of the currency divided by the futures price of the currency.

(a) The relationship between the futures price F_t and the spot price S_t at time t is

$$F_t = S_t e^{(r - r_f)(T - t)}$$

Suppose that the hedge ratio is h. The price obtained with hedging is

$$h(F_0 - F_t) + S_t$$

where F_0 is the initial futures price. This is

$$hF_0 + S_t - hS_t e^{(r - r_f)(T - t)}$$

If $h = e^{(r_f - r)(T - t)}$, this reduces to hF_0 and a zero variance hedge is obtained.

(b) When t is one day, h is approximately $e^{(r_f - r)T} = S_0 / F_0$. The appropriate hedge ratio is therefore S_0 / F_0.

(c) When a futures contract is used for hedging, the price movements in each day should in theory be hedged separately. This is because the daily settlement means that a futures contract is closed out and rewritten at the end of each day. From (b) the correct hedge ratio at any given time is, therefore, S/F where S is the spot price and F is the futures price. Suppose there is an exposure to N units of the foreign currency and M units of the foreign currency underlie one futures contract. With a hedge ratio of 1 we should trade N/M contracts. With a hedge ratio of S/F we should trade

$$\frac{SN}{FM}$$

contracts. In other words we should calculate the number of contracts that should be traded as the dollar value of our exposure divided by the dollar value of one futures contract. (This is not the same as the dollar value of our exposure divided by the dollar value of the assets underlying one futures contract.) Since a futures contract is settled daily, we should in theory rebalance our hedge daily so that the outstanding number of futures contracts is always $(SN)/(FM)$. This is known as tailing the hedge. (See Chapter 3.)

CHAPTER 6
Interest Rate Futures

Problem 6.1.
A U.S. Treasury bond pays a 7% coupon on January 7 and July 7. How much interest accrues per $100 of principal to the bond holder between July 7, 2011 and August 9, 2011? How would your answer be different if it were a corporate bond?

There are 33 calendar days between July 7, 2011 and August 9, 2011. There are 184 calendar days between July 7, 2011 and January 7, 2011. The interest earned per $100 of principal is therefore $3.5 \times 33/184 = \$0.6277$. For a corporate bond we assume 32 days between July 7 and August 9, 2011 and 180 days between July 7, 2011 and January 7, 2011. The interest earned is $3.5 \times 32/180 = \$0.6222$.

Problem 6.2.
It is January 9, 2013. The price of a Treasury bond with a 12% coupon that matures on October 12, 2020, is quoted as 102-07. What is the cash price?

There are 89 days between October 12, 2012, and January 9, 2013. There are 182 days between October 12, 2012, and April 12, 2013. The cash price of the bond is obtained by adding the accrued interest to the quoted price. The quoted price is $102\frac{7}{32}$ or 102.21875. The cash price is therefore

$$102.21875 + \frac{89}{182} \times 6 = \$105.15$$

Problem 6.3.
How is the conversion factor of a bond calculated by the CME Group? How is it used?

The conversion factor for a bond is equal to the quoted price the bond would have per dollar of principal on the first day of the delivery month on the assumption that the interest rate for all maturities equals 6% per annum (with semiannual compounding). The bond maturity and the times to the coupon payment dates are rounded down to the nearest three months for the purposes of the calculation. The conversion factor defines how much an investor with a short bond futures contract receives when bonds are delivered. If the conversion factor is 1.2345 the amount investor receives is calculated by multiplying 1.2345 by the most recent futures price and adding accrued interest.

Problem 6.4.
A Eurodollar futures price changes from 96.76 to 96.82. What is the gain or loss to an investor who is long two contracts?

The Eurodollar futures price has increased by 6 basis points. The investor makes a gain per contract of $25 \times 6 = \$150$ or $300 in total.

Problem 6.5.
What is the purpose of the convexity adjustment made to Eurodollar futures rates? Why is the convexity adjustment necessary?

Suppose that a Eurodollar futures quote is 95.00. This gives a futures rate of 5% for the three-month period covered by the contract. The convexity adjustment is the amount by which futures rate has to be reduced to give an estimate of the forward rate for the period. The convexity adjustment is necessary because a) the futures contract is settled daily and b) the futures contract expires at the beginning of the three months. Both of these lead to the futures rate being greater than the forward rate.

Problem 6.6.
The 350-day LIBOR rate is 3% with continuous compounding and the forward rate calculated from a Eurodollar futures contract that matures in 350 days is 3.2% with continuous compounding. Estimate the 440-day zero rate.

From equation (6.4) the rate is
$$\frac{3.2 \times 90 + 3 \times 350}{440} = 3.0409$$
or 3.0409%.

Problem 6.7.
It is January 30. You are managing a bond portfolio worth $6 million. The duration of the portfolio in six months will be 8.2 years. The September Treasury bond futures price is currently 108-15, and the cheapest-to-deliver bond will have a duration of 7.6 years in September. How should you hedge against changes in interest rates over the next six months?

The value of a contract is $108\frac{15}{32} \times 1,000 = \$108,468.75$. The number of contracts that should be shorted is
$$\frac{6,000,000}{108,468.75} \times \frac{8.2}{7.6} = 59.7$$
Rounding to the nearest whole number, 60 contracts should be shorted. The position should be closed out at the end of July.

Problem 6.8.
The price of a 90-day Treasury bill is quoted as 10.00. What continuously compounded return (on an actual/365 basis) does an investor earn on the Treasury bill for the 90-day period?

The cash price of the Treasury bill is
$$100 - \frac{90}{360} \times 10 = \$97.50$$

The annualized continuously compounded return is
$$\frac{365}{90} \ln\left(1 + \frac{2.5}{97.5}\right) = 10.27\%$$

Problem 6.9.
It is May 5, 2011. The quoted price of a government bond with a 12% coupon that matures on July 27, 2014, is 110-17. What is the cash price?

The number of days between January 27, 2011 and May 5, 2011 is 98. The number of days between January 27, 2011 and July 27, 2011 is 181. The accrued interest is therefore

$$6 \times \frac{98}{181} = 3.2486$$

The quoted price is 110.5312. The cash price is therefore

$$110.5312 + 3.2486 = 113.7798$$

or $113.78.

Problem 6.10.

Suppose that the Treasury bond futures price is 101-12. Which of the following four bonds is cheapest to deliver?

Bond	Price	Conversion Factor
1	125-05	1.2131
2	142-15	1.3792
3	115-31	1.1149
4	144-02	1.4026

The cheapest-to-deliver bond is the one for which

$$\text{Quoted Price} - \text{Futures Price} \times \text{Conversion Factor}$$

is least. Calculating this factor for each of the 4 bonds we get

$$\text{Bond 1}: 125.15625 - 101.375 \times 1.2131 = 2.178$$
$$\text{Bond 2}: 142.46875 - 101.375 \times 1.3792 = 2.652$$
$$\text{Bond 3}: 115.96875 - 101.375 \times 1.1149 = 2.946$$
$$\text{Bond 4}: 144.06250 - 101.375 \times 1.4026 = 1.874$$

Bond 4 is therefore the cheapest to deliver.

Problem 6.11.

It is July 30, 2013. The cheapest-to-deliver bond in a September 2013 Treasury bond futures contract is a 13% coupon bond, and delivery is expected to be made on September 30, 2013. Coupon payments on the bond are made on February 4 and August 4 each year. The term structure is flat, and the rate of interest with semiannual compounding is 12% per annum. The conversion factor for the bond is 1.5. The current quoted bond price is $110. Calculate the quoted futures price for the contract.

There are 176 days between February 4 and July 30 and 181 days between February 4 and August 4. The cash price of the bond is, therefore:

$$110 + \frac{176}{181} \times 6.5 = 116.32$$

The rate of interest with continuous compounding is $2\ln 1.06 = 0.1165$ or 11.65% per annum. A coupon of 6.5 will be received in 5 days ($= 0.01366$ years) time. The present value of the coupon is

$$6.5e^{-0.01366 \times 0.1165} = 6.490$$

The futures contract lasts for 62 days ($= 0.1694$ years). The cash futures price if the contract were written on the 13% bond would be

$$(116.32 - 6.490)e^{0.1694 \times 0.1165} = 112.02$$

At delivery there are 57 days of accrued interest. The quoted futures price if the contract were written on the 13% bond would therefore be

$$112.02 - 6.5 \times \frac{57}{184} = 110.01$$

Taking the conversion factor into account the quoted futures price should be:

$$\frac{110.01}{1.5} = 73.34$$

Problem 6.12.

An investor is looking for arbitrage opportunities in the Treasury bond futures market. What complications are created by the fact that the party with a short position can choose to deliver any bond with a maturity of over 15 years?

If the bond to be delivered and the time of delivery were known, arbitrage would be straightforward. When the futures price is too high, the arbitrageur buys bonds and shorts an equivalent number of bond futures contracts. When the futures price is too low, the arbitrageur shorts bonds and goes long an equivalent number of bond futures contracts. Uncertainty as to which bond will be delivered introduces complications. The bond that appears cheapest-to-deliver now may not in fact be cheapest-to-deliver at maturity. In the case where the futures price is too high, this is not a major problem since the party with the short position (i.e., the arbitrageur) determines which bond is to be delivered. In the case where the futures price is too low, the arbitrageur's position is far more difficult since he or she does not know which bond to short; it is unlikely that a profit can be locked in for all possible outcomes.

Problem 6.13.

Suppose that the nine-month LIBOR interest rate is 8% per annum and the six-month LIBOR interest rate is 7.5% per annum (both with actual/365 and continuous compounding). Estimate the three-month Eurodollar futures price quote for a contract maturing in six months.

The forward interest rate for the time period between months 6 and 9 is 9% per annum with continuous compounding. This is because 9% per annum for three months when combined with $7\frac{1}{2}$% per annum for six months gives an average interest rate of 8% per annum for the nine-month period.
With quarterly compounding the forward interest rate is

$$4(e^{0.09/4} - 1) = 0.09102$$

or 9.102%. This assumes that the day count is actual/actual. With a day count of actual/360 the rate is $9.102 \times 360 / 365 = 8.977$. The three-month Eurodollar quote for a contract maturing in six months is therefore

$$100 - 8.977 = 91.02$$

Problem 6.14.

Suppose that the 300-day LIBOR zero rate is 4% and Eurodollar quotes for contracts maturing in 300, 398 and 489 days are 95.83, 95.62, and 95.48. Calculate 398-day and 489-day LIBOR zero rates. Assume no difference between forward and futures rates for the purposes of your calculations.

The forward rates calculated form the first two Eurodollar futures are 4.17% and 4.38%. These are expressed with an actual/360 day count and quarterly compounding. With

continuous compounding and an actual/365 day count they are
(365/90)ln(1+0.0417/4)=4.2060% and (365/90)ln(1+0.0438/4)= 4.4167%. It follows from equation (6.4) that the 398 day rate is
(4×300+4.2060×98)/398=4.0507
or 4.0507%. The 489 day rate is
(4.0507×398+4.4167× 91)/489=4.1188
or 4.1188%. We are assuming that the first futures rate applies to 98 days rather than the usual 91 days. The third futures quote is not needed.

Problem 6.15.

Suppose that a bond portfolio with a duration of 12 years is hedged using a futures contract in which the underlying asset has a duration of four years. What is likely to be the impact on the hedge of the fact that the 12-year rate is less volatile than the four-year rate?

Duration-based hedging procedures assume parallel shifts in the yield curve. Since the 12-year rate tends to move by less than the 4-year rate, the portfolio manager may find that he or she is over-hedged.

Problem 6.16.

Suppose that it is February 20 and a treasurer realizes that on July 17 the company will have to issue $5 million of commercial paper with a maturity of 180 days. If the paper were issued today, the company would realize $4,820,000. (In other words, the company would receive $4,820,000 for its paper and have to redeem it at $5,000,000 in 180 days' time.) The September Eurodollar futures price is quoted as 92.00. How should the treasurer hedge the company's exposure?

The company treasurer can hedge the company's exposure by shorting Eurodollar futures contracts. The Eurodollar futures position leads to a profit if rates rise and a loss if they fall. The duration of the commercial paper is twice that of the Eurodollar deposit underlying the Eurodollar futures contract. The contract price of a Eurodollar futures contract is 980,000. The number of contracts that should be shorted is, therefore,

$$\frac{4,820,000}{980,000} \times 2 = 9.84$$

Rounding to the nearest whole number 10 contracts should be shorted.

Problem 6.17.

On August 1 a portfolio manager has a bond portfolio worth $10 million. The duration of the portfolio in October will be 7.1 years. The December Treasury bond futures price is currently 91-12 and the cheapest-to-deliver bond will have a duration of 8.8 years at maturity. How should the portfolio manager immunize the portfolio against changes in interest rates over the next two months?

The treasurer should short Treasury bond futures contract. If bond prices go down, this futures position will provide offsetting gains. The number of contracts that should be shorted is

$$\frac{10,000,000 \times 7.1}{91,375 \times 8.8} = 88.30$$

Rounding to the nearest whole number 88 contracts should be shorted.

Problem 6.18.
How can the portfolio manager change the duration of the portfolio to 3.0 years in Problem 6.17?

The answer in Problem 6.17 is designed to reduce the duration to zero. To reduce the duration from 7.1 to 3.0 instead of from 7.1 to 0, the treasurer should short

$$\frac{4.1}{7.1} \times 88.30 = 50.99$$

or 51 contracts.

Problem 6.19.
Between October 30, 2012, and November 1, 2012, you have a choice between owning a U.S. government bond paying a 12% coupon and a U.S. corporate bond paying a 12% coupon. Consider carefully the day count conventions discussed in this chapter and decide which of the two bonds you would prefer to own. Ignore the risk of default.

You would prefer to own the Treasury bond. Under the 30/360 day count convention there is one day between October 30 and November 1. Under the actual/actual (in period) day count convention, there are two days. Therefore you would earn approximately twice as much interest by holding the Treasury bond.

Problem 6.20.
Suppose that a Eurodollar futures quote is 88 for a contract maturing in 60 days. What is the LIBOR forward rate for the 60- to 150-day period? Ignore the difference between futures and forwards for the purposes of this question.

The Eurodollar futures contract price of 88 means that the Eurodollar futures rate is 12% per annum with quarterly compounding. This is the forward rate for the 60- to 150-day period with quarterly compounding and an actual/360 day count convention.

Problem 6.21.
The three-month Eurodollar futures price for a contract maturing in six years is quoted as 95.20. The standard deviation of the change in the short-term interest rate in one year is 1.1%. Estimate the forward LIBOR interest rate for the period between 6.00 and 6.25 years in the future.

Using the notation of Section 6.3, $\sigma = 0.011$, $t_1 = 6$, and $t_2 = 6.25$. The convexity adjustment is

$$\frac{1}{2} \times 0.011^2 \times 6 \times 6.25 = 0.002269$$

or about 23 basis points. The futures rate is 4.8% with quarterly compounding and an actual/360 day count. This becomes $4.8 \times 365 / 360 = 4.867\%$ with an actual/actual day count. It is $4\ln(1 + .04867 / 4) = 4.84\%$ with continuous compounding. The forward rate is therefore $4.84 - 0.23 = 4.61\%$ with continuous compounding.

Problem 6.22.
Explain why the forward interest rate is less than the corresponding futures interest rate calculated from a Eurodollar futures contract.

Suppose that the contracts apply to the interest rate between times T_1 and T_2. There are two reasons for a difference between the forward rate and the futures rate. The first is that the futures contract is settled daily whereas the forward contract is settled once at time T_2. The second is that without daily settlement a futures contract would be settled at time T_1 not T_2. Both reasons tend to make the futures rate greater than the forward rate.

CHAPTER 7
Swaps

Problem 7.1.
Companies A and B have been offered the following rates per annum on a $20 million five-year loan:

	Fixed Rate	*Floating Rate*
Company A	5.0%	LIBOR+0.1%
Company B	6.4%	LIBOR+0.6%

Company A requires a floating-rate loan; company B requires a fixed-rate loan. Design a swap that will net a bank, acting as intermediary, 0.1% per annum and that will appear equally attractive to both companies.

A has an apparent comparative advantage in fixed-rate markets but wants to borrow floating. B has an apparent comparative advantage in floating-rate markets but wants to borrow fixed. This provides the basis for the swap. There is a 1.4% per annum differential between the fixed rates offered to the two companies and a 0.5% per annum differential between the floating rates offered to the two companies. The total gain to all parties from the swap is therefore $1.4 - 0.5 = 0.9\%$ per annum. Because the bank gets 0.1% per annum of this gain, the swap should make each of A and B 0.4% per annum better off. This means that it should lead to A borrowing at LIBOR -0.3% and to B borrowing at 6.0%. The appropriate arrangement is therefore as shown in Figure S7.1.

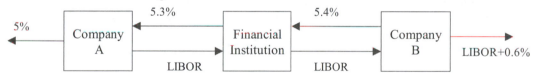

Figure S7.1   Swap for Problem 7.1

Problem 7.2.
Company X wishes to borrow U.S. dollars at a fixed rate of interest. Company Y wishes to borrow Japanese yen at a fixed rate of interest. The amounts required by the two companies are roughly the same at the current exchange rate. The companies have been quoted the following interest rates, which have been adjusted for the impact of taxes:

	Yen	Dollars
Company X	5.0%	9.6%
Company Y	6.5%	10.0%

Design a swap that will net a bank, acting as intermediary, 50 basis points per annum. Make the swap equally attractive to the two companies and ensure that all foreign exchange risk is assumed by the bank.

X has a comparative advantage in yen markets but wants to borrow dollars. Y has a comparative advantage in dollar markets but wants to borrow yen. This provides the basis for the swap. There is a 1.5% per annum differential between the yen rates and a 0.4% per annum differential between the dollar rates. The total gain to all parties from the swap is therefore $1.5 - 0.4 = 1.1\%$ per annum. The bank requires 0.5% per annum, leaving 0.3% per annum for each of X and Y. The swap should lead to X borrowing dollars at $9.6 - 0.3 = 9.3\%$ per annum and to Y borrowing yen at $6.5 - 0.3 = 6.2\%$ per annum. The appropriate arrangement is therefore as shown in Figure S7.2. All foreign exchange risk is borne by the bank.

Figure S7.2   Swap for Problem 7.2

Problem 7.3.

A $100 million interest rate swap has a remaining life of 10 months. Under the terms of the swap, six-month LIBOR is exchanged for 7% per annum (compounded semiannually). The average of the bid–offer rate being exchanged for six-month LIBOR in swaps of all maturities is currently 5% per annum with continuous compounding. The six-month LIBOR rate was 4.6% per annum two months ago. What is the current value of the swap to the party paying floating? What is its value to the party paying fixed?

In four months $3.5 million ($= 0.5 \times 0.07 \times \$100$ million) will be received and $2.3 million ($= 0.5 \times 0.046 \times \$100$ million) will be paid. (We ignore day count issues.) In 10 months $3.5 million will be received, and the LIBOR rate prevailing in four months' time will be paid. The value of the fixed-rate bond underlying the swap is

$3.5e^{-0.05 \times 4/12} + 103.5e^{-0.05 \times 10/12} = \$102.718$ million

The value of the floating-rate bond underlying the swap is

$(100 + 2.3)e^{-0.05 \times 4/12} = \$100.609$ million

The value of the swap to the party paying floating is $\$102.718 - \$100.609 = \$2.109$ million. The value of the swap to the party paying fixed is –$2.109 million.

These results can also be derived by decomposing the swap into forward contracts. Consider the party paying floating. The first forward contract involves paying $2.3 million and receiving $3.5 million in four months. It has a value of $1.2e^{-0.05 \times 4/12} = \$1.180$ million. To value the second forward contract, we note that the forward interest rate is 5% per annum with continuous compounding, or 5.063% per annum with semiannual compounding. The value of the forward contract is

$100 \times (0.07 \times 0.5 - 0.05063 \times 0.5)e^{-0.05 \times 10/12} = \$0.929$ million

The total value of the forward contracts is therefore $\$1.180 + \$0.929 = \$2.109$ million.

Problem 7.4.
Explain what a swap rate is. What is the relationship between swap rates and par yields?

A swap rate for a particular maturity is the average of the bid and offer fixed rates that a market maker is prepared to exchange for LIBOR in a standard plain vanilla swap with that maturity. The swap rate for a particular maturity is the LIBOR/swap par yield for that maturity.

Problem 7.5.
A currency swap has a remaining life of 15 months. It involves exchanging interest at 10% on £20 million for interest at 6% on $30 million once a year. The term structure of interest rates in both the United Kingdom and the United States is currently flat, and if the swap were negotiated today the interest rates exchanged would be 4% in dollars and 7% in sterling. All interest rates are quoted with annual compounding. The current exchange rate (dollars per pound sterling) is 1.8500. What is the value of the swap to the party paying sterling? What is the value of the swap to the party paying dollars?

The swap involves exchanging the sterling interest of 20×0.10 or £2 million for the dollar interest of $30 \times 0.06 = \$1.8$ million. The principal amounts are also exchanged at the end of the life of the swap. The value of the sterling bond underlying the swap is

$$\frac{2}{(1.07)^{1/4}} + \frac{22}{(1.07)^{5/4}} = 22.182 \text{ million pounds}$$

The value of the dollar bond underlying the swap is

$$\frac{1.8}{(1.04)^{1/4}} + \frac{31.8}{(1.04)^{5/4}} = \$32.061 \text{ million}$$

The value of the swap to the party paying sterling is therefore
$32.061 - (22.182 \times 1.85) = -\$8.976$ million

The value of the swap to the party paying dollars is +$8.976 million. The results can also be obtained by viewing the swap as a portfolio of forward contracts. The continuously compounded interest rates in sterling and dollars are 6.766% per annum and 3.922% per annum. The 3-month and 15-month forward exchange rates are $1.85e^{(0.03922-0.06766) \times 0.25} = 1.8369$ and $1.85e^{(0.03922-0.06766) \times 1.25} = 1.7854$. The values of the two forward contracts corresponding to the exchange of interest for the party paying sterling are therefore
$(1.8 - 2 \times 1.8369)e^{-0.03922 \times 0.25} = -\$1.855$ million
and
$(1.8 - 2 \times 1.7854)e^{-0.03922 \times 1.25} = -\$1.686$ million
The value of the forward contract corresponding to the exchange of principals is
$(30 - 20 \times 1.7854)e^{-0.03922 \times 1.25} = -\$5.435$ million
The total value of the swap is $-\$1.855 - \$1.686 - \$5.435 = -\$8.976$ million.

Problem 7.6.
Explain the difference between the credit risk and the market risk in a financial contract.

Credit risk arises from the possibility of a default by the counterparty. Market risk arises from movements in market variables such as interest rates and exchange rates. A complication is that the credit risk in a swap is contingent on the values of market variables. A company's position in a swap has credit risk only when the value of the swap to the company is positive.

Problem 7.7.
A corporate treasurer tells you that he has just negotiated a five-year loan at a competitive fixed rate of interest of 5.2%. The treasurer explains that he achieved the 5.2% rate by borrowing at six-month LIBOR plus 150 basis points and swapping LIBOR for 3.7%. He goes on to say that this was possible because his company has a comparative advantage in the floating-rate market. What has the treasurer overlooked?

The rate is not truly fixed because, if the company's credit rating declines, it will not be able to roll over its floating rate borrowings at LIBOR plus 150 basis points. The effective fixed borrowing rate then increases. Suppose for example that the treasurer's spread over LIBOR increases from 150 basis points to 200 basis points. The borrowing rate increases from 5.2% to 5.7%.

Problem 7.8.
Explain why a bank is subject to credit risk when it enters into two offsetting swap contracts.

At the start of the swap, both contracts have a value of approximately zero. As time passes, it is likely that the swap values will change, so that one swap has a positive value to the bank and the other has a negative value to the bank. If the counterparty on the other side of the positive-value swap defaults, the bank still has to honor its contract with the other counterparty. It is liable to lose an amount equal to the positive value of the swap.

Problem 7.9.
Companies X and Y have been offered the following rates per annum on a $5 million 10-year investment:

	Fixed Rate	Floating Rate
Company X	8.0%	LIBOR
Company Y	8.8%	LIBOR

Company X requires a fixed-rate investment; company Y requires a floating-rate investment. Design a swap that will net a bank, acting as intermediary, 0.2% per annum and will appear equally attractive to X and Y.

The spread between the interest rates offered to X and Y is 0.8% per annum on fixed rate investments and 0.0% per annum on floating rate investments. This means that the total apparent benefit to all parties from the swap is 0.8% per annum. Of this 0.2% per annum will go to the bank. This leaves 0.3% per annum for each of X and Y. In other words, company X should be able to get a fixed-rate return of 8.3% per annum while company Y should be able to get a floating-rate return LIBOR + 0.3% per annum. The required swap is shown in Figure S7.3. The bank earns 0.2%, company X earns 8.3%, and company Y earns LIBOR + 0.3%.

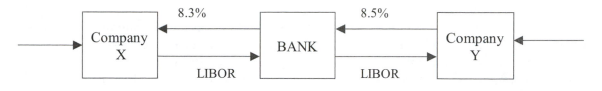

Figure S7.3 Swap for Problem 7.9

Problem 7.10.

A financial institution has entered into an interest rate swap with company X. Under the terms of the swap, it receives 10% per annum and pays six-month LIBOR on a principal of $10 million for five years. Payments are made every six months. Suppose that company X defaults on the sixth payment date (end of year 3) when the interest rate (with semiannual compounding) is 8% per annum for all maturities. What is the loss to the financial institution? Assume that six-month LIBOR was 9% per annum halfway through year 3.

At the end of year 3 the financial institution was due to receive $500,000 ($= 0.5 \times 10\%$ of $10 million) and pay $450,000 ($= 0.5 \times 9\%$ of $10 million). The immediate loss is therefore $50,000. To value the remaining swap we assume than forward rates are realized. All forward rates are 8% per annum. The remaining cash flows are therefore valued on the assumption that the floating payment is $0.5 \times 0.08 \times 10,000,000 = \$400,000$ and the net payment that would be received is $500,000 - 400,000 = \$100,000$. The total cost of default is therefore the cost of foregoing the following cash flows:

3 year:	$50,000
3.5 year:	$100,000
4 year:	$100,000
4.5 year:	$100,000
5 year:	$100,000

Discounting these cash flows to year 3 at 4% per six months we obtain the cost of the default as $413,000.

Problem 7.11.

Companies A and B face the following interest rates (adjusted for the differential impact of taxes):

	A	B
US dollars (floating rate)	LIBOR+0.5%	LIBOR+1.0%
Canadian dollars (fixed rate)	5.0%	6.5%

Assume that A wants to borrow U.S. dollars at a floating rate of interest and B wants to borrow Canadian dollars at a fixed rate of interest. A financial institution is planning to arrange a swap and requires a 50-basis-point spread. If the swap is equally attractive to A and B, what rates of interest will A and B end up paying?

Company A has a comparative advantage in the Canadian dollar fixed-rate market. Company B has a comparative advantage in the U.S. dollar floating-rate market. (This may be because of their tax positions.) However, company A wants to borrow in the U.S. dollar floating-rate market and company B wants to borrow in the Canadian dollar fixed-rate market. This gives rise to the swap opportunity.

The differential between the U.S. dollar floating rates is 0.5% per annum, and the differential between the Canadian dollar fixed rates is 1.5% per annum. The difference between the differentials is 1% per annum. The total potential gain to all parties from the swap is therefore 1% per annum, or 100 basis points. If the financial intermediary requires 50 basis points, each of A and B can be made 25 basis points better off. Thus a swap can be designed so that it provides A with U.S. dollars at LIBOR + 0.25% per annum, and B with Canadian dollars at 6.25% per annum. The swap is shown in Figure S7.4.

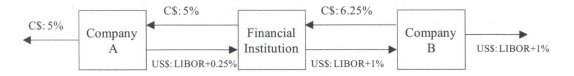

Figure S7.4   Swap for Problem 7.11

Principal payments flow in the opposite direction to the arrows at the start of the life of the swap and in the same direction as the arrows at the end of the life of the swap. The financial institution would be exposed to some foreign exchange risk which could be hedged using forward contracts.

Problem 7.12.

A financial institution has entered into a 10-year currency swap with company Y. Under the terms of the swap, the financial institution receives interest at 3% per annum in Swiss francs and pays interest at 8% per annum in U.S. dollars. Interest payments are exchanged once a year. The principal amounts are 7 million dollars and 10 million francs. Suppose that company Y declares bankruptcy at the end of year 6, when the exchange rate is $0.80 per franc. What is the cost to the financial institution? Assume that, at the end of year 6, the interest rate is 3% per annum in Swiss francs and 8% per annum in U.S. dollars for all maturities. All interest rates are quoted with annual compounding.

When interest rates are compounded annually

$$F_0 = S_0 \left(\frac{1+r}{1+r_f} \right)^T$$

where F_0 is the T-year forward rate, S_0 is the spot rate, r is the domestic risk-free rate, and r_f is the foreign risk-free rate. As $r = 0.08$ and $r_f = 0.03$, the spot and forward exchange rates at the end of year 6 are

Spot:	0.8000
1 year forward:	0.8388
2 year forward:	0.8796
3 year forward:	0.9223
4 year forward:	0.9670

The value of the swap at the time of the default can be calculated on the assumption that forward rates are realized. The cash flows lost as a result of the default are therefore as follows:

Year	Dollar Paid	CHF Received	Forward Rate	Dollar Equiv of CHF Received	Cash Flow Lost
6	560,000	300,000	0.8000	240,000	-320,000
7	560,000	300,000	0.8388	251,600	-308,400
8	560,000	300,000	0.8796	263,900	-296,100
9	560,000	300,000	0.9223	276,700	-283,300
10	7,560,000	10,300,000	0.9670	9,960,100	2,400,100

Discounting the numbers in the final column to the end of year 6 at 8% per annum, the cost of the default is $679,800.

Note that, if this were the only contract entered into by company Y, it would make no sense for the company to default at the end of year six as the exchange of payments at that time has a positive value to company Y. In practice, company Y is likely to be defaulting and declaring bankruptcy for reasons unrelated to this particular contract and payments on the contract are likely to stop when bankruptcy is declared.

Problem 7.13.

After it hedges its foreign exchange risk using forward contracts, is the financial institution's average spread in Figure 7.11 likely to be greater than or less than 20 basis points? Explain your answer.

The financial institution will have to buy 1.1% of the AUD principal in the forward market for each year of the life of the swap. Since AUD interest rates are higher than dollar interest rates, AUD is at a discount in forward markets. This means that the AUD purchased for year 2 is less expensive than that purchased for year 1; the AUD purchased for year 3 is less expensive than that purchased for year 2; and so on. This works in favor of the financial institution and means that its spread increases with time. The spread is always above 20 basis points.

Problem 7.14.

"Companies with high credit risks are the ones that cannot access fixed-rate markets directly. They are the companies that are most likely to be paying fixed and receiving floating in an interest rate swap." Assume that this statement is true. Do you think it increases or decreases the risk of a financial institution's swap portfolio? Assume that companies are most likely to default when interest rates are high.

Consider a plain-vanilla interest rate swap involving two companies X and Y. We suppose that X is paying fixed and receiving floating while Y is paying floating and receiving fixed. The quote suggests that company X will usually be less creditworthy than company Y. (Company X might be a BBB-rated company that has difficulty in accessing fixed-rate markets directly; company Y might be a AAA-rated company that has no difficulty accessing fixed or floating rate markets.) Presumably company X wants fixed-rate funds and company Y wants floating-rate funds.

The financial institution will realize a loss if company Y defaults when rates are high or if company X defaults when rates are low. These events are relatively unlikely since (a) Y is unlikely to default in any circumstances and (b) defaults are less likely to happen when rates are low. For the purposes of illustration, suppose that the probabilities of various events are as follows:

Default by Y: 0.001

Default by X:	0.010
Rates high when default occurs:	0.7
Rates low when default occurs:	0.3

The probability of a loss is
$$0.001 \times 0.7 + 0.010 \times 0.3 = 0.0037$$
If the roles of X and Y in the swap had been reversed the probability of a loss would be
$$0.001 \times 0.3 + 0.010 \times 0.7 = 0.0073$$
Assuming companies are more likely to default when interest rates are high, the above argument shows that the observation in quotes has the effect of decreasing the risk of a financial institution's swap portfolio. It is worth noting that the assumption that defaults are more likely when interest rates are high is open to question. The assumption is motivated by the thought that high interest rates often lead to financial difficulties for corporations. However, there is often a time lag between interest rates being high and the resultant default. When the default actually happens interest rates may be relatively low.

Problem 7.15.
Why is the expected loss from a default on a swap less than the expected loss from the default on a loan with the same principal?

In an interest-rate swap a financial institution's exposure depends on the difference between a fixed-rate of interest and a floating-rate of interest. It has no exposure to the notional principal. In a loan the whole principal can be lost.

Problem 7.16.
A bank finds that its assets are not matched with its liabilities. It is taking floating-rate deposits and making fixed-rate loans. How can swaps be used to offset the risk?

The bank is paying a floating-rate on the deposits and receiving a fixed-rate on the loans. It can offset its risk by entering into interest rate swaps (with other financial institutions or corporations) in which it contracts to pay fixed and receive floating.

Problem 7.17.
Explain how you would value a swap that is the exchange of a floating rate in one currency for a fixed rate in another currency.

The floating payments can be valued in currency A by (i) assuming that the forward rates are realized, and (ii) discounting the resulting cash flows at appropriate currency A discount rates. Suppose that the value is V_A. The fixed payments can be valued in currency B by discounting them at the appropriate currency B discount rates. Suppose that the value is V_B. If Q is the current exchange rate (number of units of currency A per unit of currency B), the value of the swap in currency A is $V_A - QV_B$. Alternatively, it is $V_A/Q - V_B$ in currency B.

Problem 7.18.
The LIBOR zero curve is flat at 5% (continuously compounded) out to 1.5 years. Swap rates for 2- and 3-year semiannual pay swaps are 5.4% and 5.6%, respectively. Estimate the LIBOR zero rates for maturities of 2.0, 2.5, and 3.0 years. (Assume that the 2.5-year swap rate is the average of the 2- and 3-year swap rates.)

The two-year swap rate is 5.4%. This means that a two-year LIBOR bond paying a semiannual coupon at the rate of 5.4% per annum sells for par. If R_2 is the two-year LIBOR zero rate

$$2.7e^{-0.05\times0.5} + 2.7e^{-0.05\times1.0} + 2.7e^{-0.05\times1.5} + 102.7e^{-R_2\times2.0} = 100$$

Solving this gives $R_2 = 0.05342$. The 2.5-year swap rate is assumed to be 5.5%. This means that a 2.5-year LIBOR bond paying a semiannual coupon at the rate of 5.5% per annum sells for par. If $R_{2.5}$ is the 2.5-year LIBOR zero rate

$$2.75e^{-0.05\times0.5} + 2.75e^{-0.05\times1.0} + 2.75e^{-0.05\times1.5} + 2.75e^{-0.05342\times2.0} + 102.75e^{-R_{2.5}\times2.5} = 100$$

Solving this gives $R_{2.5} = 0.05442$. The 3-year swap rate is 5.6%. This means that a 3-year LIBOR bond paying a semiannual coupon at the rate of 5.6% per annum sells for par. If R_3 is the three-year LIBOR zero rate

$$2.8e^{-0.05\times0.5} + 2.8e^{-0.05\times1.0} + 2.8e^{-0.05\times1.5} + 2.8e^{-0.05342\times2.0} + 2.8e^{-0.05442\times2.5}$$
$$+102.8e^{-R_3\times3.0} = 100$$

Solving this gives $R_3 = 0.05544$. The zero rates for maturities 2.0, 2.5, and 3.0 years are therefore 5.342%, 5.442%, and 5.544%, respectively.

Chapter 8
Securitization and the Credit Crisis of 2007

Problem 8.1
What was the role of GNMA (Ginnie Mae) in the mortgage-backed securities market of the 1970s?

GNMA guaranteed qualifying mortgages against default and created securities that were sold to investors.

Problem 8.2
Explain what is meant by a) an ABS and b) an ABS CDO.

An ABS is a set of tranches created from a portfolio of mortgages or other assets. An ABS CDO is an ABS created from particular tranches (e.g. the BBB tranches) of a number of different ABSs.

Problem 8.3
What is a mezzanine tranche?

The mezzanine tranche of an ABS or ABS CDO is a tranche that is in the middle as far as seniority goes. It is ranks below the senior tranches and therefore absorbs losses before they do. It ranks above the equity tranche (so that the equity tranche absorbs losses before it does).

Problem 8.4
What is the waterfall in a securitization?

The waterfall defines how the cash flows from the underlying assets are allocated to the tranches. In a typical arrangement, cash flows are first used to pay the senior tranches their promised return. The cash flows (if any) that are left over are used to provide the mezzanine tranches with their promised returns. The cash flows (if any) that are left over are then used to provide the equity tranches with their promised returns. Any residual cash flows are used to pay down the principal on the senior tranches.

Problem 8.5
What are the numbers in Table 8.1 for a loss rate of a) 12% and b) 15%?

Losses on underlying assets	Losses to mezzanine tranche of ABS	Losses to equity tranche of ABS CDO	Losses to mezzanine tranche of ABS CDO	Losses to senior tranche of ABS CDO
12%	46.7%	100%	100%	17.9%
15%	66.7%	100%	100%	48.7%

Problem 8.6
What is a subprime mortgage?

A subprime mortgage is a mortgage where the risk of default is higher than normal. This may be because the borrower has a poor credit history or the ratio of the loan to value is high or both.

Problem 8.7

Why do you think the increase in house prices during the 2000 to 2007 period is referred to as a bubble?

The increase in the price of houses was caused by unsustainable factors.

Problem 8.8.

Why did mortgage lenders frequently not check on information provided by potential borrowers on mortgage application forms during the 2000 to 2007 period?

Subprime mortgages were frequently securitized. The only information that was retained during the securitization process was the applicant's FICO score and the loan-to-value ratio of the mortgage.

Problem 8.9.

How were the risks in ABS CDOs misjudged by the market?

Investors underestimated how high the default correlations between mortgages would be in stressed market conditions. Investors also did not always realize that the tranches underlying ABS CDOs were usually quite thin so that they were either totally wiped out or untouched. There was an unfortunate tendency to assume that a tranche with a particular rating could be considered to be the same as a bond with that rating. This assumption is not valid for the reasons just mentioned.

Problem 8.10.

What is meant by the term "agency costs"? How did agency costs play a role in the credit crisis?

"Agency costs" is a term used to describe the costs in a situation where the interests of two parties are not perfectly aligned. There were potential agency costs between a) the originators of mortgages and investors and b) employees of banks who earned bonuses and the banks themselves.

Problem 8.11.

How is an ABS CDO created? What was the motivation to create ABS CDOs?

Typically an ABS CDO is created from the BBB-rated tranches of an ABS. This is because it is difficult to find investors in a direct way for the BBB-rated tranches of an ABS.

Problem 8.12.

Explain the impact of an increase in default correlation on the risks of the senior tranche of an ABS. What is its impact on the risks of the equity tranche?

As default correlation increases, the senior tranche of a CDO becomes more risky because it is more likely to suffer losses. It therefore becomes less valuable. As default correlation increases, the equity tranche becomes more valuable. To understand why this is so, note that in the limit when there is perfect correlation there is a high probability that there will be no defaults and the equity tranche will suffer no losses.

Problem 8.13.
Explain why the AAA-rated tranche of an ABS CDO is more risky than the AAA-rated tranche of an ABS.

A moderately high default rate will wipe out the tranches underlying the ABS CDO so that the AAA-rated tranche of the ABS CDO is also wiped out. A moderately high default rate will at worst wipe out only part of the AAA-rated tranche of an ABS.

Problem 8.14.
Explain why the end-of-year bonus is sometimes referred to as "short-term compensation."

The end-of-year bonus usually reflects performance during the year. This type of compensation tends to lead traders and other employees of banks to focus on their next bonus and therefore have a short-term time horizon for their decision making.

CHAPTER 9
Mechanics of Options Markets

Problem 9.1.
An investor buys a European put on a share for $3. The stock price is $42 and the strike price is $40. Under what circumstances does the investor make a profit? Under what circumstances will the option be exercised? Draw a diagram showing the variation of the investor's profit with the stock price at the maturity of the option.

The investor makes a profit if the price of the stock on the expiration date is less than $37. In these circumstances the gain from exercising the option is greater than $3. The option will be exercised if the stock price is less than $40 at the maturity of the option. The variation of the investor's profit with the stock price in Figure S9.1.

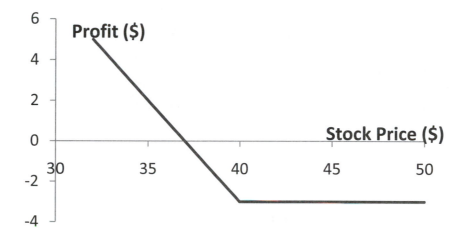

Figure S9.1   Investor's profit in Problem 9.1

Problem 9.2.
An investor sells a European call on a share for $4. The stock price is $47 and the strike price is $50. Under what circumstances does the investor make a profit? Under what circumstances will the option be exercised? Draw a diagram showing the variation of the investor's profit with the stock price at the maturity of the option.

The investor makes a profit if the price of the stock is below $54 on the expiration date. If the stock price is below $50, the option will not be exercised, and the investor makes a profit of $4. If the stock price is between $50 and $54, the option is exercised and the investor makes a profit between $0 and $4. The variation of the investor's profit with the stock price is as shown in Figure S9.2.

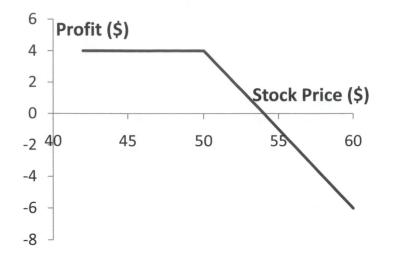

Figure S9.2   Investor's profit in Problem 9.2

Problem 9.3.
An investor sells a European call option with strike price of K and maturity T and buys a put with the same strike price and maturity. Describe the investor's position.

The payoff to the investor is
$$-\max\left(S_T-K,\,0\right)+\max\left(K-S_T,\,0\right)$$

This is $K-S_T$ in all circumstances. The investor's position is the same as a short position in a forward contract with delivery price K.

Problem 9.4.
Explain why margins are required when clients write options but not when they buy options.

When an investor buys an option, cash must be paid up front. There is no possibility of future liabilities and therefore no need for a margin account. When an investor sells an option, there are potential future liabilities. To protect against the risk of a default, margins are required.

Problem 9.5.
A stock option is on a February, May, August, and November cycle. What options trade on (a) April 1 and (b) May 30?

On April 1 options trade with expiration months of April, May, August, and November. On May 30 options trade with expiration months of June, July, August, and November.

Problem 9.6.
A company declares a 2-for-1 stock split. Explain how the terms change for a call option with a strike price of $60.

The strike price is reduced to $30, and the option gives the holder the right to purchase twice as many shares.

Problem 9.7.

"Employee stock options issued by a company are different from regular exchange-traded call options on the company's stock because they can affect the capital structure of the company." Explain this statement.

The exercise of employee stock options usually leads to new shares being issued by the company and sold to the employee. This changes the amount of equity in the capital structure. When a regular exchange-traded option is exercised no new shares are issued and the company's capital structure is not affected.

Problem 9.8.

A corporate treasurer is designing a hedging program involving foreign currency options. What are the pros and cons of using (a) the NASDAQ OMX and (b) the over-the-counter market for trading?

The NASDAQ OMX offers options with standard strike prices and times to maturity. Options in the over-the-counter market have the advantage that they can be tailored to meet the precise needs of the treasurer. Their disadvantage is that they expose the treasurer to some credit risk. Exchanges organize their trading so that there is virtually no credit risk.

Problem 9.9.

Suppose that a European call option to buy a share for $100.00 costs $5.00 and is held until maturity. Under what circumstances will the holder of the option make a profit? Under what circumstances will the option be exercised? Draw a diagram illustrating how the profit from a long position in the option depends on the stock price at maturity of the option.

Ignoring the time value of money, the holder of the option will make a profit if the stock price at maturity of the option is greater than $105. This is because the payoff to the holder of the option is, in these circumstances, greater than the $5 paid for the option. The option will be exercised if the stock price at maturity is greater than $100. Note that if the stock price is between $100 and $105 the option is exercised, but the holder of the option takes a loss overall. The profit from a long position is as shown in Figure S9.3.

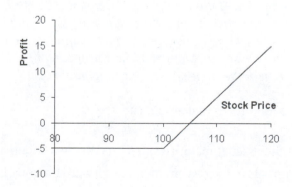

Figure S9.3   Profit from long position in Problem 9.9

Problem 9.10.

Suppose that a European put option to sell a share for $60 costs $8 and is held until maturity. Under what circumstances will the seller of the option (the party with the short position) make a profit? Under what circumstances will the option be exercised? Draw a diagram illustrating how the profit from a short position in the option depends on the stock price at maturity of the option.

Ignoring the time value of money, the seller of the option will make a profit if the stock price at maturity is greater than $52.00. This is because the cost to the seller of the option is in these circumstances less than the price received for the option. The option will be exercised if the stock price at maturity is less than $60.00. Note that if the stock price is between $52.00 and $60.00 the seller of the option makes a profit even though the option is exercised. The profit from the short position is as shown in Figure S9.4.

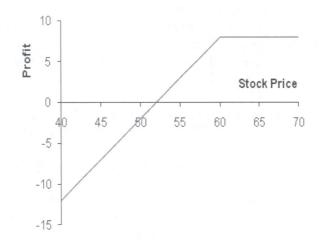

Figure S9.4   Profit from short position in Problem 9.10

Problem 9.11.

Describe the terminal value of the following portfolio: a newly entered-into long forward contract on an asset and a long position in a European put option on the asset with the same maturity as the forward contract and a strike price that is equal to the forward price of the asset at the time the portfolio is set up. Show that the European put option has the same value as a European call option with the same strike price and maturity.

The terminal value of the long forward contract is:

$$S_T - F_0$$

where S_T is the price of the asset at maturity and F_0 is the forward price of the asset at the time the portfolio is set up. (The delivery price in the forward contract is also F_0.)

The terminal value of the put option is:

$$\max (F_0 - S_T, 0)$$

The terminal value of the portfolio is therefore

$$S_T - F_0 + \max(F_0 - S_T, 0)$$
$$= \max(0, S_T - F_0]$$

This is the same as the terminal value of a European call option with the same maturity as the forward contract and an exercise price equal to F_0. This result is illustrated in the Figure S9.5.

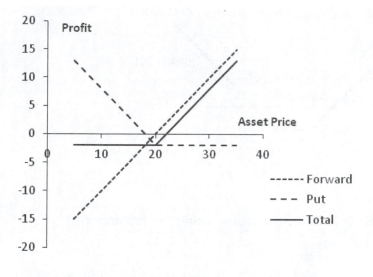

Figure S9.5   Profit from portfolio in Problem 9.11

We have shown that the forward contract plus the put is worth the same as a call with the same strike price and time to maturity as the put. The forward contract is worth zero at the time the portfolio is set up. It follows that the put is worth the same as the call at the time the portfolio is set up.

Problem 9.12.
A trader buys a call option with a strike price of $45 and a put option with a strike price of $40. Both options have the same maturity. The call costs $3 and the put costs $4. Draw a diagram showing the variation of the trader's profit with the asset price.

Figure S9.6 shows the variation of the trader's position with the asset price. We can divide the alternative asset prices into three ranges:

a) When the asset price less than $40, the put option provides a payoff of $40 - S_T$ and the call option provides no payoff. The options cost $7 and so the total profit is $33 - S_T$.

b) When the asset price is between $40 and $45, neither option provides a payoff. There is a net loss of $7.

c) When the asset price greater than $45, the call option provides a payoff of $S_T - 45$ and the put option provides no payoff. Taking into account the $7 cost of the options, the total profit is $S_T - 52$.

The trader makes a profit (ignoring the time value of money) if the stock price is less than $33 or greater than $52. This type of trading strategy is known as a strangle and is discussed in Chapter 11.

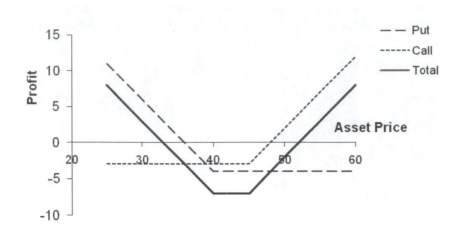

Figure S9.6   Profit from trading strategy in Problem 9.12

Problem 9.13.
Explain why an American option is always worth at least as much as a European option on the same asset with the same strike price and exercise date.

The holder of an American option has all the same rights as the holder of a European option and more. It must therefore be worth at least as much. If it were not, an arbitrageur could short the European option and take a long position in the American option.

Problem 9.14.
Explain why an American option is always worth at least as much as its intrinsic value.

The holder of an American option has the right to exercise it immediately. The American option must therefore be worth at least as much as its intrinsic value. If it were not an arbitrageur could lock in a sure profit by buying the option and exercising it immediately.

Problem 9.15.
Explain carefully the difference between writing a put option and buying a call option.

Writing a put gives a payoff of $\min(S_T - K, 0)$. Buying a call gives a payoff of $\max(S_T - K, 0)$. In both cases the potential payoff is $S_T - K$. The difference is that for a written put the counterparty chooses whether you get the payoff (and will allow you to get it only when it is negative to you). For a long call you decide whether you get the payoff (and you choose to get it when it is positive to you.)

Problem 9.16.
The treasurer of a corporation is trying to choose between options and forward contracts to hedge the corporation's foreign exchange risk. Discuss the advantages and disadvantages of each.

Forward contracts lock in the exchange rate that will apply to a particular transaction in the future. Options provide insurance that the exchange rate will not be worse than some level. The advantage of a forward contract is that uncertainty is eliminated as far as possible. The disadvantage is that the outcome with hedging can be significantly worse than the outcome with no hedging. This disadvantage is not as marked with options. However, unlike forward contracts, options involve an up-front cost.

Problem 9.17.
Consider an exchange-traded call option contract to buy 500 shares with a strike price of $40 and maturity in four months. Explain how the terms of the option contract change when there is
   a) *A 10% stock dividend*
   b) *A 10% cash dividend*
   c) *A 4-for-1 stock split*

a) The option contract becomes one to buy $500 \times 1.1 = 550$ shares with an exercise price $40/1.1 = 36.36$.
b) There is no effect. The terms of an options contract are not normally adjusted for cash dividends.
c) The option contract becomes one to buy $500 \times 4 = 2,000$ shares with an exercise price of $40/4 = \$10$.

Problem 9.18.
"If most of the call options on a stock are in the money, it is likely that the stock price has risen rapidly in the last few months." Discuss this statement.

The exchange has certain rules governing when trading in a new option is initiated. These mean that the option is close-to-the-money when it is first traded. If all call options are in the money it is therefore likely that the stock price has increased since trading in the option began.

Problem 9.19.
What is the effect of an unexpected cash dividend on (a) a call option price and (b) a put option price?

An unexpected cash dividend would reduce the stock price on the ex-dividend date. This stock price reduction would not be anticipated by option holders. As a result there would be a reduction in the value of a call option and an increase the value of a put option. (Note that the terms of an option are adjusted for cash dividends only in exceptional circumstances.)

Problem 9.20.
Options on General Motors stock are on a March, June, September, and December cycle. What options trade on (a) March 1, (b) June 30, and (c) August 5?

   a) March, April, June and September
   b) July, August, September, December
   c) August, September, December, March.
Longer dated options may also trade.

Problem 9.21.
Explain why the market maker's bid-offer spread represents a real cost to options investors.

A "fair" price for the option can reasonably be assumed to be half way between the bid and the offer price quoted by a market maker. An investor typically buys at the market maker's offer and sells at the market maker's bid. Each time he or she does this there is a hidden cost equal to half the bid-offer spread.

Problem 9.22.
A United States investor writes five naked call option contracts. The option price is $3.50, the strike price is $60.00, and the stock price is $57.00. What is the initial margin requirement?

The two calculations are necessary to determine the initial margin. The first gives
$$500 \times (3.5 + 0.2 \times 57 - 3) = 5,950$$
The second gives
$$500 \times (3.5 + 0.1 \times 57) = 4,600$$
The initial margin is the greater of these, or $5,950. Part of this can be provided by the initial amount of $500 \times 3.5 = \$1,750$ received for the options.

CHAPTER 10
Properties of Stock Options

Problem 10.1.
List the six factors affecting stock option prices.

The six factors affecting stock option prices are the stock price, strike price, risk-free interest rate, volatility, time to maturity, and dividends.

Problem 10.2.
What is a lower bound for the price of a four-month call option on a non-dividend-paying stock when the stock price is $28, the strike price is $25, and the risk-free interest rate is 8% per annum?

The lower bound is

$$28 - 25e^{-0.08 \times 0.3333} = \$3.66$$

Problem 10.3.
What is a lower bound for the price of a one-month European put option on a non-dividend-paying stock when the stock price is $12, the strike price is $15, and the risk-free interest rate is 6% per annum?

The lower bound is

$$15e^{-0.06 \times 0.08333} - 12 = \$2.93$$

Problem 10.4.
Give two reasons that the early exercise of an American call option on a non-dividend-paying stock is not optimal. The first reason should involve the time value of money. The second reason should apply even if interest rates are zero.

Delaying exercise delays the payment of the strike price. This means that the option holder is able to earn interest on the strike price for a longer period of time. Delaying exercise also provides insurance against the stock price falling below the strike price by the expiration date. Assume that the option holder has an amount of cash K and that interest rates are zero. When the option is exercised early it is worth S_T at expiration. Delaying exercise means that it will be worth $\max(K, S_T)$ at expiration.

Problem 10.5.
"The early exercise of an American put is a trade-off between the time value of money and the insurance value of a put." Explain this statement.

An American put when held in conjunction with the underlying stock provides insurance. It guarantees that the stock can be sold for the strike price, K. If the put is exercised early, the insurance ceases. However, the option holder receives the strike price immediately and is able to earn interest on it between the time of the early exercise and the expiration date.

Problem 10.6.

Why is an American call option on a dividend-paying stock is always worth at least as much as its intrinsic value. Is the same true of a European call option? Explain your answer.

An American call option can be exercised at any time. If it is exercised its holder gets the intrinsic value. It follows that an American call option must be worth at least its intrinsic value. A European call option can be worth less than its intrinsic value. Consider, for example, the situation where a stock is expected to provide a very high dividend during the life of an option. The price of the stock will decline as a result of the dividend. Because the European option can be exercised only after the dividend has been paid, its value may be less than the intrinsic value today.

Problem 10.7.

The price of a non-dividend paying stock is $19 and the price of a three-month European call option on the stock with a strike price of $20 is $1. The risk-free rate is 4% per annum. What is the price of a three-month European put option with a strike price of $20?

In this case, $c = 1$, $T = 0.25$, $S_0 = 19$, $K = 20$, and $r = 0.04$. From put–call parity

$$p = c + Ke^{-rT} - S_0$$

or

$$p = 1 + 20e^{-0.04 \times 0.25} - 19 = 1.80$$

so that the European put price is $1.80.

Problem 10.8.

Explain why the arguments leading to put–call parity for European options cannot be used to give a similar result for American options.

When early exercise is not possible, we can argue that two portfolios that are worth the same at time T must be worth the same at earlier times. When early exercise is possible, the argument falls down. Suppose that $P + S > C + Ke^{-rT}$. This situation does not lead to an arbitrage opportunity. If we buy the call, short the put, and short the stock, we cannot be sure of the result because we do not know when the put will be exercised.

Problem 10.9.

What is a lower bound for the price of a six-month call option on a non-dividend-paying stock when the stock price is $80, the strike price is $75, and the risk-free interest rate is 10% per annum?

The lower bound is

$$80 - 75e^{-0.1 \times 0.5} = \$8.66$$

Problem 10.10

What is a lower bound for the price of a two-month European put option on a non-dividend-paying stock when the stock price is $58, the strike price is $65, and the risk-free interest rate is 5% per annum?

The lower bound is

$$65e^{-0.05 \times 2/12} - 58 = \$6.46$$

Problem 10.11.

A four-month European call option on a dividend-paying stock is currently selling for $5. The stock price is $64, the strike price is $60, and a dividend of $0.80 is expected in one month. The risk-free interest rate is 12% per annum for all maturities. What opportunities are there for an arbitrageur?

The present value of the strike price is $60e^{-0.12\times4/12} = \$57.65$. The present value of the dividend is $0.80e^{-0.12\times1/12} = 0.79$. Because
$$5 < 64 - 57.65 - 0.79$$
the condition in equation (10.8) is violated. An arbitrageur should buy the option and short the stock. This generates $64 - 5 = \$59$. The arbitrageur invests $0.79 of this at 12% for one month to pay the dividend of $0.80 in one month. The remaining $58.21 is invested for four months at 12%. Regardless of what happens a profit will materialize.

If the stock price declines below $60 in four months, the arbitrageur loses the $5 spent on the option but gains on the short position. The arbitrageur shorts when the stock price is $64, has to pay dividends with a present value of $0.79, and closes out the short position when the stock price is $60 or less. Because $57.65 is the present value of $60, the short position generates at least $64 - 57.65 - 0.79 = \$5.56$ in present value terms. The present value of the arbitrageur's gain is therefore at least $5.56 - 5.00 = \$0.56$.

If the stock price is above $60 at the expiration of the option, the option is exercised. The arbitrageur buys the stock for $60 in four months and closes out the short position. The present value of the $60 paid for the stock is $57.65 and as before the dividend has a present value of $0.79. The gain from the short position and the exercise of the option is therefore exactly $64 - 57.65 - 0.79 = \$5.56$. The arbitrageur's gain in present value terms is exactly $5.56 - 5.00 = \$0.56$.

Problem 10.12.

A one-month European put option on a non-dividend-paying stock is currently selling for $2.50. The stock price is $47, the strike price is $50, and the risk-free interest rate is 6% per annum. What opportunities are there for an arbitrageur?

In this case the present value of the strike price is $50e^{-0.06\times1/12} = 49.75$. Because
$$2.5 < 49.75 - 47.00$$
the condition in equation (10.5) is violated. An arbitrageur should borrow $49.50 at 6% for one month, buy the stock, and buy the put option. This generates a profit in all circumstances. If the stock price is above $50 in one month, the option expires worthless, but the stock can be sold for at least $50. A sum of $50 received in one month has a present value of $49.75 today. The strategy therefore generates profit with a present value of at least $0.25.

If the stock price is below $50 in one month the put option is exercised and the stock owned is sold for exactly $50 (or $49.75 in present value terms). The trading strategy therefore generates a profit of exactly $0.25 in present value terms.

Problem 10.13.

Give an intuitive explanation of why the early exercise of an American put becomes more attractive as the risk-free rate increases and volatility decreases.

The early exercise of an American put is attractive when the interest earned on the strike price is greater than the insurance element lost. When interest rates increase, the value of the interest earned on the strike price increases making early exercise more attractive. When volatility decreases, the insurance element is less valuable. Again this makes early exercise more attractive.

Problem 10.14.

The price of a European call that expires in six months and has a strike price of $30 is $2. The underlying stock price is $29, and a dividend of $0.50 is expected in two months and again in five months. The term structure is flat, with all risk-free interest rates being 10%. What is the price of a European put option that expires in six months and has a strike price of $30?

Using the notation in the chapter, put-call parity [equation (10.10)] gives
$$c + Ke^{-rT} + D = p + S_0$$
or
$$p = c + Ke^{-rT} + D - S_0$$
In this case
$$p = 2 + 30e^{-0.1\times6/12} + (0.5e^{-0.1\times2/12} + 0.5e^{-0.1\times5/12}) - 29 = 2.51$$
In other words the put price is $2.51.

Problem 10.15.

Explain the arbitrage opportunities in Problem 10.14 if the European put price is $3.

If the put price is $3.00, it is too high relative to the call price. An arbitrageur should buy the call, short the put and short the stock. This generates $-2 + 3 + 29 = \$30$ in cash which is invested at 10%. Regardless of what happens a profit with a present value of $3.00 - 2.51 = \$0.49$ is locked in.

If the stock price is above $30 in six months, the call option is exercised, and the put option expires worthless. The call option enables the stock to be bought for $30, or $30e^{-0.10\times6/12} = \$28.54$ in present value terms. The dividends on the short position cost $0.5e^{-0.1\times2/12} + 0.5e^{-0.1\times5/12} = \$0.97$ in present value terms so that there is a profit with a present value of $30 - 28.54 - 0.97 = \$0.49$.

If the stock price is below $30 in six months, the put option is exercised and the call option expires worthless. The short put option leads to the stock being bought for $30, or $30e^{-0.10\times6/12} = \$28.54$ in present value terms. The dividends on the short position cost $0.5e^{-0.1\times2/12} + 0.5e^{-0.1\times5/12} = \$0.97$ in present value terms so that there is a profit with a present value of $30 - 28.54 - 0.97 = \$0.49$.

Problem 10.16.

The price of an American call on a non-dividend-paying stock is $4. The stock price is $31, the strike price is $30, and the expiration date is in three months. The risk-free interest rate is 8%. Derive upper and lower bounds for the price of an American put on the same stock with the same strike price and expiration date.

From equation (10.7)
$$S_0 - K \le C - P \le S_0 - Ke^{-rT}$$
In this case
$$31 - 30 \le 4 - P \le 31 - 30e^{-0.08\times0.25}$$
or
$$1.00 \le 4.00 - P \le 1.59$$

or
$$2.41 \le P \le 3.00$$
Upper and lower bounds for the price of an American put are therefore $2.41 and $3.00.

Problem 10.17.
Explain carefully the arbitrage opportunities in Problem 10.16 if the American put price is greater than the calculated upper bound.

If the American put price is greater than $3.00 an arbitrageur can sell the American put, short the stock, and buy the American call. This realizes at least $3 + 31 - 4 = \$30$ which can be invested at the risk-free interest rate. At some stage during the 3-month period either the American put or the American call will be exercised. The arbitrageur then pays $30, receives the stock and closes out the short position. The cash flows to the arbitrageur are $+\$30$ at time zero and $-\$30$ at some future time. These cash flows have a positive present value.

Problem 10.18.
Prove the result in equation (10.7). (Hint: For the first part of the relationship consider (a) a portfolio consisting of a European call plus an amount of cash equal to K and (b) a portfolio consisting of an American put option plus one share.)

As in the text we use c and p to denote the European call and put option price, and C and P to denote the American call and put option prices. Because $P \ge p$, it follows from put–call parity that
$$P \ge c + Ke^{-rT} - S_0$$
and since $c = C$,
$$P \ge C + Ke^{-rT} - S_0$$
or
$$C - P \le S_0 - Ke^{-rT}$$

For a further relationship between C and P, consider
Portfolio I: One European call option plus an amount of cash equal to K.
Portfolio J: One American put option plus one share.
Both options have the same exercise price and expiration date. Assume that the cash in portfolio I is invested at the risk-free interest rate. If the put option is not exercised early portfolio J is worth
$$\max(S_T, K)$$
at time T. Portfolio I is worth
$$\max(S_T - K, 0) + Ke^{rT} = \max(S_T, K) - K + Ke^{rT}$$
at this time. Portfolio I is therefore worth more than portfolio J. Suppose next that the put option in portfolio J is exercised early, say, at time τ. This means that portfolio J is worth K at time τ. However, even if the call option were worthless, portfolio I would be worth $Ke^{r\tau}$ at time τ. It follows that portfolio I is worth at least as much as portfolio J in all circumstances. Hence
$$c + K \ge P + S_0$$
Since $c = C$,
$$C + K \ge P + S_0$$
or

$$C - P \geq S_0 - K$$

Combining this with the other inequality derived above for $C - P$, we obtain

$$S_0 - K \leq C - P \leq S_0 - Ke^{-rT}$$

Problem 10.19.
Prove the result in equation (10.11). (Hint: For the first part of the relationship consider (a) a portfolio consisting of a European call plus an amount of cash equal to $D + K$ and (b) a portfolio consisting of an American put option plus one share.)

As in the text we use c and p to denote the European call and put option price, and C and P to denote the American call and put option prices. The present value of the dividends will be denoted by D. As shown in the answer to Problem 10.18, when there are no dividends

$$C - P \leq S_0 - Ke^{-rT}$$

Dividends reduce C and increase P. Hence this relationship must also be true when there are dividends.

For a further relationship between C and P, consider

Portfolio I: one European call option plus an amount of cash equal to $D + K$

Portfolio J: one American put option plus one share

Both options have the same exercise price and expiration date. Assume that the cash in portfolio I is invested at the risk-free interest rate. If the put option is not exercised early, portfolio J is worth

$$\max(S_T, K) + De^{rT}$$

at time T. Portfolio I is worth

$$\max(S_T - K, 0) + (D + K)e^{rT} = \max(S_T, K) + De^{rT} + Ke^{rT} - K$$

at this time. Portfolio I is therefore worth more than portfolio J. Suppose next that the put option in portfolio J is exercised early, say, at time τ. This means that portfolio J is worth at most $K + De^{r\tau}$ at time τ. However, even if the call option were worthless, portfolio I would be worth $(D + K)e^{r\tau}$ at time τ. It follows that portfolio I is worth more than portfolio J in all circumstances. Hence

$$c + D + K \geq P + S_0$$

Because $C \geq c$

$$C - P \geq S_0 - D - K$$

Problem 10.20.
Consider a five-year call option on a non-dividend-paying stock granted to employees. The option can be exercised at any time after the end of the first year. Unlike a regular exchange-traded call option, the employee stock option cannot be sold. What is the likely impact of this restriction on early exercise?

An employee stock option may be exercised early because the employee needs cash or because he or she is uncertain about the company's future prospects. Regular call options can be sold in the market in either of these two situations, but employee stock options cannot be sold. In theory an employee can short the company's stock as an alternative to exercising. In practice this is not usually encouraged and may even be illegal for senior managers.

Problem 10.21.
Use the software DerivaGem to verify that Figures 10.1 and 10.2 are correct.

70

The graphs can be produced from the first worksheet in DerivaGem. Select Equity as the Underlying Type. Select Black-Scholes as the Option Type. Input stock price as 50, volatility as 30%, risk-free rate as 5%, time to exercise as 1 year, and exercise price as 50. Leave the dividend table blank because we are assuming no dividends. Select the button corresponding to call. Do not select the implied volatility button. Hit the *Enter* key and click on calculate. DerivaGem will show the price of the option as 7.15562248. Move to the Graph Results on the right hand side of the worksheet. Enter Option Price for the vertical axis and Asset price for the horizontal axis. Choose the minimum strike price value as 10 (software will not accept 0) and the maximum strike price value as 100. Hit *Enter* and click on *Draw Graph*. This will produce Figure 10.1a. Figures 10.1c, 10.1e, 10.2a, and 10.2c can be produced similarly by changing the horizontal axis. By selecting put instead of call and recalculating the rest of the figures can be produced. You are encouraged to experiment with this worksheet. Try different parameter values and different types of options.

CHAPTER 11
Trading Strategies Involving Options

Problem 11.1.
What is meant by a protective put? What position in call options is equivalent to a protective put?

A protective put consists of a long position in a put option combined with a long position in the underlying shares. It is equivalent to a long position in a call option plus a certain amount of cash. This follows from put–call parity:

$$p + S_0 = c + Ke^{-rT} + D$$

Problem 11.2.
Explain two ways in which a bear spread can be created.

A bear spread can be created using two call options with the same maturity and different strike prices. The investor shorts the call option with the lower strike price and buys the call option with the higher strike price. A bear spread can also be created using two put options with the same maturity and different strike prices. In this case, the investor shorts the put option with the lower strike price and buys the put option with the higher strike price.

Problem 11.3.
When is it appropriate for an investor to purchase a butterfly spread?

A butterfly spread involves a position in options with three different strike prices (K_1, K_2, and K_3). A butterfly spread should be purchased when the investor considers that the price of the underlying stock is likely to stay close to the central strike price, K_2.

Problem 11.4.
Call options on a stock are available with strike prices of $15, $17\frac{1}{2}$, and $20 and expiration dates in three months. Their prices are $4, $2, and $\frac{1}{2}$, respectively. Explain how the options can be used to create a butterfly spread. Construct a table showing how profit varies with stock price for the butterfly spread.

An investor can create a butterfly spread by buying call options with strike prices of $15 and $20 and selling two call options with strike prices of $17\frac{1}{2}$. The initial investment is $4 + \frac{1}{2} - 2 \times 2 = \$\frac{1}{2}$. The following table shows the variation of profit with the final stock price:

Stock Price, S_T	Profit
$S_T < 15$	$-\frac{1}{2}$
$15 < S_T < 17\frac{1}{2}$	$(S_T - 15) - \frac{1}{2}$
$17\frac{1}{2} < S_T < 20$	$(20 - S_T) - \frac{1}{2}$
$S_T > 20$	$-\frac{1}{2}$

Problem 11.5.
What trading strategy creates a reverse calendar spread?

A reverse calendar spread is created by buying a short-maturity option and selling a long-maturity option, both with the same strike price.

Problem 11.6.
What is the difference between a strangle and a straddle?

Both a straddle and a strangle are created by combining a long position in a call with a long position in a put. In a straddle the two have the same strike price and expiration date. In a strangle they have different strike prices and the same expiration date.

Problem 11.7.
A call option with a strike price of $50 costs $2. A put option with a strike price of $45 costs $3. Explain how a strangle can be created from these two options. What is the pattern of profits from the strangle?

A strangle is created by buying both options. The pattern of profits is as follows:

Stock Price, S_T	Profit
$S_T < 45$	$(45 - S_T) - 5$
$45 < S_T < 50$	-5
$S_T > 50$	$(S_T - 50) - 5$

Problem 11.8.
Use put–call parity to relate the initial investment for a bull spread created using calls to the initial investment for a bull spread created using puts.

A bull spread using calls provides a profit pattern with the same general shape as a bull spread using puts (see Figures 11.2 and 11.3 in the text). Define p_1 and c_1 as the prices of put and call with strike price K_1 and p_2 and c_2 as the prices of a put and call with strike price K_2. From put-call parity

$$p_1 + S = c_1 + K_1 e^{-rT}$$

$$p_2 + S = c_2 + K_2 e^{-rT}$$

Hence:

$$p_1 - p_2 = c_1 - c_2 - (K_2 - K_1)e^{-rT}$$

This shows that the initial investment when the spread is created from puts is less than the initial investment when it is created from calls by an amount $(K_2 - K_1)e^{-rT}$. In fact as mentioned in the text the initial investment when the bull spread is created from puts is negative, while the initial investment when it is created from calls is positive.
The profit when calls are used to create the bull spread is higher than when puts are used by

$(K_2 - K_1)(1 - e^{-rT})$. This reflects the fact that the call strategy involves an additional risk-free investment of $(K_2 - K_1)e^{-rT}$ over the put strategy. This earns interest of
$(K_2 - K_1)e^{-rT}(e^{rT} - 1) = (K_2 - K_1)(1 - e^{-rT})$.

Problem 11.9.
Explain how an aggressive bear spread can be created using put options.

An aggressive bull spread using call options is discussed in the text. Both of the options used have relatively high strike prices. Similarly, an aggressive bear spread can be created using put options. Both of the options should be out of the money (that is, they should have relatively low strike prices). The spread then costs very little to set up because both of the puts are worth close to zero. In most circumstances the spread will provide zero payoff. However, there is a small chance that the stock price will fall fast so that on expiration both options will be in the money. The spread then provides a payoff equal to the difference between the two strike prices, $K_2 - K_1$.

Problem 11.10.
Suppose that put options on a stock with strike prices $30 and $35 cost $4 and $7, respectively. How can the options be used to create (a) a bull spread and (b) a bear spread? Construct a table that shows the profit and payoff for both spreads.

A bull spread is created by buying the $30 put and selling the $35 put. This strategy gives rise to an initial cash inflow of $3. The outcome is as follows:

Stock Price	Payoff	Profit
$S_T \geq 35$	0	3
$30 \leq S_T < 35$	$S_T - 35$	$S_T - 32$
$S_T < 30$	-5	-2

A bear spread is created by selling the $30 put and buying the $35 put. This strategy costs $3 initially. The outcome is as follows:

Stock Price	Payoff	Profit
$S_T \geq 35$	0	-3
$30 \leq S_T < 35$	$35 - S_T$	$32 - S_T$
$S_T < 30$	5	2

Problem 11.11.
Use put–call parity to show that the cost of a butterfly spread created from European puts is identical to the cost of a butterfly spread created from European calls.

Define c_1, c_2, and c_3 as the prices of calls with strike prices K_1, K_2 and K_3. Define p_1, p_2 and p_3 as the prices of puts with strike prices K_1, K_2 and K_3. With the usual notation

$$c_1 + K_1 e^{-rT} = p_1 + S$$

$$c_2 + K_2 e^{-rT} = p_2 + S$$

$$c_3 + K_3 e^{-rT} = p_3 + S$$

Hence

$$c_1 + c_3 - 2c_2 + (K_1 + K_3 - 2K_2)e^{-rT} = p_1 + p_3 - 2p_2$$

Because $K_2 - K_1 = K_3 - K_2$, it follows that $K_1 + K_3 - 2K_2 = 0$ and

$$c_1 + c_3 - 2c_2 = p_1 + p_3 - 2p_2$$

The cost of a butterfly spread created using European calls is therefore exactly the same as the cost of a butterfly spread created using European puts.

Problem 11.12.

A call with a strike price of $60 costs $6. A put with the same strike price and expiration date costs $4. Construct a table that shows the profit from a straddle. For what range of stock prices would the straddle lead to a loss?

A straddle is created by buying both the call and the put. This strategy costs $10. The profit/loss is shown in the following table:

Stock Price	Payoff	Profit
$S_T > 60$	$S_T - 60$	$S_T - 70$
$S_T \leq 60$	$60 - S_T$	$50 - S_T$

This shows that the straddle will lead to a loss if the final stock price is between $50 and $70.

Problem 11.13.

Construct a table showing the payoff from a bull spread when puts with strike prices K_1 and K_2 are used $(K_2 > K_1)$.

The bull spread is created by buying a put with strike price K_1 and selling a put with strike price K_2. The payoff is calculated as follows:

Stock Price	Payoff from Long Put	Payoff from Short Put	Total Payoff
$S_T \geq K_2$	0	0	0
$K_1 < S_T < K_2$	0	$S_T - K_2$	$-(K_2 - S_T)$
$S_T \leq K_1$	$K_1 - S_T$	$S_T - K_2$	$-(K_2 - K_1)$

Problem 11.14.

An investor believes that there will be a big jump in a stock price, but is uncertain as to the direction. Identify six different strategies the investor can follow and explain the differences among them.

Possible strategies are:
    Strangle
    Straddle

Strip
Strap
Reverse calendar spread
Reverse butterfly spread

The strategies all provide positive profits when there are large stock price moves. A strangle is less expensive than a straddle, but requires a bigger move in the stock price in order to provide a positive profit. Strips and straps are more expensive than straddles but provide bigger profits in certain circumstances. A strip will provide a bigger profit when there is a large downward stock price move. A strap will provide a bigger profit when there is a large upward stock price move. In the case of strangles, straddles, strips and straps, the profit increases as the size of the stock price movement increases. By contrast in a reverse calendar spread and a reverse butterfly spread there is a maximum potential profit regardless of the size of the stock price movement.

Problem 11.15.
How can a forward contract on a stock with a particular delivery price and delivery date be created from options?

Suppose that the delivery price is K and the delivery date is T. The forward contract is created by buying a European call and selling a European put when both options have strike price K and exercise date T. This portfolio provides a payoff of $S_T - K$ under all circumstances where S_T is the stock price at time T. Suppose that F_0 is the forward price. If $K = F_0$, the forward contract that is created has zero value. This shows that the price of a call equals the price of a put when the strike price is F_0.

Problem 11.16.
"A box spread comprises four options. Two can be combined to create a long forward position and two can be combined to create a short forward position." Explain this statement.

A box spread is a bull spread created using calls and a bear spread created using puts. With the notation in the text it consists of a) a long call with strike K_1, b) a short call with strike K_2, c) a long put with strike K_2, and d) a short put with strike K_1. a) and d) give a long forward contract with delivery price K_1; b) and c) give a short forward contract with delivery price K_2. The two forward contracts taken together give the payoff of $K_2 - K_1$.

Problem 11.17.
What is the result if the strike price of the put is higher than the strike price of the call in a strangle?

The result is shown in Figure S11.1. The profit pattern from a long position in a call and a put when the put has a higher strike price than a call is much the same as when the call has a higher strike price than the put. Both the initial investment and the final payoff are much higher in the first case

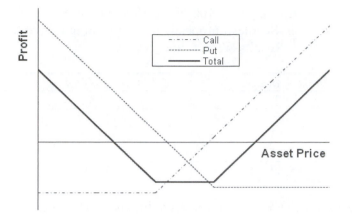

Figure S11.1 Profit Pattern in Problem 11.17

Problem 11.18.

One Australian dollar is currently worth $0.64. A one-year butterfly spread is set up using European call options with strike prices of $0.60, $0.65, and $0.70. The risk-free interest rates in the United States and Australia are 5% and 4% respectively, and the volatility of the exchange rate is 15%. Use the DerivaGem software to calculate the cost of setting up the butterfly spread position. Show that the cost is the same if European put options are used instead of European call options.

To use DerivaGem select the first worksheet and choose Currency as the Underlying Type. Select Black--Scholes European as the Option Type. Input exchange rate as 0.64, volatility as 15%, risk-free rate as 5%, foreign risk-free interest rate as 4%, time to exercise as 1 year, and exercise price as 0.60. Select the button corresponding to call. Do not select the implied volatility button. Hit the Enter key and click on calculate. DerivaGem will show the price of the option as 0.0618. Change the exercise price to 0.65, hit Enter, and click on calculate again. DerivaGem will show the value of the option as 0.0352. Change the exercise price to 0.70, hit Enter, and click on calculate. DerivaGem will show the value of the option as 0.0181.

Now select the button corresponding to put and repeat the procedure. DerivaGem shows the values of puts with strike prices 0.60, 0.65, and 0.70 to be 0.0176, 0.0386, and 0.0690, respectively.

The cost of setting up the butterfly spread when calls are used is therefore
$$0.0618 + 0.0181 - 2 \times 0.0352 = 0.0095$$
The cost of setting up the butterfly spread when puts are used is
$$0.0176 + 0.0690 - 2 \times 0.0386 = 0.0094$$
Allowing for rounding errors these two are the same.

Problem 11.19

An index provides a dividend yield of 1% and has a volatility of 20%. The risk-free interest rate is 4%. How long does a principal-protected note, created as in Example 11.1, have to last for it to be profitable to the bank? Use DerivaGem.

Assume that the investment in the index is initially $100. (This is a scaling factor that makes no difference to the result.) DerivaGem can be used to value an option on the index with the index level equal to 100, the volatility equal to 20%, the risk-free rate equal to 4%, the dividend yield equal to 1%, and the exercise price equal to 100. For different times to maturity, T, we value a call option (using Black-Scholes European) and the amount available to buy the call option, which is $100-100e^{-0.04 \times T}$. Results are as follows:

Time to maturity, T	Funds Available	Value of Option
1	3.92	9.32
2	7.69	13.79
5	18.13	23.40
10	32.97	33.34
11	35.60	34.91

This table shows that the answer is between 10 and 11 years. Continuing the calculations we find that if the life of the principal-protected note is 10.35 year or more, it is profitable for the bank. (Excel's Solver can be used in conjunction with the DerivaGem functions to facilitate calculations.)

CHAPTER 12
Binomial Trees

Problem 12.1.
A stock price is currently $40. It is known that at the end of one month it will be either $42 or $38. The risk-free interest rate is 8% per annum with continuous compounding. What is the value of a one-month European call option with a strike price of $39?

Consider a portfolio consisting of
-1: Call option
$+\Delta$: Shares
If the stock price rises to $42, the portfolio is worth $42\Delta - 3$. If the stock price falls to $38, it is worth 38Δ. These are the same when
$$42\Delta - 3 = 38\Delta$$
or $\Delta = 0.75$. The value of the portfolio in one month is 28.5 for both stock prices. Its value today must be the present value of 28.5, or $28.5e^{-0.08\times0.08333} = 28.31$. This means that
$$-f + 40\Delta = 28.31$$
where f is the call price. Because $\Delta = 0.75$, the call price is $40 \times 0.75 - 28.31 = \$1.69$. As an alternative approach, we can calculate the probability, p, of an up movement in a risk-neutral world. This must satisfy:
$$42p + 38(1-p) = 40e^{0.08\times0.08333}$$
so that
$$4p = 40e^{0.08\times0.08333} - 38$$
or $p = 0.5669$. The value of the option is then its expected payoff discounted at the risk-free rate:
$$[3\times0.5669 + 0\times0.4331]e^{-0.08\times0.08333} = 1.69$$
or $1.69. This agrees with the previous calculation.

Problem 12.2.
Explain the no-arbitrage and risk-neutral valuation approaches to valuing a European option using a one-step binomial tree.

In the no-arbitrage approach, we set up a riskless portfolio consisting of a position in the option and a position in the stock. By setting the return on the portfolio equal to the risk-free interest rate, we are able to value the option. When we use risk-neutral valuation, we first choose probabilities for the branches of the tree so that the expected return on the stock equals the risk-free interest rate. We then value the option by calculating its expected payoff and discounting this expected payoff at the risk-free interest rate.

Problem 12.3.
What is meant by the delta of a stock option?

The delta of a stock option measures the sensitivity of the option price to the price of the stock when small changes are considered. Specifically, it is the ratio of the change in the price of the stock option to the change in the price of the underlying stock.

Problem 12.4.

A stock price is currently $50. It is known that at the end of six months it will be either $45 or $55. The risk-free interest rate is 10% per annum with continuous compounding. What is the value of a six-month European put option with a strike price of $50?

Consider a portfolio consisting of
-1: Put option
$+\Delta$: Shares
If the stock price rises to $55, this is worth 55Δ. If the stock price falls to $45, the portfolio is worth $45\Delta - 5$. These are the same when
$$45\Delta - 5 = 55\Delta$$
or $\Delta = -0.50$. The value of the portfolio in six months is -27.5 for both stock prices. Its value today must be the present value of -27.5, or $-27.5e^{-0.1\times0.5} = -26.16$. This means that
$$-f + 50\Delta = -26.16$$
where f is the put price. Because $\Delta = -0.50$, the put price is $1.16. As an alternative approach we can calculate the probability, p, of an up movement in a risk-neutral world. This must satisfy:
$$55p + 45(1-p) = 50e^{0.1\times0.5}$$
so that
$$10p = 50e^{0.1\times0.5} - 45$$
or $p = 0.7564$. The value of the option is then its expected payoff discounted at the risk-free rate:
$$[0 \times 0.7564 + 5 \times 0.2436]e^{-0.1\times0.5} = 1.16$$
or $1.16. This agrees with the previous calculation.

Problem 12.5.

A stock price is currently $100. Over each of the next two six-month periods it is expected to go up by 10% or down by 10%. The risk-free interest rate is 8% per annum with continuous compounding. What is the value of a one-year European call option with a strike price of $100?

In this case $u = 1.10$, $d = 0.90$, $\Delta t = 0.5$, and $r = 0.08$, so that
$$p = \frac{e^{0.08\times0.5} - 0.90}{1.10 - 0.90} = 0.7041$$
The tree for stock price movements is shown in Figure S12.1. We can work back from the end of the tree to the beginning, as indicated in the diagram, to give the value of the option as $9.61. The option value can also be calculated directly from equation (12.10):
$$[0.7041^2 \times 21 + 2 \times 0.7041 \times 0.2959 \times 0 + 0.2959^2 \times 0]e^{-2\times0.08\times0.5} = 9.61$$
or $9.61.

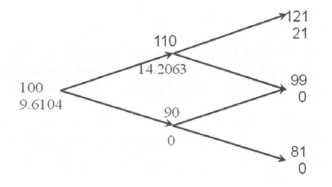

Figure S12.1   Tree for Problem 12.5

Problem 12.6.

For the situation considered in Problem 12.5, what is the value of a one-year European put option with a strike price of $100? Verify that the European call and European put prices satisfy put–call parity.

Figure S12.2 shows how we can value the put option using the same tree as in Problem 12.5. The value of the option is $1.92. The option value can also be calculated directly from equation (12.10):

$$e^{-2\times0.08\times0.5}[0.7041^2\times0+2\times0.7041\times0.2959\times1+0.2959^2\times19]=1.92$$

or $1.92. The stock price plus the put price is $100+1.92 = \$101.92$. The present value of the strike price plus the call price is $100e^{-0.08\times1}+9.61 = \$101.92$. These are the same, verifying that put–call parity holds.

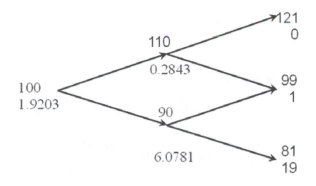

Figure S12.2   Tree for Problem 12.6

Problem 12.7.

What are the formulas for u and d in terms of volatility?

$u = e^{\sigma\sqrt{\Delta t}}$ and $d = e^{-\sigma\sqrt{\Delta t}}$

Problem 12.8.

Consider the situation in which stock price movements during the life of a European option are governed by a two-step binomial tree. Explain why it is not possible to set up a position in the stock and the option that remains riskless for the whole of the life of the option.

The riskless portfolio consists of a short position in the option and a long position in Δ shares. Because Δ changes during the life of the option, this riskless portfolio must also change.

Problem 12.9.

A stock price is currently $50. It is known that at the end of two months it will be either $53 or $48. The risk-free interest rate is 10% per annum with continuous compounding. What is the value of a two-month European call option with a strikeprice of $49? Use no-arbitrage arguments.

At the end of two months the value of the option will be either $4 (if the stock price is $53) or $0 (if the stock price is $48). Consider a portfolio consisting of:

$$+\Delta \quad : \quad \text{shares}$$

$$-1 \quad : \quad \text{option}$$

The value of the portfolio is either 48Δ or $53\Delta - 4$ in two months. If

$$48\Delta = 53\Delta - 4$$

i.e.,

$$\Delta = 0.8$$

the value of the portfolio is certain to be 38.4. For this value of Δ the portfolio is therefore riskless. The current value of the portfolio is:

$$0.8 \times 50 - f$$

where f is the value of the option. Since the portfolio must earn the risk-free rate of interest

$$(0.8 \times 50 - f)e^{0.10 \times 2/12} = 38.4$$

i.e.,

$$f = 2.23$$

The value of the option is therefore $2.23.

This can also be calculated directly from equations (12.2) and (12.3). $u = 1.06$, $d = 0.96$ so that

$$p = \frac{e^{0.10 \times 2/12} - 0.96}{1.06 - 0.96} = 0.5681$$

and

$$f = e^{-0.10 \times 2/12} \times 0.5681 \times 4 = 2.23$$

Problem 12.10.

A stock price is currently $80. It is known that at the end of four months it will be either $75 or $85. The risk-free interest rate is 5% per annum with continuous compounding. What is the value of a four-month European put option with a strike price of $80? Use no-arbitrage arguments.

At the end of four months the value of the option will be either $5 (if the stock price is $75) or $0 (if the stock price is $85). Consider a portfolio consisting of:

$$-\Delta \quad : \quad \text{shares}$$

$$+1 \quad : \quad \text{option}$$

(Note: The delta, Δ of a put option is negative. We have constructed the portfolio so that it is $+1$ option and $-\Delta$ shares rather than -1 option and $+\Delta$ shares so that the initial investment is positive.)

The value of the portfolio is either -85Δ or $-75\Delta + 5$ in four months. If

$$-85\Delta = -75\Delta + 5$$

i.e.,

$$\Delta = -0.5$$

the value of the portfolio is certain to be 42.5. For this value of Δ the portfolio is therefore riskless. The current value of the portfolio is:

$$0.5 \times 80 + f$$

where f is the value of the option. Since the portfolio is riskless

$$(0.5 \times 80 + f)e^{0.05 \times 4/12} = 42.5$$

i.e.,

$$f = 1.80$$

The value of the option is therefore $1.80.

This can also be calculated directly from equations (12.2) and (12.3). $u = 1.0625$, $d = 0.9375$ so that

$$p = \frac{e^{0.05 \times 4/12} - 0.9375}{1.0625 - 0.9375} = 0.6345$$

$1 - p = 0.3655$ and

$$f = e^{-0.05 \times 4/12} \times 0.3655 \times 5 = 1.80$$

Problem 12.11.
A stock price is currently $40. It is known that at the end of three months it will be either $45 or $35. The risk-free rate of interest with quarterly compounding is 8% per annum. Calculate the value of a three-month European put option on the stock with an exercise price of $40. Verify that no-arbitrage arguments and risk-neutral valuation arguments give the same answers.

At the end of three months the value of the option is either $5 (if the stock price is $35) or $0 (if the stock price is $45).

Consider a portfolio consisting of:

$$-\Delta \quad : \quad \text{shares}$$

$$+1 \quad : \quad \text{option}$$

(Note: The delta, Δ, of a put option is negative. We have constructed the portfolio so that it is $+1$ option and $-\Delta$ shares rather than -1 option and $+\Delta$ shares so that the initial investment is positive.)

The value of the portfolio is either $-35\Delta + 5$ or -45Δ. If:

$$-35\Delta + 5 = -45\Delta$$

i.e.,

$$\Delta = -0.5$$

the value of the portfolio is certain to be 22.5. For this value of Δ the portfolio is therefore riskless. The current value of the portfolio is

$$-40\Delta + f$$

where f is the value of the option. Since the portfolio must earn the risk-free rate of interest

$$(40 \times 0.5 + f) \times 1.02 = 22.5$$

Hence

$$f = 2.06$$

i.e., the value of the option is $2.06.

This can also be calculated using risk-neutral valuation. Suppose that p is the probability of an upward stock price movement in a risk-neutral world. We must have

$$45p + 35(1 - p) = 40 \times 1.02$$

i.e.,

$$10p = 5.8$$

or:

$$p = 0.58$$

The expected value of the option in a risk-neutral world is:

$$0 \times 0.58 + 5 \times 0.42 = 2.10$$

This has a present value of

$$\frac{2.10}{1.02} = 2.06$$

This is consistent with the no-arbitrage answer.

Problem 12.12.

A stock price is currently $50. Over each of the next two three-month periods it is expected to go up by 6% or down by 5%. The risk-free interest rate is 5% per annum with continuous compounding. What is the value of a six-month European call option with a strike price of $51?

A tree describing the behavior of the stock price is shown in Figure S12.3. The risk-neutral probability of an up move, p, is given by

$$p = \frac{e^{0.05 \times 3/12} - 0.95}{1.06 - 0.95} = 0.5689$$

There is a payoff from the option of $56.18 - 51 = 5.18$ for the highest final node (which corresponds to two up moves) zero in all other cases. The value of the option is therefore

$$5.18 \times 0.5689^2 \times e^{-0.05 \times 6/12} = 1.635$$

This can also be calculated by working back through the tree as indicated in Figure S12.3. The value of the call option is the lower number at each node in the figure.

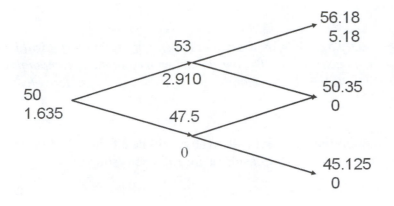

Figure S12.3 Tree for Problem 12.12

Problem 12.13.

For the situation considered in Problem 12.12, what is the value of a six-month European put option with a strike price of $51? Verify that the European call and European put prices satisfy put–call parity. If the put option were American, would it ever be optimal to exercise it early at any of the nodes on the tree?

The tree for valuing the put option is shown in Figure S12.4. We get a payoff of $51 - 50.35 = 0.65$ if the middle final node is reached and a payoff of $51 - 45.125 = 5.875$ if the lowest final node is reached. The value of the option is therefore

$$(0.65 \times 2 \times 0.5689 \times 0.4311 + 5.875 \times 0.4311^2)e^{-0.05 \times 6/12} = 1.376$$

This can also be calculated by working back through the tree as indicated in Figure S12.4. The value of the put plus the stock price is

$$1.376 + 50 = 51.376$$

The value of the call plus the present value of the strike price is

$$1.635 + 51e^{-0.05 \times 6/12} = 51.376$$

This verifies that put–call parity holds
To test whether it worth exercising the option early we compare the value calculated for the option at each node with the payoff from immediate exercise. At node C the payoff from immediate exercise is $51 - 47.5 = 3.5$. Because this is greater than 2.8664, the option should be exercised at this node. The option should not be exercised at either node A or node B.

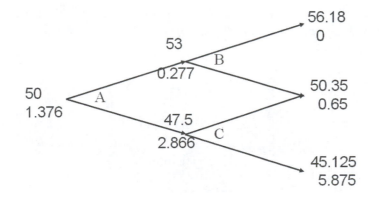

Figure S12.4 Tree for Problem 12.13

Problem 12.14.

A stock price is currently $25. It is known that at the end of two months it will be either $23 or $27. The risk-free interest rate is 10% per annum with continuous compounding. Suppose S_T is the stock price at the end of two months. What is the value of a derivative that pays off S_T^2 at this time?

At the end of two months the value of the derivative will be either 529 (if the stock price is 23) or 729 (if the stock price is 27). Consider a portfolio consisting of:

$$+\Delta \quad : \quad \text{shares}$$
$$-1 \quad : \quad \text{derivative}$$

The value of the portfolio is either $27\Delta - 729$ or $23\Delta - 529$ in two months. If

$$27\Delta - 729 = 23\Delta - 529$$

i.e.,

$$\Delta = 50$$

the value of the portfolio is certain to be 621. For this value of Δ the portfolio is therefore riskless. The current value of the portfolio is:

$$50 \times 25 - f$$

where f is the value of the derivative. Since the portfolio must earn the risk-free rate of interest

$$(50 \times 25 - f)e^{0.10 \times 2/12} = 621$$

i.e.,

$$f = 639.3$$

The value of the option is therefore $639.3.
This can also be calculated directly from equations (12.2) and (12.3). $u = 1.08$, $d = 0.92$ so that

$$p = \frac{e^{0.10 \times 2/12} - 0.92}{1.08 - 0.92} = 0.6050$$

and

$$f = e^{-0.10 \times 2/12}(0.6050 \times 729 + 0.3950 \times 529) = 639.3$$

Problem 12.15.

Calculate u, d, and p when a binomial tree is constructed to value an option on a foreign currency. The tree step size is one month, the domestic interest rate is 5% per annum, the foreign interest rate is 8% per annum, and the volatility is 12% per annum.

In this case

$$a = e^{(0.05-0.08) \times 1/12} = 0.9975$$

$$u = e^{0.12\sqrt{1/12}} = 1.0352$$

$$d = 1/u = 0.9660$$

$$p = \frac{0.9975 - 0.9660}{1.0352 - 0.9660} = 0.4553$$

CHAPTER 13
Wiener Processes and Itô's Lemma

Problem 13.1.
What would it mean to assert that the temperature at a certain place follows a Markov process? Do you think that temperatures do, in fact, follow a Markov process?

Imagine that you have to forecast the future temperature from a) the current temperature, b) the history of the temperature in the last week, and c) a knowledge of seasonal averages and seasonal trends. If temperature followed a Markov process, the history of the temperature in the last week would be irrelevant.

To answer the second part of the question you might like to consider the following scenario for the first week in May:
1. Monday to Thursday are warm days; today, Friday, is a very cold day.
2. Monday to Friday are all very cold days.

What is your forecast for the weekend? If you are more pessimistic in the case of the second scenario, temperatures do not follow a Markov process.

Problem 13.2.
Can a trading rule based on the past history of a stock's price ever produce returns that are consistently above average? Discuss.

The first point to make is that any trading strategy can, just because of good luck, produce above average returns. The key question is whether a trading strategy *consistently* outperforms the market when adjustments are made for risk. It is certainly possible that a trading strategy could do this. However, when enough investors know about the strategy and trade on the basis of the strategy, the profit will disappear.

As an illustration of this, consider a phenomenon known as the small firm effect. Portfolios of stocks in small firms appear to have outperformed portfolios of stocks in large firms when appropriate adjustments are made for risk. Research was published about this in the early 1980s and mutual funds were set up to take advantage of the phenomenon. There is some evidence that this has resulted in the phenomenon disappearing.

Problem 13.3.
A company's cash position, measured in millions of dollars, follows a generalized Wiener process with a drift rate of 0.5 per quarter and a variance rate of 4.0 per quarter. How high does the company's initial cash position have to be for the company to have a less than 5% chance of a negative cash position by the end of one year?

Suppose that the company's initial cash position is x. The probability distribution of the cash position at the end of one year is

$$\varphi(x + 4 \times 0.5, 4 \times 4) = \varphi(x + 2.0, 16)$$

where $\varphi(m, v)$ is a normal probability distribution with mean m and variance v. The probability of a negative cash position at the end of one year is

$$N\left(-\frac{x + 2.0}{4}\right)$$

where $N(x)$ is the cumulative probability that a standardized normal variable (with mean zero and standard deviation 1.0) is less than x. From normal distribution tables

$$N\left(-\frac{x+2.0}{4}\right) = 0.05$$

when:

$$-\frac{x+2.0}{4} = -1.6449$$

i.e., when $x = 4.5796$. The initial cash position must therefore be $4.58 million.

Problem 13.4.

Variables X_1 and X_2 follow generalized Wiener processes with drift rates μ_1 and μ_2 and variances σ_1^2 and σ_2^2. What process does $X_1 + X_2$ follow if:

    (a) *The changes in X_1 and X_2 in any short interval of time are uncorrelated?*

    (b) *There is a correlation ρ between the changes in X_1 and X_2 in any short interval of time?*

(a) Suppose that X_1 and X_2 equal a_1 and a_2 initially. After a time period of length T, X_1 has the probability distribution

$$\varphi(a_1 + \mu_1 T, \sigma_1^2 T)$$

and X_2 has a probability distribution

$$\varphi(a_2 + \mu_2 T, \sigma_2^2 T)$$

From the property of sums of independent normally distributed variables, $X_1 + X_2$ has the probability distribution

$$\varphi\left(a_1 + \mu_1 T + a_2 + \mu_2 T, \sigma_1^2 T + \sigma_2^2 T\right)$$

i.e.,

$$\varphi\left[a_1 + a_2 + (\mu_1 + \mu_2)T, (\sigma_1^2 + \sigma_2^2)T\right]$$

This shows that $X_1 + X_2$ follows a generalized Wiener process with drift rate $\mu_1 + \mu_2$ and variance rate $\sigma_1^2 + \sigma_2^2$.

(b) In this case the change in the value of $X_1 + X_2$ in a short interval of time Δt has the probability distribution:

$$\varphi\left[(\mu_1 + \mu_2)\Delta t, (\sigma_1^2 + \sigma_2^2 + 2\rho\sigma_1\sigma_2)\Delta t\right]$$

If μ_1, μ_2, σ_1, σ_2 and ρ are all constant, arguments similar to those in Section 13.2 show that the change in a longer period of time T is

$$\varphi\left[(\mu_1 + \mu_2)T, (\sigma_1^2 + \sigma_2^2 + 2\rho\sigma_1\sigma_2)T\right]$$

The variable, $X_1 + X_2$, therefore follows a generalized Wiener process with drift rate

88

$\mu_1 + \mu_2$ and variance rate $\sigma_1^2 + \sigma_2^2 + 2\rho\sigma_1\sigma_2$.

Problem 13.5.

Consider a variable, S, that follows the process

$$dS = \mu\,dt + \sigma\,dz$$

For the first three years, $\mu = 2$ and $\sigma = 3$; for the next three years, $\mu = 3$ and $\sigma = 4$. If the initial value of the variable is 5, what is the probability distribution of the value of the variable at the end of year six?

The change in S during the first three years has the probability distribution

$$\varphi(2\times 3,\ 9\times 3) = \varphi(6,\ 27)$$

The change during the next three years has the probability distribution

$$\varphi(3\times 3,\ 16\times 3) = \varphi(9,\ 48)$$

The change during the six years is the sum of a variable with probability distribution $\varphi(6, 27)$ and a variable with probability distribution $\varphi(9, 48)$. The probability distribution of the change is therefore

$$\varphi(6+9, 27+48)$$

$$= \varphi(15, 75)$$

Since the initial value of the variable is 5, the probability distribution of the value of the variable at the end of year six is

$$\varphi(20, 75)$$

Problem 13.6.

Suppose that G is a function of a stock price, S and time. Suppose that σ_S and σ_G are the volatilities of S and G. Show that when the expected return of S increases by $\lambda\sigma_S$, the growth rate of G increases by $\lambda\sigma_G$, where λ is a constant.

From Itô's lemma

$$\sigma_G G = \frac{\partial G}{\partial S}\sigma_S S$$

Also the drift of G is

$$\frac{\partial G}{\partial S}\mu S + \frac{\partial G}{\partial t} + \frac{1}{2}\frac{\partial^2 G}{\partial S^2}\sigma^2 S^2$$

where μ is the expected return on the stock. When μ increases by $\lambda\sigma_S$, the drift of G increases by

$$\frac{\partial G}{\partial S} \lambda \sigma_s S$$

or

$$\lambda \sigma_G G$$

The growth rate of G, therefore, increases by $\lambda \sigma_G$.

Problem 13.7.

Stock A and stock B both follow geometric Brownian motion. Changes in any short interval of time are uncorrelated with each other. Does the value of a portfolio consisting of one of stock A and one of stock B follow geometric Brownian motion? Explain your answer.

Define S_A, μ_A and σ_A as the stock price, expected return and volatility for stock A. Define S_B, μ_B and σ_B as the stock price, expected return and volatility for stock B. Define ΔS_A and ΔS_B as the change in S_A and S_B in time Δt. Since each of the two stocks follows geometric Brownian motion,

$$\Delta S_A = \mu_A S_A \Delta t + \sigma_A S_A \varepsilon_A \sqrt{\Delta t}$$

$$\Delta S_B = \mu_B S_B \Delta t + \sigma_B S_B \varepsilon_B \sqrt{\Delta t}$$

where ε_A and ε_B are independent random samples from a normal distribution.

$$\Delta S_A + \Delta S_B = (\mu_A S_A + \mu_B S_B)\Delta t + (\sigma_A S_A \varepsilon_A + \sigma_B S_B \varepsilon_B)\sqrt{\Delta t}$$

This *cannot* be written as

$$\Delta S_A + \Delta S_B = \mu(S_A + S_B)\Delta t + \sigma(S_A + S_B)\varepsilon\sqrt{\Delta t}$$

for any constants μ and σ. (Neither the drift term nor the stochastic term correspond.) Hence the value of the portfolio does not follow geometric Brownian motion.

Problem 13.8.

The process for the stock price in equation (13.8) is
$$\Delta S = \mu S \, \Delta t + \sigma S \varepsilon \sqrt{\Delta t}$$
where μ and σ are constant. Explain carefully the difference between this model and each of the following:

$$\Delta S = \mu \, \Delta t + \sigma \varepsilon \sqrt{\Delta t}$$
$$\Delta S = \mu S \, \Delta t + \sigma \varepsilon \sqrt{\Delta t}$$
$$\Delta S = \mu \, \Delta t + \sigma S \varepsilon \sqrt{\Delta t}$$

Why is the model in equation (13.8) a more appropriate model of stock price behavior than any of these three alternatives?

In:

$$\Delta S = \mu S \Delta t + \sigma S \varepsilon \sqrt{\Delta t}$$

the expected increase in the stock price and the variability of the stock price are constant when both are expressed as a proportion (or as a percentage) of the stock price
In:

$$\Delta S = \mu \Delta t + \sigma \varepsilon \sqrt{\Delta t}$$

the expected increase in the stock price and the variability of the stock price are constant in absolute terms. For example, if the expected growth rate is $5 per annum when the stock price is $25, it is also $5 per annum when it is $100. If the standard deviation of weekly stock price movements is $1 when the price is $25, it is also $1 when the price is $100.
In:

$$\Delta S = \mu S \Delta t + \sigma \varepsilon \sqrt{\Delta t}$$

the expected increase in the stock price is a constant proportion of the stock price while the variability is constant in absolute terms.
In:

$$\Delta S = \mu \Delta t + \sigma S \varepsilon \sqrt{\Delta t}$$

the expected increase in the stock price is constant in absolute terms while the variability of the proportional stock price change is constant.
The model:

$$\Delta S = \mu S \Delta t + \sigma S \varepsilon \sqrt{\Delta t}$$

is the most appropriate one since it is most realistic to assume that the expected *percentage return* and the variability of the *percentage return* in a short interval are constant.

Problem 13.9.

It has been suggested that the short-term interest rate, r, follows the stochastic process

$$dr = a(b - r)\, dt + rc\, dz$$

where a, b, and c are positive constants and dz is a Wiener process. Describe the nature of this process.

The drift rate is $a(b - r)$. Thus, when the interest rate is above b the drift rate is negative and, when the interest rate is below b, the drift rate is positive. The interest rate is therefore continually pulled towards the level b. The rate at which it is pulled toward this level is a. A volatility equal to c is superimposed upon the "pull" or the drift.

Suppose $a = 0.4$, $b = 0.1$ and $c = 0.15$ and the current interest rate is 20% per annum. The interest rate is pulled towards the level of 10% per annum. This can be regarded as a long run average. The current drift is -4% per annum so that the expected rate at the end of one year is about 16% per annum. (In fact it is slightly greater than this, because as the interest rate decreases, the "pull" decreases.) Superimposed upon the drift is a volatility of 15% per annum.

Problem 13.10.

Suppose that a stock price, S, follows geometric Brownian motion with expected return μ and volatility σ:

91

$$dS = \mu S\,dt + \sigma S\,dz$$

What is the process followed by the variable S^n? Show that S^n also follows geometric Brownian motion.

If $G(S,t) = S^n$ then $\partial G / \partial t = 0$, $\partial G / \partial S = nS^{n-1}$, and $\partial^2 G / \partial S^2 = n(n-1)S^{n-2}$. Using Itô's lemma:

$$dG = [\mu nG + \frac{1}{2}n(n-1)\sigma^2 G]\,dt + \sigma nG\,dz$$

This shows that $G = S^n$ follows geometric Brownian motion where the expected return is

$$\mu n + \frac{1}{2}n(n-1)\sigma^2$$

and the volatility is $n\sigma$. The stock price S has an expected return of μ and the expected value of S_T is $S_0 e^{\mu T}$. The expected value of S_T^n is

$$S_0^n e^{[\mu n + \frac{1}{2}n(n-1)\sigma^2]T}$$

Problem 13.11.

Suppose that x is the yield to maturity with continuous compounding on a zero-coupon bond that pays off \$1 at time T. Assume that x follows the process

$$dx = a(x_0 - x)\,dt + sx\,dz$$

where a, x_0, and s are positive constants and dz is a Wiener process. What is the process followed by the bond price?

The process followed by B, the bond price, is from Itô's lemma:

$$dB = \left[\frac{\partial B}{\partial x}a(x_0 - x) + \frac{\partial B}{\partial t} + \frac{1}{2}\frac{\partial^2 B}{\partial x^2}s^2 x^2\right]dt + \frac{\partial B}{\partial x}sx\,dz$$

Since:

$$B = e^{-x(T-t)}$$

the required partial derivatives are

$$\frac{\partial B}{\partial t} = xe^{-x(T-t)} = xB$$

$$\frac{\partial B}{\partial x} = -(T-t)e^{-x(T-t)} = -(T-t)B$$

$$\frac{\partial^2 B}{\partial x^2} = (T-t)^2 e^{-x(T-t)} = (T-t)^2 B$$

Hence:

$$dB = \left[-a(x_0 - x)(T-t) + x + \frac{1}{2}s^2 x^2 (T-t)^2\right]B\,dt - sx(T-t)B\,dz$$

Problem 13.12

A stock whose price is $30 has an expected return of 9% and a volatility of 20%. In Excel simulate the stock price path over 5 years using monthly time steps and random samples from a normal distribution. Chart the simulated stock price path. By hitting F9 observe how the path changes as the random sample change.

The process is

$$\Delta S = 0.09 \times S \times \Delta t + 0.20 \times S \times \varepsilon \times \sqrt{\Delta t}$$

Where Δt is the length of the time step (=1/12) and ε is a random sample from a standard normal distribution.

CHAPTER 14
The Black-Scholes-Merton Model

Problem 14.1.
What does the Black–Scholes–Merton stock option pricing model assume about the probability distribution of the stock price in one year? What does it assume about the continuously compounded rate of return on the stock during the year?

The Black–Scholes–Merton option pricing model assumes that the probability distribution of the stock price in 1 year (or at any other future time) is lognormal. It assumes that the continuously compounded rate of return on the stock during the year is normally distributed.

Problem 14.2.
The volatility of a stock price is 30% per annum. What is the standard deviation of the percentage price change in one trading day?

The standard deviation of the percentage price change in time Δt is $\sigma\sqrt{\Delta t}$ where σ is the volatility. In this problem $\sigma = 0.3$ and, assuming 252 trading days in one year, $\Delta t = 1/252 = 0.004$ so that $\sigma\sqrt{\Delta t} = 0.3\sqrt{0.004} = 0.019$ or 1.9%.

Problem 14.3.
Explain the principle of risk-neutral valuation.

The price of an option or other derivative when expressed in terms of the price of the underlying stock is independent of risk preferences. Options therefore have the same value in a risk-neutral world as they do in the real world. We may therefore assume that the world is risk neutral for the purposes of valuing options. This simplifies the analysis. In a risk-neutral world all securities have an expected return equal to risk-free interest rate. Also, in a risk-neutral world, the appropriate discount rate to use for expected future cash flows is the risk-free interest rate.

Problem 14.4.
Calculate the price of a three-month European put option on a non-dividend-paying stock with a strike price of $50 when the current stock price is $50, the risk-free interest rate is 10% per annum, and the volatility is 30% per annum.

In this case $S_0 = 50$, $K = 50$, $r = 0.1$, $\sigma = 0.3$, $T = 0.25$, and

$$d_1 = \frac{\ln(50/50) + (0.1 + 0.09/2)0.25}{0.3\sqrt{0.25}} = 0.2417$$

$$d_2 = d_1 - 0.3\sqrt{0.25} = 0.0917$$

The European put price is

$$50N(-0.0917)e^{-0.1\times0.25} - 50N(-0.2417)$$

$$= 50 \times 0.4634e^{-0.1\times0.25} - 50 \times 0.4045 = 2.37$$

or $2.37.

Problem 14.5.

What difference does it make to your calculations in Problem 14.4 if a dividend of $1.50 is expected in two months?

In this case we must subtract the present value of the dividend from the stock price before using Black–Scholes-Merton. Hence the appropriate value of S_0 is

$$S_0 = 50 - 1.50e^{-0.1667 \times 0.1} = 48.52$$

As before $K = 50$, $r = 0.1$, $\sigma = 0.3$, and $T = 0.25$. In this case

$$d_1 = \frac{\ln(48.52/50) + (0.1 + 0.09/2)0.25}{0.3\sqrt{0.25}} = 0.0414$$

$$d_2 = d_1 - 0.3\sqrt{0.25} = -0.1086$$

The European put price is

$$50N(0.1086)e^{-0.1 \times 0.25} - 48.52N(-0.0414)$$

$$= 50 \times 0.5432e^{-0.1 \times 0.25} - 48.52 \times 0.4835 = 3.03$$

or $3.03.

Problem 14.6.

What is implied volatility? How can it be calculated?

The implied volatility is the volatility that makes the Black–Scholes-Merton price of an option equal to its market price. It is calculated using an iterative procedure.

Problem 14.7.

A stock price is currently $40. Assume that the expected return from the stock is 15% and its volatility is 25%. What is the probability distribution for the rate of return (with continuous compounding) earned over a two-year period?

In this case $\mu = 0.15$ and $\sigma = 0.25$. From equation (14.7) the probability distribution for the rate of return over a one-year period with continuous compounding is:

$$\varphi\left(0.15 - \frac{0.25^2}{2}, \frac{0.25^2}{2}\right)$$

i.e.,

$$\varphi(0.11875, 0.03125)$$

The expected value of the return is 11.875% per annum and the standard deviation is 17.7% per annum.

Problem 14.8.

A stock price has an expected return of 16% and a volatility of 35%. The current price is $38.
  a) *What is the probability that a European call option on the stock with an exercise price of $40 and a maturity date in six months will be exercised?*
  b) *What is the probability that a European put option on the stock with the same exercise price and maturity will be exercised?*

a) The required probability is the probability of the stock price being above \$40 in six months time. Suppose that the stock price in six months is S_T

$$\ln S_T \sim \varphi(\ln 38 + (0.16 - \frac{0.35^2}{2})0.5, 0.35^2 \times 0.5)$$

i.e.,

$$\ln S_T \sim \varphi(3.687, 0.247^2)$$

Since $\ln 40 = 3.689$, the required probability is

$$1 - N\left(\frac{3.689 - 3.687}{0.247}\right) = 1 - N(0.008)$$

From normal distribution tables $N(0.008) = 0.5032$ so that the required probability is 0.4968.

b) In this case the required probability is the probability of the stock price being less than \$40 in six months time. It is

$$1 - 0.4968 = 0.5032$$

Problem 14.9.

Using the notation in the chapter, prove that a 95% confidence interval for S_T is between

$$S_0 e^{(\mu - \sigma^2/2)T - 1.96\sigma\sqrt{T}} \quad \text{and} \quad S_0 e^{(\mu - \sigma^2/2)T + 1.96\sigma\sqrt{T}}$$

From equation (14.3):

$$\ln S_T \sim \varphi[\ln S_0 + (\mu - \frac{\sigma^2}{2})T, \sigma^2 T]$$

95% confidence intervals for $\ln S_T$ are therefore

$$\ln S_0 + (\mu - \frac{\sigma^2}{2})T - 1.96\sigma\sqrt{T}$$

and

$$\ln S_0 + (\mu - \frac{\sigma^2}{2})T + 1.96\sigma\sqrt{T}$$

95% confidence intervals for S_T are therefore

$$e^{\ln S_0 + (\mu - \sigma^2/2)T - 1.96\sigma\sqrt{T}} \quad \text{and} \quad e^{\ln S_0 + (\mu - \sigma^2/2)T + 1.96\sigma\sqrt{T}}$$

i.e.

$$S_0 e^{(\mu - \sigma^2/2)T - 1.96\sigma\sqrt{T}} \quad \text{and} \quad S_0 e^{(\mu - \sigma^2/2)T + 1.96\sigma\sqrt{T}}$$

Problem 14.10.

A portfolio manager announces that the average of the returns realized in each of the last 10 years is 20% per annum. In what respect is this statement misleading?

This problem relates to the material in Section 14.3. The statement is misleading in that a certain sum of money, say \$1000, when invested for 10 years in the fund would have realized a return (with annual compounding) of less than 20% per annum.
The average of the returns realized in each year is always greater than the return per annum (with annual compounding) realized over 10 years. The first is an arithmetic average of the returns in each year; the second is a geometric average of these returns.

Problem 14.11.

Assume that a non-dividend-paying stock has an expected return of μ and a volatility of σ. An innovative financial institution has just announced that it will trade a derivative that pays off a dollar amount equal to $\ln S_T$ at time T where S_T denotes the values of the stock price at time T.

    a) *Use risk-neutral valuation to calculate the price of the derivative at time t in term of the stock price, S, at time t*

    b) *Confirm that your price satisfies the differential equation (14.16)*

a) At time t, the expected value of $\ln S_T$ is from equation (14.3)
$$\ln S + (\mu - \sigma^2 / 2)(T - t)$$
In a risk-neutral world the expected value of $\ln S_T$ is therefore
$$\ln S + (r - \sigma^2 / 2)(T - t)$$
Using risk-neutral valuation the value of the derivative at time t is
$$e^{-r(T-t)}[\ln S + (r - \sigma^2 / 2)(T - t)]$$

b) If
$$f = e^{-r(T-t)}[\ln S + (r - \sigma^2 / 2)(T - t)]$$
then
$$\frac{\partial f}{\partial t} = re^{-r(T-t)}[\ln S + (r - \sigma^2 / 2)(T - t)] - e^{-r(T-t)}\left(r - \sigma^2 / 2\right)$$
$$\frac{\partial f}{\partial S} = \frac{e^{-r(T-t)}}{S}$$
$$\frac{\partial^2 f}{\partial S^2} = -\frac{e^{-r(T-t)}}{S^2}$$

The left-hand side of the Black-Scholes-Merton differential equation is
$$e^{-r(T-t)}\left[r \ln S + r(r - \sigma^2 / 2)(T - t) - (r - \sigma^2 / 2) + r - \sigma^2 / 2\right]$$
$$= e^{-r(T-t)}\left[r \ln S + r(r - \sigma^2 / 2)(T - t)\right]$$
$$= rf$$
Hence the differential equation is satisfied.

Problem 14.12.

Consider a derivative that pays off S_T^n at time T where S_T is the stock price at that time.

When the stock price follows geometric Brownian motion, it can be shown that its price at time t $(t \leq T)$ has the form
$$h(t,T)S^n$$
where S is the stock price at time t and h is a function only of t and T.

(a) By substituting into the Black–Scholes–Merton partial differential equation derive an ordinary differential equation satisfied by $h(t,T)$.

(b) What is the boundary condition for the differential equation for $h(t,T)$?

(c) Show that
$$h(t,T) = e^{[0.5\sigma^2 n(n-1) + r(n-1)](T-t)}$$
where r is the risk-free interest rate and σ is the stock price volatility.

If $G(S,t) = h(t,T)S^n$ then $\partial G / \partial t = h_t S^n$, $\partial G / \partial S = hnS^{n-1}$, and $\partial^2 G / \partial S^2 = hn(n-1)S^{n-2}$ where $h_t = \partial h / \partial t$. Substituting into the Black–Scholes–Merton differential equation we obtain

$$h_t + rhn + \frac{1}{2}\sigma^2 hn(n-1) = rh$$

The derivative is worth S^n when $t = T$. The boundary condition for this differential equation is therefore $h(T,T) = 1$

The equation

$$h(t,T) = e^{[0.5\sigma^2 n(n-1) + r(n-1)](T-t)}$$

satisfies the boundary condition since it collapses to $h = 1$ when $t = T$. It can also be shown that it satisfies the differential equation in (a). Alternatively we can solve the differential equation in (a) directly. The differential equation can be written

$$\frac{h_t}{h} = -r(n-1) - \frac{1}{2}\sigma^2 n(n-1)$$

The solution to this is

$$\ln h = [r(n-1) + \frac{1}{2}\sigma^2 n(n-1)](T-t)$$

or

$$h(t,T) = e^{[0.5\sigma^2 n(n-1) + r(n-1)](T-t)}$$

Problem 14.13.
What is the price of a European call option on a non-dividend-paying stock when the stock price is $52, the strike price is $50, the risk-free interest rate is 12% per annum, the volatility is 30% per annum, and the time to maturity is three months?

In this case $S_0 = 52$, $K = 50$, $r = 0.12$, $\sigma = 0.30$ and $T = 0.25$.

$$d_1 = \frac{\ln(52/50) + (0.12 + 0.3^2/2)0.25}{0.30\sqrt{0.25}} = 0.5365$$

$$d_2 = d_1 - 0.30\sqrt{0.25} = 0.3865$$

The price of the European call is

$$52N(0.5365) - 50e^{-0.12\times0.25}N(0.3865)$$

$$= 52 \times 0.7042 - 50e^{-0.03} \times 0.6504$$

$$= 5.06$$

or $5.06.

Problem 14.14.
What is the price of a European put option on a non-dividend-paying stock when the stock price is $69, the strike price is $70, the risk-free interest rate is 5% per annum, the volatility is 35% per annum, and the time to maturity is six months?

In this case $S_0 = 69$, $K = 70$, $r = 0.05$, $\sigma = 0.35$ and $T = 0.5$.

$$d_1 = \frac{\ln(69/70) + (0.05 + 0.35^2/2) \times 0.5}{0.35\sqrt{0.5}} = 0.1666$$

$$d_2 = d_1 - 0.35\sqrt{0.5} = -0.0809$$

The price of the European put is

$$70e^{-0.05 \times 0.5} N(0.0809) - 69 N(-0.1666)$$

$$= 70e^{-0.025} \times 0.5323 - 69 \times 0.4338$$

$$= 6.40$$

or $6.40.

Problem 14.15.

Consider an American call option on a stock. The stock price is $70, the time to maturity is eight months, the risk-free rate of interest is 10% per annum, the exercise price is $65, and the volatility is 32%. A dividend of $1 is expected after three months and again after six months. Show that it can never be optimal to exercise the option on either of the two dividend dates. Use DerivaGem to calculate the price of the option.

Using the notation of Section 14.12, $D_1 = D_2 = 1$, $K(1 - e^{-r(T-t_2)}) = 65(1 - e^{-0.1 \times 0.1667}) = 1.07$, and $K(1 - e^{-r(t_2-t_1)}) = 65(1 - e^{-0.1 \times 0.25}) = 1.60$. Since

$$D_1 < K(1 - e^{-r(T-t_2)})$$

and

$$D_2 < K(1 - e^{-r(t_2-t_1)})$$

It is never optimal to exercise the call option early. DerivaGem shows that the value of the option is 10.94.

Problem 14.16.

A call option on a non-dividend-paying stock has a market price of $2.50. The stock price is $15, the exercise price is $13, the time to maturity is three months, and the risk-free interest rate is 5% per annum. What is the implied volatility?

In the case $c = 2.5$, $S_0 = 15$, $K = 13$, $T = 0.25$, $r = 0.05$. The implied volatility must be calculated using an iterative procedure.
A volatility of 0.2 (or 20% per annum) gives $c = 2.20$. A volatility of 0.3 gives $c = 2.32$. A volatility of 0.4 gives $c = 2.507$. A volatility of 0.39 gives $c = 2.487$. By interpolation the implied volatility is about 0.396 or 39.6% per annum.
The implied volatility can also be calculated using DerivaGem. Select equity as the Underlying Type in the first worksheet. Select Black-Scholes European as the Option Type. Input stock price as 15, the risk-free rate as 5%, time to exercise as 0.25, and exercise price as 13. Leave the dividend table blank because we are assuming no dividends. Select the button corresponding to call. Select the implied volatility button. Input the Price as 2.5 in the second half of the option data table. Hit the *Enter* key and click on calculate. DerivaGem will show the volatility of the option as 39.64%.

Problem 14.17.

With the notation used in this chapter
  (a) *What is $N'(x)$?*
  (b) *Show that $SN'(d_1) = Ke^{-r(T-t)} N'(d_2)$, where S is the stock price at time t*

$$d_1 = \frac{\ln(S/K) + (r + \sigma^2/2)(T-t)}{\sigma\sqrt{T-t}}$$

$$d_2 = \frac{\ln(S/K) + (r - \sigma^2/2)(T-t)}{\sigma\sqrt{T-t}}$$

(c) *Calculate* $\partial d_1 / \partial S$ *and* $\partial d_2 / \partial S$.

(d) *Show that when*

$$c = SN(d_1) - Ke^{-r(T-t)}N(d_2)$$

$$\frac{\partial c}{\partial t} = -rKe^{-r(T-t)}N(d_2) - SN'(d_1)\frac{\sigma}{2\sqrt{T-t}}$$

where c *is the price of a call option on a non-dividend-paying stock.*

(e) *Show that* $\partial c / \partial S = N(d_1)$.

(f) *Show that the* c *satisfies the Black–Scholes–Merton differential equation.*

(g) *Show that* c *satisfies the boundary condition for a European call option, i.e., that*
$c = \max(S - K, 0)$ *as* $t \longrightarrow T$

(a) Since $N(x)$ is the cumulative probability that a variable with a standardized normal distribution will be less than x, $N'(x)$ is the probability density function for a standardized normal distribution, that is,

$$N'(x) = \frac{1}{\sqrt{2\pi}}e^{-\frac{x^2}{2}}$$

(b)
$$N'(d_1) = N'(d_2 + \sigma\sqrt{T-t})$$

$$= \frac{1}{\sqrt{2\pi}}\exp\left[-\frac{d_2^2}{2} - \sigma d_2\sqrt{T-t} - \frac{1}{2}\sigma^2(T-t)\right]$$

$$= N'(d_2)\exp\left[-\sigma d_2\sqrt{T-t} - \frac{1}{2}\sigma^2(T-t)\right]$$

Because

$$d_2 = \frac{\ln(S/K) + (r - \sigma^2/2)(T-t)}{\sigma\sqrt{T-t}}$$

it follows that

$$\exp\left[-\sigma d_2\sqrt{T-t} - \frac{1}{2}\sigma^2(T-t)\right] = \frac{Ke^{-r(T-t)}}{S}$$

As a result

$$SN'(d_1) = Ke^{-r(T-t)}N'(d_2)$$

which is the required result.

(c)
$$d_1 = \frac{\ln\frac{S}{K} + (r + \frac{\sigma^2}{2})(T-t)}{\sigma\sqrt{T-t}}$$

$$= \frac{\ln S - \ln K + (r + \frac{\sigma^2}{2})(T-t)}{\sigma\sqrt{T-t}}$$

Hence

$$\frac{\partial d_1}{\partial S} = \frac{1}{S\sigma\sqrt{T-t}}$$

Similarly

$$d_2 = \frac{\ln S - \ln K + (r - \frac{\sigma^2}{2})(T-t)}{\sigma\sqrt{T-t}}$$

and

$$\frac{\partial d_2}{\partial S} = \frac{1}{S\sigma\sqrt{T-t}}$$

Therefore:

$$\frac{\partial d_1}{\partial S} = \frac{\partial d_2}{\partial S}$$

(d)

$$c = SN(d_1) - Ke^{-r(T-t)}N(d_2)$$

$$\frac{\partial c}{\partial t} = SN'(d_1)\frac{\partial d_1}{\partial t} - rKe^{-r(T-t)}N(d_2) - Ke^{-r(T-t)}N'(d_2)\frac{\partial d_2}{\partial t}$$

From (b):

$$SN'(d_1) = Ke^{-r(T-t)}N'(d_2)$$

Hence

$$\frac{\partial c}{\partial t} = -rKe^{-r(T-t)}N(d_2) + SN'(d_1)\left(\frac{\partial d_1}{\partial t} - \frac{\partial d_2}{\partial t}\right)$$

Since

$$d_1 - d_2 = \sigma\sqrt{T-t}$$

$$\frac{\partial d_1}{\partial t} - \frac{\partial d_2}{\partial t} = \frac{\partial}{\partial t}(\sigma\sqrt{T-t})$$

$$= -\frac{\sigma}{2\sqrt{T-t}}$$

Hence

$$\frac{\partial c}{\partial t} = -rKe^{-r(T-t)}N(d_2) - SN'(d_1)\frac{\sigma}{2\sqrt{T-t}}$$

(e) From differentiating the Black–Scholes–Merton formula for a call price we obtain

$$\frac{\partial c}{\partial S} = N(d_1) + SN'(d_1)\frac{\partial d_1}{\partial S} - Ke^{-r(T-t)}N'(d_2)\frac{\partial d_2}{dS}$$

From the results in (b) and (c) it follows that

$$\frac{\partial c}{\partial S} = N(d_1)$$

(f) Differentiating the result in (e) and using the result in (c), we obtain

$$\frac{\partial^2 c}{\partial S^2} = N'(d_1)\frac{\partial d_1}{\partial S}$$

$$= N'(d_1)\frac{1}{S\sigma\sqrt{T-t}}$$

From the results in d) and e)

$$\frac{\partial c}{\partial t} + rS\frac{\partial c}{\partial S} + \frac{1}{2}\sigma^2 S^2 \frac{\partial^2 c}{\partial S^2} = -rKe^{-r(T-t)}N(d_2) - SN'(d_1)\frac{\sigma}{2\sqrt{T-t}}$$

$$+ rSN(d_1) + \frac{1}{2}\sigma^2 S^2 N'(d_1)\frac{1}{S\sigma\sqrt{T-t}}$$

$$= r[SN(d_1) - Ke^{-r(T-t)}N(d_2)]$$

$$= rc$$

This shows that the Black-Scholes-Merton formula for a call option does indeed satisfy the Black-Scholes-Merton differential equation

(g)   Consider what happens in the formula for c in part (d) as t approaches T. If $S > K$ d_1 and d_2 tend to infinity and $N(d_1)$ and $N(d_2)$ tend to 1. If $S < K$, d_1 and d_2 tend to zero. It follows that the formula for c tends to $\max(S - K, 0)$.

Problem 14.18.
Show that the Black–Scholes–Merton formulas for call and put options satisfy put–call parity.

The Black-Scholes-Merton formula for a European call option is
$$c = S_0 N(d_1) - Ke^{-rT}N(d_2)$$
so that
$$c + Ke^{-rT} = S_0 N(d_1) - Ke^{-rT}N(d_2) + Ke^{-rT}$$
or
$$c + Ke^{-rT} = S_0 N(d_1) + Ke^{-rT}[1 - N(d_2)]$$
or
$$c + Ke^{-rT} = S_0 N(d_1) + Ke^{-rT}N(-d_2)$$
The Black–Scholes–Merton formula for a European put option is
$$p = Ke^{-rT}N(-d_2) - S_0 N(-d_1)$$
so that
$$p + S_0 = Ke^{-rT}N(-d_2) - S_0 N(-d_1) + S_0$$
or
$$p + S_0 = Ke^{-rT}N(-d_2) + S_0[1 - N(-d_1)]$$
or
$$p + S_0 = Ke^{-rT}N(-d_2) + S_0 N(d_1)$$
This shows that the put–call parity result
$$c + Ke^{-rT} = p + S_0$$
holds.

Problem 14.19.
A stock price is currently $50 and the risk-free interest rate is 5%. Use the DerivaGem

©2012 Pearson Education, Inc. Publishing as Prentice Hall.

software to translate the following table of European call options on the stock into a table of implied volatilities, assuming no dividends. Are the option prices consistent with the assumptions underlying Black–Scholes–Merton?

Stock Price	Maturity = 3 months	Maturity = 6 months	Maturity = 12 months
45	7.00	8.30	10.50
50	3.50	5.20	7.50
55	1.60	2.90	5.10

Using DerivaGem we obtain the following table of implied volatilities

Stock Price	Maturity = 3 months	Maturity = 6 months	Maturity = 12 months
45	37.78	34.99	34.02
50	32.12	32.78	32.03
55	31.98	30.77	30.45

To calculate first number, select equity as the Underlying Type in the first worksheet. Select Black-Scholes European as the Option Type. Input stock price as 50, the risk-free rate as 5%, time to exercise as 0.25, and exercise price as 45. Leave the dividend table blank because we are assuming no dividends. Select the button corresponding to call. Select the implied volatility button. Input the Price as 7.0 in the second half of the option data table. Hit the *Enter* key and click on calculate. DerivaGem will show the volatility of the option as 37.78%. Change the strike price and time to exercise and recompute to calculate the rest of the numbers in the table.

The option prices are not exactly consistent with Black–Scholes–Merton. If they were, the implied volatilities would be all the same. We usually find in practice that low strike price options on a stock have significantly higher implied volatilities than high strike price options on the same stock. This phenomenon is discussed in Chapter 19.

Problem 14.20.
Explain carefully why Black's approach to evaluating an American call option on a dividend-paying stock may give an approximate answer even when only one dividend is anticipated. Does the answer given by Black's approach understate or overstate the true option value? Explain your answer.

Black's approach in effect assumes that the holder of option must decide at time zero whether it is a European option maturing at time t_n (the final ex-dividend date) or a European option maturing at time T. In fact the holder of the option has more flexibility than this. The holder can choose to exercise at time t_n if the stock price at that time is above some level but not otherwise. Furthermore, if the option is not exercised at time t_n, it can still be exercised at time T.

It appears that Black's approach should understate the true option value. This is because the holder of the option has more alternative strategies for deciding when to exercise the option than the two strategies implicitly assumed by the approach. These alternative strategies add value to the option.

However, this is not the whole story! The standard approach to valuing either an American or a European option on a stock paying a single dividend applies the volatility to the stock price less the present value of the dividend. (The procedure for valuing an American option is explained in Chapter 20.) Black's approach when considering exercise just prior to the dividend date applies the volatility to the stock price itself. Black's approach therefore assumes more stock price variability than the standard approach in some of its calculations. In some circumstances it can give a higher price than the standard approach.

Problem 14.21.
Consider an American call option on a stock. The stock price is $50, the time to maturity is 15 months, the risk-free rate of interest is 8% per annum, the exercise price is $55, and the volatility is 25%. Dividends of $1.50 are expected in 4 months and 10 months. Show that it can never be optimal to exercise the option on either of the two dividend dates. Calculate the price of the option.

With the notation in the text
$$D_1 = D_2 = 1.50, \quad t_1 = 0.3333, \quad t_2 = 0.8333, \quad T = 1.25, \quad r = 0.08 \quad \text{and} \quad K = 55$$

$$K\left[1 - e^{-r(T-t_2)}\right] = 55(1 - e^{-0.08 \times 0.4167}) = 1.80$$

Hence
$$D_2 < K\left[1 - e^{-r(T-t_2)}\right]$$

Also:
$$K\left[1 - e^{-r(t_2-t_1)}\right] = 55(1 - e^{-0.08 \times 0.5}) = 2.16$$

Hence:
$$D_1 < K\left[1 - e^{-r(t_2-t_1)}\right]$$

It follows from the conditions established in Section 14.12 that the option should never be exercised early.

The present value of the dividends is
$$1.5e^{-0.3333 \times 0.08} + 1.5e^{-0.8333 \times 0.08} = 2.864$$

The option can be valued using the European pricing formula with:
$$S_0 = 50 - 2.864 = 47.136, \quad K = 55, \quad \sigma = 0.25, \quad r = 0.08, \quad T = 1.25$$

$$d_1 = \frac{\ln(47.136/55) + (0.08 + 0.25^2/2)1.25}{0.25\sqrt{1.25}} = -0.0545$$

$$d_2 = d_1 - 0.25\sqrt{1.25} = -0.3340$$

$$N(d_1) = 0.4783, \quad N(d_2) = 0.3692$$

and the call price is
$$47.136 \times 0.4783 - 55e^{-0.08 \times 1.25} \times 0.3692 = 4.17$$

or $4.17.

Problem 14.22.
Show that the probability that a European call option will be exercised in a risk-neutral world is, with the notation introduced in this chapter, $N(d_2)$. What is an expression for the value of a derivative that pays off $100 if the price of a stock at time T is greater than K?

The probability that the call option will be exercised is the probability that $S_T > K$ where S_T is the stock price at time T. In a risk neutral world

$$\ln S_T \sim \varphi[\ln S_0 + (r - \sigma^2/2)T, \sigma^2 T]$$

The probability that $S_T > K$ is the same as the probability that $\ln S_T > \ln K$. This is

$$1 - N\left[\frac{\ln K - \ln S_0 - (r - \sigma^2/2)T}{\sigma\sqrt{T}}\right]$$

$$= N\left[\frac{\ln(S_0/K) + (r - \sigma^2/2)T}{\sigma\sqrt{T}}\right]$$

$$= N(d_2)$$

The expected value at time T in a risk neutral world of a derivative security which pays off $100 when $S_T > K$ is therefore

$$100N(d_2)$$

From risk neutral valuation the value of the security at time t is

$$100e^{-rT}N(d_2)$$

Problem 14.23.

Show that S^{-2r/σ^2} could be the price of a traded derivative security.

If $f = S^{-2r/\sigma^2}$ then

$$\frac{\partial f}{\partial S} = -\frac{2r}{\sigma^2}S^{-2r/\sigma^2 - 1}$$

$$\frac{\partial^2 f}{\partial S^2} = \left(\frac{2r}{\sigma^2}\right)\left(\frac{2r}{\sigma^2} + 1\right)S^{-2r/\sigma^2 - 2}$$

$$\frac{\partial f}{\partial t} = 0$$

$$\frac{\partial f}{\partial t} + rS\frac{\partial f}{\partial S} + \frac{1}{2}\sigma^2 S^2 \frac{\partial^2 f}{\partial S^2} = rS^{-2r/\sigma^2} = rf$$

This shows that the Black-Scholes-Merton equation is satisfied. S^{-2r/σ^2} could therefore be the price of a traded security.

Problem 14.24.
A company has an issue of executive stock options outstanding. Should dilution be taken into account when the options are valued? Explain you answer.

The answer is no. If markets are efficient they have already taken potential dilution into account in determining the stock price. This argument is explained in Business Snapshot 14.3.

Problem 14.25.
A company's stock price is $50 and 10 million shares are outstanding. The company is

considering giving its employees three million at-the-money five-year call options. Option exercises will be handled by issuing more shares. The stock price volatility is 25%, the five-year risk-free rate is 5% and the company does not pay dividends. Estimate the cost to the company of the employee stock option issue.

The Black-Scholes-Merton price of the option is given by setting $S_0 = 50$, $K = 50$, $r = 0.05$, $\sigma = 0.25$, and $T = 5$. It is 16.252. From an analysis similar to that in Section 14.10 the cost to the company of the options is

$$\frac{10}{10+3} \times 16.252 = 12.5$$

or about \$12.5 per option. The total cost is therefore 3 million times this or \$37.5 million. If the market perceives no benefits from the options the stock price will fall by \$3.75.

CHAPTER 15
Employee Stock Options

Problem 15.1.
Why was it attractive for companies to grant at-the-money stock options prior to 2005? What changed in 2005?

Prior to 2005 companies did not have to expense at-the-money options on the income statement. They merely had to report the value of the options in notes to the accounts. FAS 123 and IAS 2 required the fair value of the options to be reported as a cost on the income statement starting in 2005.

Problem 15.2.
What are the main differences between a typical employee stock option and an American call option traded on an exchange or in the over-the-counter market?

The main differences are a) employee stock options last much longer than the typical exchange-traded or over-the-counter option, b) there is usually a vesting period during which they cannot be exercised, c) the options cannot be sold by the employee, d) if the employee leaves the company the options usually either expire worthless or have to be exercised immediately, and e) exercise of the options usually leads to the company issuing more shares.

Problem 15.3.
Explain why employee stock options on a non-dividend-paying stock are frequently exercised before the end of their lives whereas an exchange-traded call option on such a stock is never exercised early.

It is always better for the option holder to sell a call option on a non-dividend -paying stock rather than exercise it. Employee stock options cannot be sold and so the only way an employee can monetize the option is to exercise the option and sell the stock.

Problem 15.4.
"Stock option grants are good because they motivate executives to act in the best interests of shareholders." Discuss this viewpoint.

This is questionable. Executives benefit from share price increases but do not bear the costs of share price decreases. Employee stock options are liable to encourage executives to take decisions that boost the value of the stock in the short term at the expense of the long term health of the company. It may even be the case that executives are encouraged to take high risks so as to maximize the value of their options.

Problem 15.5.
"Granting stock options to executives is like allowing a professional footballer to bet on the outcome of games." Discuss this viewpoint.

Professional footballers are not allowed to bet on the outcomes of games because they themselves influence the outcomes. Arguably, an executive should not be allowed to bet on the future stock price of her company because her actions influence that price. However, it could be argued that there is nothing wrong with a professional footballer betting that his team will win (but everything wrong with betting that it will lose). Similarly there is nothing wrong with an executive betting that her company will do well.

Problem 15.6.
Why did some companies backdate stock option grants in the US prior to 2002? What changed in 2002?

Backdating allowed the company to issue employee stock options with a strike price equal to the price at some previous date and claim that they were at the money. At the money options did not lead to an expense on the income statement until 2005. The amount recorded for the value of the options in the notes to the income was less than the actual cost on the true grant date. In 2002 the SEC required companies to report stock option grants within two business days of the grant date. This eliminated the possibility of backdating for companies that complied with this rule.

Problem 15.7.
In what way would the benefits of backdating be reduced if a stock option grant had to be revalued at the end of each quarter?

If a stock option grant had to be revalued each quarter the value of the option of the grant date (however determined) would become less important. Stock price movements following the reported grant date would be incorporated in the next revaluation. The total cost of the options would be independent of the stock price on the grant date.

Problem 15.8.
Explain how you would do the analysis to produce a chart such as the one in Figure 15.2.

It would be necessary to look at returns on each stock in the sample (possibly adjusted for the returns on the market and the beta of the stock) around the reported employee stock option grant date. One could designate Day 0 as the grant date and look at returns on each stock each day from Day –30 to Day +30. The returns would then be averaged across the stocks.

Problem 15.9.
On May 31 a company's stock price is $70. One million shares are outstanding. An executive exercises 100,000 stock options with a strike price of $50. What is the impact of this on the stock price?

There should be no impact on the stock price because the stock price will already reflect the dilution expected from the executive's exercise decision.

Problem 15.10.
The notes accompanying a company's financial statements say: "Our executive stock options last 10 years and vest after four years. We valued the options granted this year using the Black–Scholes–Merton model with an expected life of 5 years and a volatility of 20%. "What does this mean? Discuss the modeling approach used by the company.

The notes indicate that the Black–Scholes–Merton model was used to produce the valuation with T, the option life, being set equal to 5 years and the stock price volatility being set equal to 20%.

Problem 15.11.

In a Dutch auction of 10,000 options, bids are as follows

> *A bids $30 for 3,000*
> *B bids $33 for 2,500*
> *C bids $29 for 5,000*
> *D bids $40 for 1,000*
> *E bids $22 for 8,000*
> *F bids $35 for 6,000*

What is the result of the auction? Who buys how many at what price?

The price at which 10,000 options can be sold is $30. B, D, and F get their order completely filled at this price. A buys 500 options (out of its total bid for 3,000 options) at this price.

Problem 15.12.

A company has granted 500,000 options to its executives. The stock price and strike price are both $40. The options last for 12 years and vest after four years. The company decides to value the options using an expected life of five years and a volatility of 30% per annum. The company pays no dividends and the risk-free rate is 4%. What will the company report as an expense for the options on its income statement?

The options are valued using Black–Scholes–Merton with $S_0 = 40$, $K = 40$, $T = 5$, $\sigma = 0.3$ and $r = 0.04$. The value of each option is $13.585. The total expense reported is $500,000 \times \$13.585$ or $6.792 million.

Problem 15.13.

A company's CFO says: "The accounting treatment of stock options is crazy. We granted 10,000,000 at-the-money stock options to our employees last year when the stock price was $30. We estimated the value of each option on the grant date to be $5. At our year end the stock price had fallen to $4, but we were still stuck with a $50 million charge to the P&L." Discuss.

The problem is that under the current rules the options are valued only once—on the grant date. Arguably it would make sense to treat the options in the same way as other derivatives entered into by the company and revalue them on each reporting date. However, this does not happen under the current rules in the United States unless the options are settled in cash.

CHAPTER 16
Options on Stock Indices and Currencies

Problem 16.1.
A portfolio is currently worth $10 million and has a beta of 1.0. An index is currently standing at 800. Explain how a put option on the index with a strike of 700 can be used to provide portfolio insurance.

When the index goes down to 700, the value of the portfolio can be expected to be $10 \times (700/800) = \$8.75$ million. (This assumes that the dividend yield on the portfolio equals the dividend yield on the index.) Buying put options on $10,000,000/800 = 12,500$ times the index with a strike of 700 therefore provides protection against a drop in the value of the portfolio below $8.75 million. If each contract is on 100 times the index a total of 125 contracts would be required.

Problem 16.2.
"Once we know how to value options on a stock paying a dividend yield, we know how to value options on stock indices, currencies, and futures." Explain this statement.

A stock index is analogous to a stock paying a continuous dividend yield, the dividend yield being the dividend yield on the index. A currency is analogous to a stock paying a continuous dividend yield, the dividend yield being the foreign risk-free interest rate.

Problem 16.3.
A stock index is currently 300, the dividend yield on the index is 3% per annum, and the risk-free interest rate is 8% per annum. What is a lower bound for the price of a six-month European call option on the index when the strike price is 290?

The lower bound is given by equation 16.1 as
$$300e^{-0.03 \times 0.5} - 290e^{-0.08 \times 0.5} = 16.90$$

Problem 16.4.
A currency is currently worth $0.80 and has a volatility of 12%. The domestic and foreign risk-free interest rates are 6% and 8%, respectively. Use a two-step binomial tree to value a) a European four-month call option with a strike price of $0.79 and b) an American four-month call option with the same strike price

In this case $u = 1.0502$ and $p = 0.4538$. The tree is shown in Figure S16.1. The value of the option if it is European is $0.0235; the value of the option if it is American is $0.0250.

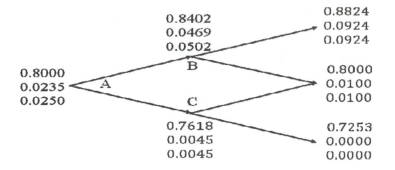

Figure S16.1   Tree to evaluate European and American put option Problem 16.4. At each node, upper number is the stock price; next number is the European put price; final number is the American put price

Problem 16.5.
Explain how corporations can use range forward contracts to hedge their foreign exchange risk when they are due to receive a certain amount of the foreign currency in the future.

A range forward contract allows a corporation to ensure that the exchange rate applicable to a transaction will not be worse that one exchange rate and will not be better than another exchange rate. In this case, a corporation would buy a put with the lower exchange rate and sell a call with the higher exchange rate.

Problem 16.6.
Calculate the value of a three-month at-the-money European call option on a stock index when the index is at 250, the risk-free interest rate is 10% per annum, the volatility of the index is 18% per annum, and the dividend yield on the index is 3% per annum.

In this case, $S_0 = 250$, $K = 250$, $r = 0.10$, $\sigma = 0.18$, $T = 0.25$, $q = 0.03$ and

$$d_1 = \frac{\ln(250/250) + (0.10 - 0.03 + 0.18^2/2)0.25}{0.18\sqrt{0.25}} = 0.2394$$

$$d_2 = d_1 - 0.18\sqrt{0.25} = 0.1494$$

and the call price is

$$250N(0.2394)e^{-0.03\times0.25} - 250N(0.1494)e^{-0.10\times0.25}$$

$$= 250\times0.5946e^{-0.03\times0.25} - 250\times0.5594e^{-0.10\times0.25}$$

or 11.15.

Problem 16.7.
Calculate the value of an eight-month European put option on a currency with a strike price of 0.50. The current exchange rate is 0.52, the volatility of the exchange rate is 12%, the domestic risk-free interest rate is 4% per annum, and the foreign risk-free interest rate is 8% per annum.

In this case $S_0 = 0.52$, $K = 0.50$, $r = 0.04$, $r_f = 0.08$, $\sigma = 0.12$, $T = 0.6667$, and

$$d_1 = \frac{\ln(0.52/0.50) + (0.04 - 0.08 + 0.12^2/2)0.6667}{0.12\sqrt{0.6667}} = 0.1771$$

$$d_2 = d_1 - 0.12\sqrt{0.6667} = 0.0791$$

and the put price is

$$0.50N(-0.0791)e^{-0.04 \times 0.6667} - 0.52N(-0.1771)e^{-0.08 \times 0.6667}$$

$$= 0.50 \times 0.4685e^{-0.04 \times 0.6667} - 0.52 \times 0.4297e^{-0.08 \times 0.6667}$$

$$= 0.0162$$

Problem 16.8.

Show that the formula in equation (16.12) for a put option to sell one unit of currency A for currency B at strike price K gives the same value as equation (16.11) for a call option to buy K units of currency B for currency A at a strike price of $1/K$.

A put option to sell one unit of currency A for K units of currency B is worth
$$Ke^{-r_B T}N(-d_2) - S_0 e^{-r_A T}N(-d_1)$$

where

$$d_1 = \frac{\ln(S_0/K) + (r_B - r_A + \sigma^2/2)T}{\sigma\sqrt{T}}$$

$$d_2 = \frac{\ln(S_0/K) + (r_B - r_A - \sigma^2/2)T}{\sigma\sqrt{T}}$$

and r_A and r_B are the risk-free rates in currencies A and B, respectively. The value of the option is measured in units of currency B. Defining $S_0^* = 1/S_0$ and $K^* = 1/K$

$$d_1 = \frac{-\ln(S_0^*/K^*) - (r_A - r_B - \sigma^2/2)T}{\sigma\sqrt{T}}$$

$$d_2 = \frac{-\ln(S_0^*/K^*) - (r_A - r_B + \sigma^2/2)T}{\sigma\sqrt{T}}$$

The put price is therefore
$$S_0 K[S_0^* e^{-r_B T}N(d_1^*) - K^* e^{-r_A T}N(d_2^*)$$

where

$$d_1^* = -d_2 = \frac{\ln(S_0^*/K^*) + (r_A - r_B + \sigma^2/2)T}{\sigma\sqrt{T}}$$

$$d_2^* = -d_1 = \frac{\ln(S_0^*/K^*) + (r_A - r_B - \sigma^2/2)T}{\sigma\sqrt{T}}$$

This shows that put option is equivalent to KS_0 call options to buy 1 unit of currency A for $1/K$ units of currency B. In this case the value of the option is measured in units of currency A. To obtain the call option value in units of currency B (thesame units as the value of the put option was measured in) we must divide by S_0. This proves the result.

Problem 16.9.
A foreign currency is currently worth $1.50. The domestic and foreign risk-free interest rates are 5% and 9%, respectively. Calculate a lower bound for the value of a six-month call option on the currency with a strike price of $1.40 if it is (a) European and (b) American.

Lower bound for European option is
$$S_0 e^{-r_f T} - K e^{-rT} = 1.5 e^{-0.09 \times 0.5} - 1.4 e^{-0.05 \times 0.5} = 0.069$$
Lower bound for American option is
$$S_0 - K = 0.10$$

Problem 16.10.
Consider a stock index currently standing at 250. The dividend yield on the index is 4% per annum, and the risk-free rate is 6% per annum. A three-month European call option on the index with a strike price of 245 is currently worth $10. What is the value of a three-month put option on the index with a strike price of 245?

In this case $S_0 = 250$, $q = 0.04$, $r = 0.06$, $T = 0.25$, $K = 245$, and $c = 10$. Using put–call parity
$$c + K e^{-rT} = p + S_0 e^{-qT}$$
or
$$p = c + K e^{-rT} - S_0 e^{-qT}$$
Substituting:
$$p = 10 + 245 e^{-0.25 \times 0.06} - 250 e^{-0.25 \times 0.04} = 3.84$$
The put price is 3.84.

Problem 16.11.
An index currently stands at 696 and has a volatility of 30% per annum. The risk-free rate of interest is 7% per annum and the index provides a dividend yield of 4% per annum. Calculate the value of a three-month European put with an exercise price of 700.

In this case $S_0 = 696$, $K = 700$, $r = 0.07$, $\sigma = 0.3$, $T = 0.25$ and $q = 0.04$. The option can be valued using equation (16.5).
$$d_1 = \frac{\ln(696 / 700) + (0.07 - 0.04 + 0.09 / 2) \times 0.25}{0.3 \sqrt{0.25}} = 0.0868$$
$$d_2 = d_1 - 0.3 \sqrt{0.25} = -0.0632$$
and
$$N(-d_1) = 0.4654, \quad N(-d_2) = 0.5252$$
The value of the put, p, is given by:
$$p = 700 e^{-0.07 \times 0.25} \times 0.5252 - 696 e^{-0.04 \times 0.25} \times 0.4654 = 40.6$$
i.e., it is $40.6.

Problem 16.12.
Show that if C is the price of an American call with exercise price K and maturity T on a stock paying a dividend yield of q, and P is the price of an American put on the same stock with the same strike price and exercise date,

$$S_0 e^{-qT} - K < C - P < S_0 - Ke^{-rT}$$

where S_0 is the stock price, r is the risk-free rate, and $r > 0$. (Hint: To obtain the first half of the inequality, consider possible values of:
Portfolio A; a European call option plus an amount K invested at the risk-free rate
Portfolio B: an American put option plus e^{-qT} of stock with dividends being reinvested in the stock
To obtain the second half of the inequality, consider possible values of:
Portfolio C: an American call option plus an amount Ke^{-rT} invested at the risk-free rate
Portfolio D: a European put option plus one stock with dividends being reinvested in the stock)

Following the hint, we first consider
Portfolio A: A European call option plus an amount K invested at the risk-free rate
Portfolio B: An American put option plus e^{-qT} of stock with dividends being reinvested in the stock.

Portfolio A is worth $c + K$ while portfolio B is worth $P + S_0 e^{-qT}$. If the put option is exercised at time $\tau (0 \leq \tau < T)$, portfolio B becomes:

$$K - S_\tau + S_\tau e^{-q(T-\tau)} \leq K$$

where S_τ is the stock price at time τ. Portfolio A is worth

$$c + Ke^{r\tau} \geq K$$

Hence portfolio A is worth at least as much as portfolio B. If both portfolios are held to maturity (time T), portfolio A is worth

$$\max(S_T - K, 0) + Ke^{rT}$$
$$= \max(S_T, K) + K(e^{rT} - 1)$$

Portfolio B is worth $\max(S_T, K)$. Hence portfolio A is worth more than portfolio B. Because portfolio A is worth at least as much as portfolio B in all circumstances

$$P + S_0 e^{-qT} \leq c + K$$

Because $c \leq C$:

$$P + S_0 e^{-qT} \leq C + K$$

or

$$S_0 e^{-qT} - K \leq C - P$$

This proves the first part of the inequality.

For the second part consider:
Portfolio C: An American call option plus an amount Ke^{-rT} invested at the risk-free rate
Portfolio D: A European put option plus one stock with dividends being reinvested in the stock.
Portfolio C is worth $C + Ke^{-rT}$ while portfolio D is worth $p + S_0$. If the call option is exercised at time $\tau (0 \leq \tau < T)$ portfolio C becomes:

$$S_\tau - K + Ke^{-r(T-\tau)} < S_\tau$$

while portfolio D is worth

$$p + S_\tau e^{q(\tau-t)} \geq S_\tau$$

Hence portfolio D is worth more than portfolio C. If both portfolios are held to maturity (time

T), portfolio C is worth $\max(S_T, K)$ while portfolio D is worth

$$\max(K - S_T, 0) + S_T e^{qT}$$
$$= \max(S_T, K) + S_T(e^{qT} - 1)$$

Hence portfolio D is worth at least as much as portfolio C.
Since portfolio D is worth at least as much as portfolio C in all circumstances:

$$C + Ke^{-rT} \leq p + S_0$$

Since $p \leq P$:

$$C + Ke^{-rT} \leq P + S_0$$

or

$$C - P \leq S_0 - Ke^{-rT}$$

This proves the second part of the inequality. Hence:

$$S_0 e^{-qT} - K \leq C - P \leq S_0 - Ke^{-rT}$$

Problem 16.13.
Show that a European call option on a currency has the same price as the corresponding European put option on the currency when the forward price equals the strike price.

This follows from put–call parity and the relationship between the forward price, F_0, and the spot price, S_0.

$$c + Ke^{-rT} = p + S_0 e^{-r_f T}$$

and

$$F_0 = S_0 e^{(r - r_f)T}$$

so that

$$c + Ke^{-rT} = p + F_0 e^{-rT}$$

If $K = F_0$ this reduces to $c = p$. The result that $c = p$ when $K = F_0$ is true for options on all underlying assets, not just options on currencies. An at-the-money option is frequently defined as one where $K = F_0$ (or $c = p$) rather than one where $K = S_0$.

Problem 16.14.
Would you expect the volatility of a stock index to be greater or less than the volatility of a typical stock? Explain your answer.

The volatility of a stock index can be expected to be less than the volatility of a typical stock. This is because some risk (i.e., return uncertainty) is diversified away when a portfolio of stocks is created. In capital asset pricing model terminology, there exists systematic and unsystematic risk in the returns from an individual stock. However, in a stock index, unsystematic risk has been diversified away and only the systematic risk contributes to volatility.

Problem 16.15.
Does the cost of portfolio insurance increase or decrease as the beta of a portfolio increases? Explain your answer.

The cost of portfolio insurance increases as the beta of the portfolio increases. This is because portfolio insurance involves the purchase of a put option on the portfolio. As beta increases, the volatility of the portfolio increases causing the cost of the put option to increase. When index options are used to provide portfolio insurance, both the number of options required and the strike price increase as beta increases.

Problem 16.16.

Suppose that a portfolio is worth $60 million and the S&P 500 is at 1200. If the value of the portfolio mirrors the value of the index, what options should be purchased to provide protection against the value of the portfolio falling below $54 million in one year's time?

If the value of the portfolio mirrors the value of the index, the index can be expected to have dropped by 10% when the value of the portfolio drops by 10%. Hence when the value of the portfolio drops to $54 million the value of the index can be expected to be 1080. This indicates that put options with an exercise price of 1080 should be purchased. The options should be on:

$$\frac{60,000,000}{1200} = \$50,000$$

times the index. Each option contract is for $100 times the index. Hence 500 contracts should be purchased.

Problem 16.17.

Consider again the situation in Problem 16.16. Suppose that the portfolio has a beta of 2.0, the risk-free interest rate is 5% per annum, and the dividend yield on both the portfolio and the index is 3% per annum. What options should be purchased to provide protection against the value of the portfolio falling below $54 million in one year's time?

When the value of the portfolio falls to $54 million the holder of the portfolio makes a capital loss of 10%. After dividends are taken into account the loss is 7% during the year. This is 12% below the risk-free interest rate. According to the capital asset pricing model, the expected excess return of the portfolio above the risk-free rate equals beta times the expected excess return of the market above the risk-free rate.
Therefore, when the portfolio provides a return 12% below the risk-free interest rate, the market's expected return is 6% below the risk-free interest rate. As the index can be assumed to have a beta of 1.0, this is also the excess expected return (including dividends) from the index. The expected return from the index is therefore -1% per annum. Since the index provides a 3% per annum dividend yield, the expected movement in the index is -4%. Thus when the portfolio's value is $54 million the expected value of the index is $0.96 \times 1200 = 1152$. Hence European put options should be purchased with an exercise price of 1152. Their maturity date should be in one year.
The number of options required is twice the number required in Problem 16.16. This is because we wish to protect a portfolio which is twice as sensitive to changes in market conditions as the portfolio in Problem 16.16. Hence options on $100,000 (or 1,000 contracts) should be purchased. To check that the answer is correct consider what happens when the value of the portfolio declines by 20% to $48 million. The return including dividends is $-$ 17%. This is 22% less than the risk-free interest rate. The index can be expected to provide a return (including dividends) which is 11% less than the risk-free interest rate, i.e. a return of -6%. The index can therefore be expected to drop by 9% to 1092. The payoff from the put options is $(1152 - 1092) \times 100,000 = \$6$ million. This is exactly what is required to restore the value of the portfolio to $54 million.

Problem 16.18.

An index currently stands at 1,500. European call and put options with a strike price of 1,400 and time to maturity of six months have market prices of 154.00 and 34.25, respectively. The six-month risk-free rate is 5%. What is the implied dividend yield?

The implied dividend yield is the value of q that satisfies the put–call parity equation. It is the value of q that solves

$$154 + 1400e^{-0.05 \times 0.5} = 34.25 + 1500e^{-0.5q}$$

This is 1.99%.

Problem 16.19.

A total return index tracks the return, including dividends, on a certain portfolio. Explain how you would value (a) forward contracts and (b) European options on the index.

A total return index behaves like a stock paying no dividends. In a risk-neutral world it can be expected to grow on average at the risk-free rate. Forward contracts and options on total return indices should be valued in the same way as forward contractsand options on non-dividend-paying stocks.

Problem 16.20.

What is the put–call parity relationship for European currency options

The put–call parity relationship for European currency options is

$$c + Ke^{-rT} = p + Se^{-r_f T}$$

To prove this result, the two portfolios to consider are:

Portfolio A: one call option plus one discount bond which will be worth K at time T

Portfolio B: one put option plus $e^{-r_f T}$ of foreign currency invested at the foreign risk-free interest rate.

Both portfolios are worth $\max(S_T, K)$ at time T. They must therefore be worth the same today. The result follows.

Problem 16.21.

Can an option on the yen-euro exchange rate be created from two options, one on the dollar-euro exchange rate, and the other on the dollar-yen exchange rate? Explain your answer.

There is no way of doing this. A natural idea is to create an option to exchange K euros for one yen from an option to exchange Y dollars for 1 yen and an option to exchange K euros for Y dollars. The problem with this is that it assumes that either both options are exercised or that neither option is exercised. There are always some circumstances where the first option is in-the-money at expiration while the second is not and vice versa.

Problem 16.22.

Prove the results in equation (16.1), (16.2), and (16.3) using the portfolios indicated.

In portfolio A, the cash, if it is invested at the risk-free interest rate, will grow to K at time T. If $S_T > K$, the call option is exercised at time T and portfolio A is worth S_T. If $S_T < K$, the call option expires worthless and the portfolio is worth K. Hence, at time T, portfolio A is worth

$$\max\left(S_T, K\right)$$

Because of the reinvestment of dividends, portfolio B becomes one share at time T. It is, therefore, worth S_T at this time. It follows that portfolio A is always worth as much as, and is sometimes worth more than, portfolio B at time T. In the absence of arbitrage opportunities, this must also be true today. Hence,

$$c + Ke^{-rT} \geq S_0 e^{-qT}$$

or

$$c \geq S_0 e^{-qT} - Ke^{-rT}$$

This proves equation (16.1).

In portfolio C, the reinvestment of dividends means that the portfolio is one put option plus one share at time T. If $S_T < K$, the put option is exercised at time T and portfolio C is worth K. If $S_T > K$, the put option expires worthless and the portfolio is worth S_T. Hence, at time T, portfolio C is worth

$$\max\left(S_T, K\right)$$

Portfolio D is worth K at time T. It follows that portfolio C is always worth as much as, and is sometimes worth more than, portfolio D at time T. In the absence of arbitrage opportunities, this must also be true today. Hence,

$$p + S_0 e^{-qT} \geq Ke^{-rT}$$

or

$$p \geq Ke^{-rT} - S_0 e^{-qT}$$

This proves equation (16.2).

Portfolios A and C are both worth $\max\left(S_T, K\right)$ at time T. They must, therefore, be worth the same today, and the put–call parity result in equation (16.3) follows.

CHAPTER 17
Futures Options

Problem 17.1
Explain the difference between a call option on yen and a call option on yen futures.

A call option on yen gives the holder the right to buy yen in the spot market at an exchange rate equal to the strike price. A call option on yen futures gives the holder the right to receive the amount by which the futures price exceeds the strike price. If the yen futures option is exercised, the holder also obtains a long position in the yen futures contract.

Problem 17.2.
Why are options on bond futures more actively traded than options on bonds?

The main reason is that a bond futures contract is a more liquid instrument than a bond. The price of a Treasury bond futures contract is known immediately from trading on the exchange. The price of a bond can be obtained only by contacting dealers.

Problem 17.3.
"A futures price is like a stock paying a dividend yield." What is the dividend yield?

A futures price behaves like a stock paying a dividend yield at the risk-free interest rate.

Problem 17.4.
A futures price is currently 50. At the end of six months it will be either 56 or 46. The risk-free interest rate is 6% per annum. What is the value of a six-month European call option with a strike price of 50?

In this case $u = 1.12$ and $d = 0.92$. The probability of an up movement in a risk-neutral world is
$$\frac{1 - 0.92}{1.12 - 0.92} = 0.4$$
From risk-neutral valuation, the value of the call is
$$e^{-0.06 \times 0.5}(0.4 \times 6 + 0.6 \times 0) = 2.33$$

Problem 17.5.
How does the put–call parity formula for a futures option differ from put–call parity for an option on a non-dividend-paying stock?

The put–call parity formula for futures options is the same as the put–call parity formula for stock options except that the stock price is replaced by $F_0 e^{-rT}$, where F_0 is the current futures price, r is the risk-free interest rate, and T is the life of the option.

Problem 17.6.
Consider an American futures call option where the futures contract and the option contract expire at the same time. Under what circumstances is the futures option worth more than the corresponding American option on the underlying asset?

The American futures call option is worth more than the corresponding American option on the underlying asset when the futures price is greater than the spot price prior to the maturity of the futures contract. This is the case when the risk-free rate is greater than the income on the asset plus the convenience yield.

Problem 17.7.
Calculate the value of a five-month European put futures option when the futures price is $19, the strike price is $20, the risk-free interest rate is 12% per annum, and the volatility of the futures price is 20% per annum.

In this case $F_0 = 19$, $K = 20$, $r = 0.12$, $\sigma = 0.20$, and $T = 0.4167$. The value of the European put futures option is

$$20N(-d_2)e^{-0.12 \times 0.4167} - 19N(-d_1)e^{-0.12 \times 0.4167}$$

where

$$d_1 = \frac{\ln(19/20) + (0.04/2)0.4167}{0.2\sqrt{0.4167}} = -0.3327$$

$$d_2 = d_1 - 0.2\sqrt{0.4167} = -0.4618$$

This is

$$e^{-0.12 \times 0.4167}[20N(0.4618) - 19N(0.3327)]$$

$$= e^{-0.12 \times 0.4167}(20 \times 0.6778 - 19 \times 0.6303)$$

$$= 1.50$$

or $1.50.

Problem 17.8.
Suppose you buy a put option contract on October gold futures with a strike price of $1200 per ounce. Each contract is for the delivery of 100 ounces. What happens if you exercise when the October futures price is $1,180?

An amount $(1,200 - 1,180) \times 100 = \$2,000$ is added to your margin account and you acquire a short futures position obligating you to sell 100 ounces of gold in October. This position is marked to market in the usual way until you choose to close it out.

Problem 17.9.
Suppose you sell a call option contract on April live cattle futures with a strike price of 90 cents per pound. Each contract is for the delivery of 40,000 pounds. What happens if the contract is exercised when the futures price is 95 cents?

In this case an amount $(0.95 - 0.90) \times 40,000 = \$2,000$ is subtracted from your margin account and you acquire a short position in a live cattle futures contract to sell 40,000 pounds of cattle in April. This position is marked to market in the usual way until you choose to close it out.

Problem 17.10.

Consider a two-month call futures option with a strike price of 40 when the risk-free interest rate is 10% per annum. The current futures price is 47. What is a lower bound for the value of the futures option if it is (a) European and (b) American?

Lower bound if option is European is
$$(F_0 - K)e^{-rT} = (47 - 40)e^{-0.1 \times 2/12} = 6.88$$
Lower bound if option is American is
$$F_0 - K = 7$$

Problem 17.11.

Consider a four-month put futures option with a strike price of 50 when the risk-free interest rate is 10% per annum. The current futures price is 47. What is a lower bound for the value of the futures option if it is (a) European and (b) American?

Lower bound if option is European is
$$(K - F_0)e^{-rT} = (50 - 47)e^{-0.1 \times 4/12} = 2.90$$
Lower bound if option is American is
$$K - F_0 = 3$$

Problem 17.12.

A futures price is currently 60 and its volatility is 30%. The risk-free interest rate is 8% per annum. Use a two-step binomial tree to calculate the value of a six-month European call option on the futures with a strike price of 60? If the call were American, would it ever be worth exercising it early?

In this case $u = e^{0.3 \times \sqrt{1/2}} = 1.1618$; $d = 1/u = 0.0.8607$; and
$$p = \frac{1 - 0.8607}{1.1618 - 0.8607} = 0.4626$$
In the tree shown in Figure S17.1 the middle number at each node is the price of the European option and the lower number is the price of the American option. The tree shows that the value of the European option is 4.3155 and the value of the American option is 4.4026. The American option should sometimes be exercised early.

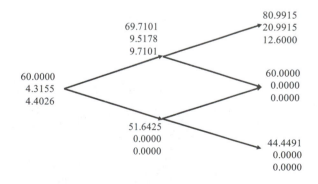

Figure S17.1 Tree to evaluate European and American call options in Problem 17.12

Problem 17.13.
In Problem 17.12 what does the binomial tree give for a six-month European put option is the value of a six-month European put option on futures with a strike price of 60? If the put were American, would it ever be worth exercising it early? Verify that the call prices calculated in Problem 17.12 and the put prices calculated here satisfy put–call parity relationships.

The parameters u, d and p are the same as in Problem 17.12. The tree in Figure S17.2 shows that the prices of the European and American put options are the same as those calculated for call options in Problem 17.12. This illustrates a symmetry that exists for at-the-money futures options. The American option should sometimes be exercised early. Because $K = F_0$ and $c = p$, the European put–call parity result holds.

$$c + Ke^{-rT} = p + F_0 e^{-rT}$$

Also because $C = P$, $F_0 e^{-rT} < K$, and $Ke^{-rT} < F_0$ the result in equation (17.2) holds. (The first expression in equation (17.2) is negative; the middle expression is zero, and the last expression is positive.)

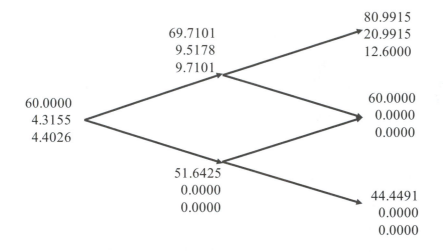

Figure S17.2 Tree to evaluate European and American put options in Problem 17.13

Problem 17.14.
A futures price is currently 25, its volatility is 30% per annum, and the risk-free interest rate is 10% per annum. What is the value of a nine-month European call on the futures with a strike price of 26?

In this case $F_0 = 25$, $K = 26$, $\sigma = 0.3$, $r = 0.1$, $T = 0.75$

$$d_1 = \frac{\ln(F_0 / K) + \sigma^2 T / 2}{\sigma \sqrt{T}} = -0.0211$$

$$d_2 = \frac{\ln(F_0 / K) - \sigma^2 T / 2}{\sigma \sqrt{T}} = -0.2809$$

$$c = e^{-0.075}[25N(-0.0211) - 26N(-0.2809)]$$

$$= e^{-0.075}[25 \times 0.4916 - 26 \times 0.3894] = 2.01$$

Problem 17.15.

A futures price is currently 70, its volatility is 20% per annum, and the risk-free interest rate is 6% per annum. What is the value of a five-month European put on the futures with a strike price of 65?

In this case $F_0 = 70$, $K = 65$, $\sigma = 0.2$, $r = 0.06$, $T = 0.4167$

$$d_1 = \frac{\ln(F_0 / K) + \sigma^2 T / 2}{\sigma \sqrt{T}} = 0.6386$$

$$d_2 = \frac{\ln(F_0 / K) - \sigma^2 T / 2}{\sigma \sqrt{T}} = 0.5095$$

$$p = e^{-0.025}[65N(-0.5095) - 70N(-0.6386)]$$

$$= e^{-0.025}[65 \times 0.3052 - 70 \times 0.2615] = 1.495$$

Problem 17.16.

Suppose that a one-year futures price is currently 35. A one-year European call option and a one-year European put option on the futures with a strike price of 34 are both priced at 2 in the market. The risk-free interest rate is 10% per annum. Identify an arbitrage opportunity.

In this case

$$c + Ke^{-rT} = 2 + 34e^{-0.1 \times 1} = 32.76$$

$$p + F_0 e^{-rT} = 2 + 35e^{-0.1 \times 1} = 33.67$$

Put-call parity shows that we should buy one call, short one put and short a futures contract. This costs nothing up front. In one year, either we exercise the call or the put is exercised against us. In either case, we buy the asset for 34 and close out the futures position. The gain on the short futures position is $35 - 34 = 1$.

Problem 17.17.

"The price of an at-the-money European call futures option always equals the price of a similar at-the-money European put futures option." Explain why this statement is true.

The put price is

$$e^{-rT}[KN(-d_2) - F_0 N(-d_1)]$$

Because $N(-x) = 1 - N(x)$ for all x the put price can also be written

$$e^{-rT}[K - KN(d_2) - F_0 + F_0 N(d_1)]$$

Because $F_0 = K$ this is the same as the call price:

$$e^{-rT}[F_0 N(d_1) - KN(d_2)]$$

This result also follows from put–call parity showing that it is not model dependent.

Problem 17.18.
Suppose that a futures price is currently 30. The risk-free interest rate is 5% per annum. A three-month American call futures option with a strike price of 28 is worth 4. Calculate bounds for the price of a three-month American put futures option with a strike price of 28.

From equation (17.2), $C - P$ must lie between
$$30e^{-0.05 \times 3/12} - 28 = 1.63$$
and
$$30 - 28e^{-0.05 \times 3/12} = 2.35$$
Because $C = 4$ we must have $1.63 < 4 - P < 2.35$ or
$$1.65 < P < 2.37$$

Problem 17.19.
Show that if C is the price of an American call option on a futures contract when the strike price is K and the maturity is T, and P is the price of an American put on the same futures contract with the same strike price and exercise date,
$$F_0 e^{-rT} - K < C - P < F_0 - Ke^{-rT}$$
where F_0 is the futures price and r is the risk-free rate. Assume that $r > 0$ and that there is no difference between forward and futures contracts. (Hint: Use an analogous approach to that indicated for Problem 16.12.)

In this case we consider
Portfolio A: A European call option on futures plus an amount K invested at the risk-free interest rate
Portfolio B: An American put option on futures plus an amount $F_0 e^{-rT}$ invested at the risk-free interest rate plus a long futures contract maturing at time T.
Following the arguments in Chapter 5 we will treat all futures contracts as forward contracts. Portfolio A is worth $c + K$ while portfolio B is worth $P + F_0 e^{-rT}$. If the put option is exercised at time $\tau \, (0 \le \tau < T)$, portfolio B is worth
$$K - F_\tau + F_0 e^{-r(T-\tau)} + F_\tau - F_0$$
$$= K + F_0 e^{-r(T-\tau)} - F_0 < K$$
at time τ where F_τ is the futures price at time τ. Portfolio A is worth
$$c + Ke^{r\tau} \ge K$$
Hence Portfolio A more than Portfolio B. If both portfolios are held to maturity (time T), Portfolio A is worth
$$\max(F_T - K, 0) + Ke^{rT}$$
$$= \max(F_T, K) + K(e^{rT} - 1)$$
Portfolio B is worth
$$\max(K - F_T, 0) + F_0 + F_T - F_0 = \max(F_T, K)$$
Hence portfolio A is worth more than portfolio B.
Because portfolio A is worth more than portfolio B in all circumstances:
$$P + F_0 e^{-r(T-t)} < c + K$$
Because $c \le C$ it follows that

124

$$P + F_0 e^{-rT} < C + K$$

or

$$F_0 e^{-rT} - K < C - P$$

This proves the first part of the inequality.

For the second part of the inequality consider:
Portfolio C: An American call futures option plus an amount Ke^{-rT} invested at the risk-free interest rate
Portfolio D: A European put futures option plus an amount F_0 invested at the risk-free interest rate plus a long futures contract.
Portfolio C is worth $C + Ke^{-rT}$ while portfolio D is worth $p + F_0$. If the call option is exercised at time $\tau (0 \leq \tau < T)$ portfolio C becomes:

$$F_\tau - K + Ke^{-r(T-\tau)} < F_\tau$$

while portfolio D is worth

$$p + F_0 e^{r\tau} + F_\tau - F_0$$
$$= p + F_0(e^{r\tau} - 1) + F_\tau \geq F_\tau$$

Hence portfolio D is worth more than portfolio C. If both portfolios are held to maturity (time T), portfolio C is worth $\max(F_T, K)$ while portfolio D is worth

$$\max(K - F_T, 0) + F_0 e^{rT} + F_T - F_0$$
$$= \max(K, F_T) + F_0(e^{rT} - 1)$$
$$> \max(K, F_T)$$

Hence portfolio D is worth more than portfolio C.
Because portfolio D is worth more than portfolio C in all circumstances

$$C + Ke^{-rT} < p + F_0$$

Because $p \leq P$ it follows that

$$C + Ke^{-rT} < P + F_0$$

or

$$C - P < F_0 - Ke^{-rT}$$

This proves the second part of the inequality. The result:

$$F_0 e^{-rT} - K < C - P < F_0 - Ke^{-rT}$$

has therefore been proved.

Problem 17.20.
Calculate the price of a three-month European call option on the spot price of silver. The three-month futures price is $12, the strike price is $13, the risk-free rate is 4%, and the volatility of the price of silver is 25%.

This has the same value as a three-month call option on silver futures where the futures contract expires in three months. It can therefore be valued using equation (17.9) with $F_0 = 12$, $K = 13$, $r = 0.04$, $\sigma = 0.25$ and $T = 0.25$. The value is 0.244.

Problem 17.21.
A corporation knows that in three months it will have $5 million to invest for 90 days at LIBOR minus 50 basis points and wishes to ensure that the rate obtained will be at least

6.5%. What position in exchange-traded interest-rate options should it take to hedge?

The rate received will be less than 6.5% when LIBOR is less than 7%. The corporation requires a three-month call option on a Eurodollar futures option with a strike price of 93. If three-month LIBOR is greater than 7% at the option maturity, the Eurodollar futures quote at option maturity will be less than 93 and there will be no payoff from the option. If the three-month LIBOR is less than 7%, one Eurodollar futures options provide a payoff of $25 per 0.01%. Each 0.01% of interest costs the corporation $125 (=5,000,000×0.0001×0.25). A total of 125/25 = 5 contracts are therefore required.

CHAPTER 18
The Greek Letters

Problem 18.1.
Explain how a stop-loss trading rule can be implemented for the writer of an out-of-the-money call option. Why does it provide a relatively poor hedge?

Suppose the strike price is 10.00. The option writer aims to be fully covered whenever the option is in the money and naked whenever it is out of the money. The option writer attempts to achieve this by buying the assets underlying the option as soon as the asset price reaches 10.00 from below and selling as soon as the asset price reaches 10.00 from above. The trouble with this scheme is that it assumes that when the asset price moves from 9.99 to 10.00, the next move will be to a price above 10.00. (In practice the next move might back to 9.99.) Similarly it assumes that when the asset price moves from 10.01 to 10.00, the next move will be to a price below 10.00. (In practice the next move might be back to 10.01.) The scheme can be implemented by buying at 10.01 and selling at 9.99. However, it is not a good hedge. The cost of the trading strategy is zero if the asset price never reaches 10.00 and can be quite high if it reaches 10.00 many times. A good hedge has the property that its cost is always very close the value of the option.

Problem 18.2.
What does it mean to assert that the delta of a call option is 0.7? How can a short position in 1,000 options be made delta neutral when the delta of each option is 0.7?

A delta of 0.7 means that, when the price of the stock increases by a small amount, the price of the option increases by 70% of this amount. Similarly, when the price of the stock decreases by a small amount, the price of the option decreases by 70% of this amount. A short position in 1,000 options has a delta of -700 and can be made delta neutral with the purchase of 700 shares.

Problem 18.3.
Calculate the delta of an at-the-money six-month European call option on a non-dividend-paying stock when the risk-free interest rate is 10% per annum and the stock price volatility is 25% per annum.

In this case, $S_0 = K$, $r = 0.1$, $\sigma = 0.25$, and $T = 0.5$. Also,

$$d_1 = \frac{\ln(S_0 / K) + (0.1 + 0.25^2 / 2)0.5}{0.25\sqrt{0.5}} = 0.3712$$

The delta of the option is $N(d_1)$ or 0.64.

Problem 18.4.
What does it mean to assert that the theta of an option position is −0.1 when time is measured in years? If a trader feels that neither a stock price nor its implied volatility will change, what type of option position is appropriate?

A theta of −0.1 means that if Δt units of time pass with no change in either the stock price or its volatility, the value of the option declines by $0.1\Delta t$. A trader who feels that neither the stock price nor its implied volatility will change should write an option with as high a negative theta as possible. Relatively short-life at-the-money options have the most negative thetas.

Problem 18.5.
What is meant by the gamma of an option position? What are the risks in the situation where the gamma of a position is large and negative and the delta is zero?

The gamma of an option position is the rate of change of the delta of the position with respect to the asset price. For example, a gamma of 0.1 would indicate that when the asset price increases by a certain small amount delta increases by 0.1 of this amount. When the gamma of an option writer's position is large and negative and the delta is zero, the option writer will lose significant amounts of money if there is a large movement (either an increase or a decrease) in the asset price.

Problem 18.6.
"The procedure for creating an option position synthetically is the reverse of the procedure for hedging the option position." Explain this statement.

To hedge an option position it is necessary to create the opposite option position synthetically. For example, to hedge a long position in a put it is necessary to create a short position in a put synthetically. It follows that the procedure for creating an option position synthetically is the reverse of the procedure for hedging the option position.

Problem 18.7.
Why did portfolio insurance not work well on October 19, 1987?

Portfolio insurance involves creating a put option synthetically. It assumes that as soon as a portfolio's value declines by a small amount the portfolio manager's position is rebalanced by either (a) selling part of the portfolio, or (b) selling index futures. On October 19, 1987, the market declined so quickly that the sort of rebalancing anticipated in portfolio insurance schemes could not be accomplished.

Problem 18.8.
The Black-Scholes-Merton price of an out-of-the-money call option with an exercise price of $40 is $4. A trader who has written the option plans to use a stop-loss strategy. The trader's plan is to buy at $40.10 and to sell at $39.90. Estimate the expected number of times the stock will be bought or sold.

The strategy costs the trader 0.10 each time the stock is bought or sold. The total expected cost of the strategy, in present value terms, must be $4. This means that the expected number of times the stock will be bought or sold is approximately 40. The expected number of times it will be bought is approximately 20 and the expected number of times it will be sold is also approximately 20. The buy and sell transactions can take place at any time during the life of the option. The above numbers are therefore only approximately correct because of the effects of discounting. Also the estimate is of the number of times the stock is bought or sold in the risk-neutral world, not the real world.

Problem 18.9.
Suppose that a stock price is currently $20 and that a call option with an exercise price of

$25 is created synthetically using a continually changing position in the stock. Consider the following two scenarios:
a) Stock price increases steadily from $20 to $35 during the life of the option.
b) Stock price oscillates wildly, ending up at $35.
Which scenario would make the synthetically created option more expensive? Explain your answer.

The holding of the stock at any given time must be $N(d_1)$. Hence the stock is bought just after the price has risen and sold just after the price has fallen. (This is the buy high sell low strategy referred to in the text.) In the first scenario the stock is continually bought. In second scenario the stock is bought, sold, bought again, sold again, etc. The final holding is the same in both scenarios. The buy, sell, buy, sell... situation clearly leads to higher costs than the buy, buy, buy... situation. This problem emphasizes one disadvantage of creating options synthetically. Whereas the cost of an option that is purchased is known up front and depends on the forecasted volatility, the cost of an option that is created synthetically is not known up front and depends on the volatility actually encountered.

Problem 18.10.
What is the delta of a short position in 1,000 European call options on silver futures? The options mature in eight months, and the futures contract underlying the option matures in nine months. The current nine-month futures price is $8 per ounce, the exercise price of the options is $8, the risk-free interest rate is 12% per annum, and the volatility of silver is 18% per annum.

The delta of a European futures call option is usually defined as the rate of change of the option price with respect to the futures price (not the spot price). It is
$$e^{-rT}N(d_1)$$
In this case $F_0 = 8$, $K = 8$, $r = 0.12$, $\sigma = 0.18$, $T = 0.6667$
$$d_1 = \frac{\ln(8/8) + (0.18^2/2) \times 0.6667}{0.18\sqrt{0.6667}} = 0.0735$$
$N(d_1) = 0.5293$ and the delta of the option is
$$e^{-0.12 \times 0.6667} \times 0.5293 = 0.4886$$
The delta of a short position in 1,000 futures options is therefore -488.6.

Problem 18.11.
In Problem 18.10, what initial position in nine-month silver futures is necessary for delta hedging? If silver itself is used, what is the initial position? If one-year silver futures are used, what is the initial position? Assume no storage costs for silver.

In order to answer this problem it is important to distinguish between the rate of change of the option with respect to the futures price and the rate of change of its price with respect to the spot price.
The former will be referred to as the futures delta; the latter will be referred to as the spot delta. The futures delta of a nine-month futures contract to buy one ounce of silver is by definition 1.0. Hence, from the answer to Problem 18.11, a long position in nine-month futures on 488.6 ounces is necessary to hedge the option position.
The spot delta of a nine-month futures contract is $e^{0.12 \times 0.75} = 1.094$ assuming no storage costs. (This is because silver can be treated in the same way as a non-dividend-paying stock when

there are no storage costs. $F_0 = S_0 e^{rT}$ so that the spot delta is the futures delta times e^{rT})

Hence the spot delta of the option position is $-488.6 \times 1.094 = -534.6$. Thus a long position in 534.6 ounces of silver is necessary to hedge the option position.

The spot delta of a one-year silver futures contract to buy one ounce of silver is $e^{0.12} = 1.1275$. Hence a long position in $e^{-0.12} \times 534.6 = 474.1$ ounces of one-year silver futures is necessary to hedge the option position.

Problem 18.12.
A company uses delta hedging to hedge a portfolio of long positions in put and call options on a currency. Which of the following would give the most favorable result?
a) *A virtually constant spot rate*
b) *Wild movements in the spot rate*
Explain your answer.

A long position in either a put or a call option has a positive gamma. From Figure 18.8, when gamma is positive the hedger gains from a large change in the stock price and loses from a small change in the stock price. Hence the hedger will fare better in case (b).

Problem 18.13.
Repeat Problem 18.12 for a financial institution with a portfolio of short positions in put and call options on a currency.

A short position in either a put or a call option has a negative gamma. From Figure 18.8, when gamma is negative the hedger gains from a small change in the stock price and loses from a large change in the stock price. Hence the hedger will fare better in case (a).

Problem 18.14.
A financial institution has just sold 1,000 seven-month European call options on the Japanese yen. Suppose that the spot exchange rate is 0.80 cent per yen, the exercise price is 0.81 cent per yen, the risk-free interest rate in the United States is 8% per annum, the risk-free interest rate in Japan is 5% per annum, and the volatility of the yen is 15% per annum. Calculate the delta, gamma, vega, theta, and rho of the financial institution's position. Interpret each number.

In this case $S_0 = 0.80$, $K = 0.81$, $r = 0.08$, $r_f = 0.05$, $\sigma = 0.15$, $T = 0.5833$

$$d_1 = \frac{\ln(0.80/0.81) + (0.08 - 0.05 + 0.15^2/2) \times 0.5833}{0.15\sqrt{0.5833}} = 0.1016$$

$$d_2 = d_1 - 0.15\sqrt{0.5833} = -0.0130$$

$$N(d_1) = 0.5405; \quad N(d_2) = 0.4998$$

The delta of one call option is $e^{-r_f T} N(d_1) = e^{-0.05 \times 0.5833} \times 0.5405 = 0.5250$.

$$N'(d_1) = \frac{1}{\sqrt{2\pi}} e^{-d_1^2/2} = \frac{1}{\sqrt{2\pi}} e^{-0.00516} = 0.3969$$

so that the gamma of one call option is

$$\frac{N'(d_1)e^{-r_f T}}{S_0 \sigma \sqrt{T}} = \frac{0.3969 \times 0.9713}{0.80 \times 0.15 \times \sqrt{0.5833}} = 4.206$$

130
©2012 Pearson Education, Inc. Publishing as Prentice Hall.

The vega of one call option is
$$S_0\sqrt{T}N'(d_1)e^{-r_fT} = 0.80\sqrt{0.5833}\times0.3969\times0.9713 = 0.2355$$
The theta of one call option is
$$-\frac{S_0N'(d_1)\sigma e^{-r_fT}}{2\sqrt{T}}+r_fS_0N(d_1)e^{-r_fT}-rKe^{-rT}N(d_2)$$
$$=-\frac{0.8\times0.3969\times0.15\times0.9713}{2\sqrt{0.5833}}$$
$$+0.05\times0.8\times0.5405\times0.9713-0.08\times0.81\times0.9544\times0.4948$$
$$=-0.0399$$
The rho of one call option is
$$KTe^{-rT}N(d_2)$$
$$=0.81\times0.5833\times0.9544\times0.4948$$
$$=0.2231$$

Delta can be interpreted as meaning that, when the spot price increases by a small amount (measured in cents), the value of an option to buy one yen increases by 0.525 times that amount. Gamma can be interpreted as meaning that, when the spot price increases by a small amount (measured in cents), the delta increases by 4.206 times that amount. Vega can be interpreted as meaning that, when the volatility (measured in decimal form) increases by a small amount, the option's value increases by 0.2355 times that amount. When volatility increases by 1% (= 0.01) the option price increases by 0.002355. Theta can be interpreted as meaning that, when a small amount of time (measured in years) passes, the option's value decreases by 0.0399 times that amount. In particular when one calendar day passes it decreases by $0.0399/365 = 0.000109$. Finally, rho can be interpreted as meaning that, when the interest rate (measured in decimal form) increases by a small amount the option's value increases by 0.2231 times that amount. When the interest rate increases by 1% (= 0.01), the options value increases by 0.002231.

Problem 18.15.
Under what circumstances is it possible to make a European option on a stock index both gamma neutral and vega neutral by adding a position in one other European option?

Assume that S_0, K, r, σ, T, q are the parameters for the option held and S_0, K^*, r, σ, T^*, q are the parameters for another option. Suppose that d_1 has its usual meaning and is calculated on the basis of the first set of parameters while d_1^* is the value of d_1 calculated on the basis of the second set of parameters. Suppose further that w of the second option are held for each of the first option held. The gamma of the portfolio is:
$$\alpha\left[\frac{N'(d_1)e^{-qT}}{S_0\sigma\sqrt{T}}+w\frac{N'(d_1^*)e^{-qT^*}}{S_0\sigma\sqrt{T^*}}\right]$$
where α is the number of the first option held.
Since we require gamma to be zero:
$$w=-\frac{N'(d_1)e^{-q(T-T^*)}}{N'(d_1^*)}\sqrt{\frac{T^*}{T}}$$
The vega of the portfolio is:

131

$$\alpha\left[S_0\sqrt{T}N'(d_1)e^{-q(T)} + wS_0\sqrt{T^*}N'(d_1^*)e^{-q(T^*)}\right]$$

Since we require vega to be zero:

$$w = -\sqrt{\frac{T}{T^*}}\frac{N'(d_1)e^{-q(T-T^*)}}{N'(d_1^*)}$$

Equating the two expressions for w

$$T^* = T$$

Hence the maturity of the option held must equal the maturity of the option used for hedging.

Problem 18.16.

A fund manager has a well-diversified portfolio that mirrors the performance of the S&P 500 and is worth $360 million. The value of the S&P 500 is 1,200, and the portfolio manager would like to buy insurance against a reduction of more than 5% in the value of the portfolio over the next six months. The risk-free interest rate is 6% per annum. The dividend yield on both the portfolio and the S&P 500 is 3%, and the volatility of the index is 30% per annum.

 a) *If the fund manager buys traded European put options, how much would the insurance cost?*
 b) *Explain carefully alternative strategies open to the fund manager involving traded European call options, and show that they lead to the same result.*
 c) *If the fund manager decides to provide insurance by keeping part of the portfolio in risk-free securities, what should the initial position be?*
 d) *If the fund manager decides to provide insurance by using nine-month index futures, what should the initial position be?*

The fund is worth $300,000 times the value of the index. When the value of the portfolio falls by 5% (to $342 million), the value of the S&P 500 also falls by 5% to 1140. The fund manager therefore requires European put options on 300,000 times the S&P 500 with exercise price 1140.

a) $S_0 = 1200$, $K = 1140$, $r = 0.06$, $\sigma = 0.30$, $T = 0.50$ and $q = 0.03$. Hence:

$$d_1 = \frac{\ln(1200/1140) + \left(0.06 - 0.03 + 0.3^2/2\right) \times 0.5}{0.3\sqrt{0.5}} = 0.4186$$

$$d_2 = d_1 - 0.3\sqrt{0.5} = 0.2064$$

$$N(d_1) = 0.6622; \quad N(d_2) = 0.5818$$

$$N(-d_1) = 0.3378; \quad N(-d_2) = 0.4182$$

The value of one put option is

$$1140e^{-rT}N(-d_2) - 1200e^{-qT}N(-d_1)$$

$$= 1140e^{-0.06\times0.5} \times 0.4182 - 1200e^{-0.03\times0.5} \times 0.3378$$

$$= 63.40$$

The total cost of the insurance is therefore
$$300,000 \times 63.40 = \$19,020,000$$

b) From put–call parity

$$S_0 e^{-qT} + p = c + Ke^{-rT}$$

or:

$$p = c - S_0 e^{-qT} + Ke^{-rT}$$

This shows that a put option can be created by selling (or shorting) e^{-qT} of the index, buying a call option and investing the remainder at the risk-free rate of interest. Applying this to the situation under consideration, the fund manager should:
1. Sell $360e^{-0.03\times0.5} = \$354.64$ million of stock
2. Buy call options on 300,000 times the S&P 500 with exercise price 1140 and maturity in six months.
3. Invest the remaining cash at the risk-free interest rate of 6% per annum.

This strategy gives the same result as buying put options directly.

c) The delta of one put option is

$$e^{-qT}[N(d_1)-1]$$
$$= e^{-0.03\times0.5}(0.6622-1)$$
$$-0.3327$$

This indicates that 33.27% of the portfolio (i.e., $119.77 million) should be initially sold and invested in risk-free securities.

d) The delta of a nine-month index futures contract is
$$e^{(r-q)T} = e^{0.03\times0.75} = 1.023$$

The spot short position required is
$$\frac{119,770,000}{1200} = 99,808$$

times the index. Hence a short position in
$$\frac{99,808}{1.023\times250} = 390$$

futures contracts is required.

Problem 18.17.
Repeat Problem 18.16 on the assumption that the portfolio has a beta of 1.5. Assume that the dividend yield on the portfolio is 4% per annum.

When the value of the portfolio goes down 5% in six months, the total return from the portfolio, including dividends, in the six months is
$$-5+2 = -3\%$$
i.e., −6% per annum. This is 12% per annum less than the risk-free interest rate. Since the portfolio has a beta of 1.5 we would expect the market to provide a return of 8% per annum less than the risk-free interest rate, i.e., we would expect the market to provide a return of −2% per annum. Since dividends on the market index are 3% per annum, we would expect

the market index to have dropped at the rate of 5% per annum or 2.5% per six months; i.e., we would expect the market to have dropped to 1170. A total of $450,000 = (1.5 \times 300,000)$ put options on the S&P 500 with exercise price 1170 and exercise date in six months are therefore required.

a) $S_0 = 1200$, $K = 1170$, $r = 0.06$, $\sigma = 0.3$, $T = 0.5$ and $q = 0.03$. Hence

$$d_1 = \frac{\ln(1200/1170) + (0.06 - 0.03 + 0.09/2) \times 0.5}{0.3\sqrt{0.5}} = 0.2961$$

$$d_2 = d_1 - 0.3\sqrt{0.5} = 0.0840$$

$$N(d_1) = 0.6164; \quad N(d_2) = 0.5335$$

$$N(-d_1) = 0.3836; \quad N(-d_2) = 0.4665$$

The value of one put option is

$$Ke^{-rT} N(-d_2) - S_0 e^{-qT} N(-d_1)$$

$$= 1170e^{-0.06 \times 0.5} \times 0.4665 - 1200e^{-0.03 \times 0.5} \times 0.3836$$

$$= 76.28$$

The total cost of the insurance is therefore

$$450,000 \times 76.28 = \$34,326,000$$

Note that this is significantly greater than the cost of the insurance in Problem 18.16.

b) As in Problem 18.16 the fund manager can 1) sell $354.64 million of stock, 2) buy call options on 450,000 times the S&P 500 with exercise price 1170 and exercise date in six months and 3) invest the remaining cash at the risk-free interest rate.

c) The portfolio is 50% more volatile than the S&P 500. When the insurance is considered as an option on the portfolio the parameters are as follows: $S_0 = 360$, $K = 342$, $r = 0.06$, $\sigma = 0.45$, $T = 0.5$ and $q = 0.04$

$$d_1 = \frac{\ln(360/342) + (0.06 - 0.04 + 0.45^2/2) \times 0.5}{0.45\sqrt{0.5}} = 0.3517$$

$$N(d_1) = 0.6374$$

The delta of the option is

$$e^{-qT}[N(d_1) - 1]$$

$$= e^{-0.04 \times 0.5}(0.6374 - 1)$$

$$= -0.355$$

This indicates that 35.5% of the portfolio (i.e., $127.8 million) should be sold and invested in riskless securities.

d) We now return to the situation considered in (a) where put options on the index are required. The delta of each put option is

$$e^{-qT}(N(d_1)-1)$$
$$=e^{-0.03\times0.5}(0.6164-1)$$
$$=-0.3779$$

The delta of the total position required in put options is $-450,000\times0.3779=-170,000$. The delta of a nine month index futures is (see Problem 18.16) 1.023. Hence a short position in

$$\frac{170,000}{1.023\times250}=665$$

index futures contracts.

Problem 18.18.

Show by substituting for the various terms in equation (18.4) that the equation is true for:
  a) *A single European call option on a non-dividend-paying stock*
  b) *A single European put option on a non-dividend-paying stock*
  c) *Any portfolio of European put and call options on a non-dividend-paying stock*

a) For a call option on a non-dividend-paying stock
$$\Delta=N(d_1)$$
$$\Gamma=\frac{N'(d_1)}{S_0\sigma\sqrt{T}}$$
$$\Theta=-\frac{S_0N'(d_1)\sigma}{2\sqrt{T}}-rKe^{-rT}N(d_2)$$
Hence the left-hand side of equation (18.4) is:
$$=-\frac{S_0N'(d_1)\sigma}{2\sqrt{T}}-rKe^{-rT}N(d_2)+rS_0N(d_1)+\frac{1}{2}\sigma S_0\frac{N'(d_1)}{\sqrt{T}}$$
$$=r[S_0N(d_1)-Ke^{-rT}N(d_2)]$$
$$=r\Pi$$

b) For a put option on a non-dividend-paying stock
$$\Delta=N(d_1)-1=-N(-d_1)$$
$$\Gamma=\frac{N'(d_1)}{S_0\sigma\sqrt{T}}$$
$$\Theta=-\frac{S_0N'(d_1)\sigma}{2\sqrt{T}}+rKe^{-rT}N(-d_2)$$
Hence the left-hand side of equation (18.4) is:
$$-\frac{S_0N'(d_1)\sigma}{2\sqrt{T}}+rKe^{-rT}N(-d_2)-rS_0N(-d_1)+\frac{1}{2}\sigma S_0\frac{N'(d_1)}{\sqrt{T}}$$
$$=r[Ke^{-rT}N(-d_2)-S_0N(-d_1)]$$
$$=r\Pi$$

c) For a portfolio of options, Π, Δ, Θ and Γ are the sums of their values for the individual options in the portfolio. It follows that equation (18.4) is true for any

135

portfolio of European put and call options.

Problem 18.19

What is the equation corresponding to equation (18.4) for (a) a portfolio of derivatives on a currency and (b) a portfolio of derivatives on a futures price?

A currency is analogous to a stock paying a continuous dividend yield at rate r_f. The differential equation for a portfolio of derivatives dependent on a currency is (see equation 16.6)

$$\frac{\partial \Pi}{\partial t} + (r - r_f)S\frac{\partial \Pi}{\partial S} + \frac{1}{2}\sigma^2 S^2 \frac{\partial^2 \Pi}{\partial S^2} = r\Pi$$

Hence

$$\Theta + (r - r_f)S\Delta + \frac{1}{2}\sigma^2 S^2 \Gamma = r\Pi$$

Similarly, for a portfolio of derivatives dependent on a futures price (see equation 17.8)

$$\Theta + \frac{1}{2}\sigma^2 S^2 \Gamma = r\Pi$$

Problem 18.20.

Suppose that $70 billion of equity assets are the subject of portfolio insurance schemes. Assume that the schemes are designed to provide insurance against the value of the assets declining by more than 5% within one year. Making whatever estimates you find necessary, use the DerivaGem software to calculate the value of the stock or futures contracts that the administrators of the portfolio insurance schemes will attempt to sell if the market falls by 23% in a single day.

We can regard the position of all portfolio insurers taken together as a single put option. The three known parameters of the option, before the 23% decline, are $S_0 = 70$, $K = 66.5$, $T = 1$. Other parameters can be estimated as $r = 0.06$, $\sigma = 0.25$ and $q = 0.03$. Then:

$$d_1 = \frac{\ln(70/66.5) + (0.06 - 0.03 + 0.25^2/2)}{0.25} = 0.4502$$

$$N(d_1) = 0.6737$$

The delta of the option is

$$e^{-qT}[N(d_1) - 1]$$
$$= e^{-0.03}(0.6737 - 1)$$
$$= -0.3167$$

This shows that 31.67% or $22.17 billion of assets should have been sold before the decline. These numbers can also be produced from DerivaGem by selecting Underlying Type and Index and Option Type as Black-Scholes European.

After the decline, $S_0 = 53.9$, $K = 66.5$, $T = 1$, $r = 0.06$, $\sigma = 0.25$ and $q = 0.03$.

$$d_1 = \frac{\ln(53.9/66.5) + (0.06 - 0.03 + 0.25^2/2)}{0.25} = -0.5953$$

$$N(d_1) = 0.2758$$

The delta of the option has dropped to

$$e^{-0.03 \times 0.5}(0.2758 - 1)$$
$$= -0.7028$$

This shows that cumulatively 70.28% of the assets originally held should be sold. An additional 38.61% of the original portfolio should be sold. The sales measured at pre-crash prices are about $27.0 billion. At post-crash prices they are about $20.8 billion.

Problem 18.21.
Does a forward contract on a stock index have the same delta as the corresponding futures contract? Explain your answer.

With our usual notation the value of a forward contract on the asset is $S_0 e^{-qT} - Ke^{-rT}$. When there is a small change, ΔS, in S_0 the value of the forward contract changes by $e^{-qT}\Delta S$. The delta of the forward contract is therefore e^{-qT}. The futures price is $S_0 e^{(r-q)T}$. When there is a small change, ΔS, in S_0 the futures price changes by $\Delta S e^{(r-q)T}$. Given the daily settlement procedures in futures contracts, this is also the immediate change in the wealth of the holder of the futures contract. The delta of the futures contract is therefore $e^{(r-q)T}$. We conclude that the deltas of a futures and forward contract are not the same. The delta of the futures is greater than the delta of the corresponding forward by a factor of e^{rT}.

Problem 18.22.
A bank's position in options on the dollar–euro exchange rate has a delta of 30,000 and a gamma of $-80,000$. Explain how these numbers can be interpreted. The exchange rate (dollars per euro) is 0.90. What position would you take to make the position delta neutral? After a short period of time, the exchange rate moves to 0.93. Estimate the new delta. What additional trade is necessary to keep the position delta neutral? Assuming the bank did set up a delta-neutral position originally, has it gained or lost money from the exchange-rate movement?

The delta indicates that when the value of the euro exchange rate increases by $0.01, the value of the bank's position increases by $0.01 \times 30,000 = \$300$. The gamma indicates that when the euro exchange rate increases by $0.01 the delta of the portfolio decreases by $0.01 \times 80,000 = 800$. For delta neutrality 30,000 euros should be shorted. When the exchange rate moves up to 0.93, we expect the delta of the portfolio to decrease by $(0.93 - 0.90) \times 80,000 = 2,400$ so that it becomes 27,600. To maintain delta neutrality, it is therefore necessary for the bank to unwind its short position 2,400 euros so that a net 27,600 have been shorted. As shown in the text (see Figure 18.8), when a portfolio is delta neutral and has a negative gamma, a loss is experienced when there is a large movement in the underlying asset price. We can conclude that the bank is likely to have lost money.

Problem 18.23.
Use the put–call parity relationship to derive, for a non-dividend-paying stock, the relationship between:
    (a) *The delta of a European call and the delta of a European put.*
    (b) *The gamma of a European call and the gamma of a European put.*
    (c) *The vega of a European call and the vega of a European put.*
    (d) *The theta of a European call and the theta of a European put.*

(a) For a non-dividend paying stock, put-call parity gives at a general time t:

$$p + S = c + Ke^{-r(T-t)}$$

Differentiating with respect to S:

$$\frac{\partial p}{\partial S} + 1 = \frac{\partial c}{\partial S}$$

or

$$\frac{\partial p}{\partial S} = \frac{\partial c}{\partial S} - 1$$

This shows that the delta of a European put equals the delta of the corresponding European call less 1.0.

(b) Differentiating with respect to S again

$$\frac{\partial^2 p}{\partial S^2} = \frac{\partial^2 c}{\partial S^2}$$

Hence the gamma of a European put equals the gamma of a European call.

(c) Differentiating the put-call parity relationship with respect to σ

$$\frac{\partial p}{\partial \sigma} = \frac{\partial c}{\partial \sigma}$$

showing that the vega of a European put equals the vega of a European call.

(d) Differentiating the put-call parity relationship with respect to t

$$\frac{\partial p}{\partial t} = rKe^{-r(T-t)} + \frac{\partial c}{\partial t}$$

This is in agreement with the thetas of European calls and puts given in Section 18.5 since $N(d_2) = 1 - N(-d_2)$.

CHAPTER 19
Volatility Smiles

Problem 19.1.
What volatility smile is likely to be observed when
- (a) *Both tails of the stock price distribution are less heavy than those of the lognormal distribution?*
- (b) *The right tail is heavier, and the left tail is less heavy, than that of a lognormal distribution?*

(a)   A smile similar to that in Figure 19.7 is observed.

(b)   An upward sloping volatility smile is observed

Problem 19.2.
What volatility smile is observed for equities?

A downward sloping volatility smile is usually observed for equities.

Problem 19.3.
What volatility smile is likely to be caused by jumps in the underlying asset price? Is the pattern likely to be more pronounced for a two-year option than for a three-month option?

Jumps tend to make both tails of the stock price distribution heavier than those of the lognormal distribution. This creates a volatility smile similar to that in Figure 19.1. The volatility smile is likely to be more pronounced for the three-month option because jumps tend to get "averaged out" over longer periods.

Problem 19.4.
A European call and put option have the same strike price and time to maturity. The call has an implied volatility of 30% and the put has an implied volatility of 25%. What trades would you do?

The put has a price that is too low relative to the call's price. The correct trading strategy is to buy the put, buy the stock, and sell the call.

Problem 19.5.
Explain carefully why a distribution with a heavier left tail and less heavy right tail than the lognormal distribution gives rise to a downward sloping volatility smile.

The heavier left tail should lead to high prices, and therefore high implied volatilities, for out-of-the-money (low-strike-price) puts. Similarly the less heavy right tail should lead to low prices, and therefore low volatilities for out-of-the-money (high-strike-price) calls. A volatility smile where volatility is a decreasing function of strike price results.

Problem 19.6.
The market price of a European call is $3.00 and its price given by Black-Scholes-Merton model with a volatility of 30% is $3.50. The price given by this Black-Scholes-Merton model

for a European put option with the same strike price and time to maturity is $1.00. What should the market price of the put option be? Explain the reasons for your answer.

With the notation in the text

$$c_{bs} + Ke^{-rT} = p_{bs} + Se^{-qT}$$

$$c_{mkt} + Ke^{-rT} = p_{mkt} + Se^{-qT}$$

It follows that

$$c_{bs} - c_{mkt} = p_{bs} - p_{mkt}$$

In this case, $c_{mkt} = 3.00$; $c_{bs} = 3.50$; and $p_{bs} = 1.00$. It follows that p_{mkt} should be 0.50.

Problem 19.7.
Explain what is meant by crashophobia.

The crashophobia argument is an attempt to explain the pronounced volatility skew in equity markets since 1987. (This was the year equity markets shocked everyone by crashing more than 20% in one day). The argument is that traders are concerned about another crash and as a result increase the price of out-of-the-money puts. This creates the volatility skew.

Problem 19.8.
A stock price is currently $20. Tomorrow, news is expected to be announced that will either increase the price by $5 or decrease the price by $5. What are the problems in using Black–Scholes-Merton to value one-month options on the stock?

The probability distribution of the stock price in one month is not lognormal. Possibly it consists of two lognormal distributions superimposed upon each other and is bimodal. Black–Scholes is clearly inappropriate, because it assumes that the stock price at any future time is lognormal.

Problem 19.9.
What volatility smile is likely to be observed for six-month options when the volatility is uncertain and positively correlated to the stock price?

When the asset price is positively correlated with volatility, the volatility tends to increase as the asset price increases, producing less heavy left tails and heavier right tails. Implied volatility then increases with the strike price.

Problem 19.10.
What problems do you think would be encountered in testing a stock option pricing model empirically?

There are a number of problems in testing an option pricing model empirically. These include the problem of obtaining synchronous data on stock prices and option prices, the problem of estimating the dividends that will be paid on the stock during the option's life, the problem of distinguishing between situations where the market is inefficient and situations where the option pricing model is incorrect, and the problems of estimating stock price volatility.

Problem 19.11.
Suppose that a central bank's policy is to allow an exchange rate to fluctuate between 0.97

and 1.03. What pattern of implied volatilities for options on the exchange rate would you expect to see?

In this case the probability distribution of the exchange rate has a thin left tail and a thin right tail relative to the lognormal distribution. We are in the opposite situation to that described for foreign currencies in Section 19.1. Both out-of-the-money and in-the-money calls and puts can be expected to have lower implied volatilities than at-the-money calls and puts. The pattern of implied volatilities is likely to be similar to Figure 19.7.

Problem 19.12.
Option traders sometimes refer to deep-out-of-the-money options as being options on volatility. Why do you think they do this?

A deep-out-of-the-money option has a low value. Decreases in its volatility reduce its value. However, this reduction is small because the value can never go below zero. Increases in its volatility, on the other hand, can lead to significant percentage increases in the value of the option. The option does, therefore, have some of the same attributes as an option on volatility.

Problem 19.13.
A European call option on a certain stock has a strike price of $30, a time to maturity of one year, and an implied volatility of 30%. A European put option on the same stock has a strike price of $30, a time to maturity of one year, and an implied volatility of 33%. What is the arbitrage opportunity open to a trader? Does the arbitrage work only when the lognormal assumption underlying Black–Scholes–Merton holds? Explain carefully the reasons for your answer.

Put–call parity implies that European put and call options have the same implied volatility. If a call option has an implied volatility of 30% and a put option has an implied volatility of 33%, the call is priced too low relative to the put. The correct trading strategy is to buy the call, sell the put and short the stock. This does not depend on the lognormal assumption underlying Black–Scholes–Merton. Put–call parity is true for any set of assumptions.

Problem 19.14.
Suppose that the result of a major lawsuit affecting a company is due to be announced tomorrow. The company's stock price is currently $60. If the ruling is favorable to the company, the stock price is expected to jump to $75. If it is unfavorable, the stock is expected to jump to $50. What is the risk-neutral probability of a favorable ruling? Assume that the volatility of the company's stock will be 25% for six months after the ruling if the ruling is favorable and 40% if it is unfavorable. Use DerivaGem to calculate the relationship between implied volatility and strike price for six-month European options on the company today. The company does not pay dividends. Assume that the six-month risk-free rate is 6%. Consider call options with strike prices of $30, $40, $50, $60, $70, and $80.

Suppose that p is the probability of a favorable ruling. The expected price of the company's stock tomorrow is

$$75p + 50(1-p) = 50 + 25p$$

This must be the price of the stock today. (We ignore the expected return to an investor over one day.) Hence

$$50 + 25p = 60$$

or $p = 0.4$.

If the ruling is favorable, the volatility, σ, will be 25%. Other option parameters are $S_0 = 75$, $r = 0.06$, and $T = 0.5$. For a value of K equal to 50, DerivaGem gives the value of a European call option price as 26.502.

If the ruling is unfavorable, the volatility, σ will be 40% Other option parameters are $S_0 = 50$, $r = 0.06$, and $T = 0.5$. For a value of K equal to 50, DerivaGem gives the value of a European call option price as 6.310.

The value today of a European call option with a strike price today is the weighted average of 26.502 and 6.310 or:

$$0.4 \times 26.502 + 0.6 \times 6.310 = 14.387$$

DerivaGem can be used to calculate the implied volatility when the option has this price. The parameter values are $S_0 = 60$, $K = 50$, $T = 0.5$, $r = 0.06$ and $c = 14.387$. The implied volatility is 47.76%.

These calculations can be repeated for other strike prices. The results are shown in the table below. The pattern of implied volatilities is shown in Figure S19.1.

Strike Price	Call Price: Favorable Outcome	Call Price: Unfavorable Outcome	Weighted Price	Implied Volatility (%)
30	45.887	21.001	30.955	46.67
40	36.182	12.437	21.935	47.78
50	26.502	6.310	14.387	47.76
60	17.171	2.826	8.564	46.05
70	9.334	1.161	4.430	43.22
80	4.159	0.451	1.934	40.36

Figure S19.1   Implied Volatilities in Problem 19.14

Problem 19.15.

An exchange rate is currently 0.8000. The volatility of the exchange rate is quoted as 12% and interest rates in the two countries are the same. Using the lognormal assumption, estimate the probability that the exchange rate in three months will be (a) less than 0.7000, (b) between 0.7000 and 0.7500, (c) between 0.7500 and 0.8000, (d) between 0.8000 and 0.8500, (e) between 0.8500 and 0.9000, and (f) greater than 0.9000. Based on the volatility smile usually observed in the market for exchange rates, which of these estimates would you expect to be too low and which would you expect to be too high?

As pointed out in Chapters 5 and 16 an exchange rate behaves like a stock that provides a dividend yield equal to the foreign risk-free rate. Whereas the growth rate in a non-dividend-paying stock in a risk-neutral world is r, the growth rate in the exchange rate in a risk-neutral world is $r - r_f$. Exchange rates have low systematic risks and so we can reasonably assume that this is also the growth rate in the real world. In this case the foreign risk-free rate equals the domestic risk-free rate ($r = r_f$). The expected growth rate in the exchange rate is therefore zero. If S_T is the exchange rate at time T its probability distribution is given by equation (14.3) with $\mu = 0$:

$$\ln S_T \sim \varphi(\ln S_0 - \sigma^2 T / 2, \sigma^2 T)$$

where S_0 is the exchange rate at time zero and σ is the volatility of the exchange rate. In this case $S_0 = 0.8000$ and $\sigma = 0.12$, and $T = 0.25$ so that

$$\ln S_T \sim \varphi(\ln 0.8 - 0.12^2 \times 0.25 / 2, 0.12^2 \times 0.25)$$

or

$$\ln S_T \sim \varphi(-0.2249, 0.06^2)$$

a) $\ln 0.70 = -0.3567$. The probability that $S_T < 0.70$ is the same as the probability that $\ln S_T < -0.3567$. It is

$$N\left(\frac{-0.3567 + 0.2249}{0.06}\right) = N(-2.1955)$$

This is 1.41%.

b) $\ln 0.75 = -0.2877$. The probability that $S_T < 0.75$ is the same as the probability that $\ln S_T < -0.2877$. It is

$$N\left(\frac{-0.2877 + 0.2249}{0.06}\right) = N(-1.0456)$$

This is 14.79%. The probability that the exchange rate is between 0.70 and 0.75 is therefore $14.79 - 1.41 = 13.38\%$.

c) $\ln 0.80 = -0.2231$. The probability that $S_T < 0.80$ is the same as the probability that $\ln S_T < -0.2231$. It is

$$N\left(\frac{-0.2231 + 0.2249}{0.06}\right) = N(0.0300)$$

This is 51.20%. The probability that the exchange rate is between 0.75 and 0.80 is therefore $51.20 - 14.79 = 36.41\%$.

d) $\ln 0.85 = -0.1625$. The probability that $S_T < 0.85$ is the same as the probability that $\ln S_T < -0.1625$. It is

$$N\left(\frac{-0.1625 + 0.2249}{0.06}\right) = N(1.0404)$$

This is 85.09%. The probability that the exchange rate is between 0.80 and 0.85 is therefore $85.09 - 51.20 = 33.89\%$.

e) $\ln 0.90 = -0.1054$. The probability that $S_T < 0.90$ is the same as the probability that $\ln S_T < -0.1054$. It is

$$N\left(\frac{-0.1054 + 0.2249}{0.06}\right) = N(1.9931)$$

This is 97.69%. The probability that the exchange rate is between 0.85 and 0.90 is therefore $97.69 - 85.09 = 12.60\%$.

f) The probability that the exchange rate is greater than 0.90 is $100 - 97.69 = 2.31\%$.

The volatility smile encountered for foreign exchange options is shown in Figure 19.1 of the text and implies the probability distribution in Figure 19.2. Figure 19.2 suggests that we would expect the probabilities in (a), (c), (d), and (f) to be too low and the probabilities in (b) and (e) to be too high.

Problem 19.16.

A stock price is $40. A six-month European call option on the stock with a strike price of $30 has an implied volatility of 35%. A six-month European call option on the stock with a strike price of $50 has an implied volatility of 28%. The six-month risk-free rate is 5% and no dividends are expected. Explain why the two implied volatilities are different. Use DerivaGem to calculate the prices of the two options. Use put–call parity to calculate the prices of six-month European put options with strike prices of $30 and $50. Use DerivaGem to calculate the implied volatilities of these two put options.

The difference between the two implied volatilities is consistent with Figure 19.3 in the text. For equities the volatility smile is downward sloping. A high strike price option has a lower implied volatility than a low strike price option. The reason is that traders consider that the probability of a large downward movement in the stock price is higher than that predicted by the lognormal probability distribution. The implied distribution assumed by traders is shown in Figure 19.4.

To use DerivaGem to calculate the price of the first option, proceed as follows. Select Equity as the Underlying Type in the first worksheet. Select Black-Scholes European as the Option Type. Input the stock price as 40, volatility as 35%, risk-free rate as 5%, time to exercise as 0.5 year, and exercise price as 30. Leave the dividend table blank because we are assuming no dividends. Select the button corresponding to call. Do not select the implied volatility button. Hit the *Enter* key and click on calculate. DerivaGem will show the price of the option as 11.155. Change the volatility to 28% and the strike price to 50. Hit the *Enter* key and click on calculate. DerivaGem will show the price of the option as 0.725.

Put–call parity is

$$c + Ke^{-rT} = p + S_0$$

so that

$$p = c + Ke^{-rT} - S_0$$

For the first option, $c = 11.155$, $S_0 = 40$, $r = 0.054$, $K = 30$, and $T = 0.5$ so that

$$p = 11.155 + 30e^{-0.05 \times 0.5} - 40 = 0.414$$

For the second option, $c = 0.725$, $S_0 = 40$, $r = 0.06$, $K = 50$, and $T = 0.5$ so that

$$p = 0.725 + 50e^{-0.05 \times 0.5} - 40 = 9.490$$

144

To use DerivaGem to calculate the implied volatility of the first put option, input the stock price as 40, the risk-free rate as 5%, time to exercise as 0.5 year, and the exercise price as 30. Input the price as 0.414 in the second half of the Option Data table. Select the buttons for a put option and implied volatility. Hit the *Enter* key and click on calculate. DerivaGem will show the implied volatility as 34.99%.

Similarly, to use DerivaGem to calculate the implied volatility of the first put option, input the stock price as 40, the risk-free rate as 5%, time to exercise as 0.5 year, and the exercise price as 50. Input the price as 9.490 in the second half of the Option Data table. Select the buttons for a put option and implied volatility. Hit the *Enter* key and click on calculate. DerivaGem will show the implied volatility as 27.99%.

These results are what we would expect. DerivaGem gives the implied volatility of a put with strike price 30 to be almost exactly the same as the implied volatility of a call with a strike price of 30. Similarly, it gives the implied volatility of a put with strike price 50 to be almost exactly the same as the implied volatility of a call with a strike price of 50.

Problem 19.17.

"The Black–Scholes–Merton model is used by traders as an interpolation tool." Discuss this view.

When plain vanilla call and put options are being priced, traders do use the Black-Scholes-Merton model as an interpolation tool. They calculate implied volatilities for the options whose prices they can observe in the market. By interpolating between strike prices and between times to maturity, they estimate implied volatilities for other options. These implied volatilities are then substituted into Black-Scholes-Merton to calculate prices for these options. In practice much of the work in producing a table such as Table 19.2 in the over-the-counter market is done by brokers. Brokers often act as intermediaries between participants in the over-the-counter market and usually have more information on the trades taking place than any individual financial institution. The brokers provide a table such as Table 19.2 to their clients as a service.

Problem 19.18

Using Table 19.2 calculate the implied volatility a trader would use for an 8-month option with $K/S_0 = 1.04$.

The implied volatility is 13.45%. We get the same answer by (a) interpolating between strike prices of 1.00 and 1.05 and then between maturities six months and one year and (b) interpolating between maturities of six months and one year and then between strike prices of 1.00 and 1.05.

CHAPTER 20
Basic Numerical Procedures

Problem 20.1.
Which of the following can be estimated for an American option by constructing a single binomial tree: delta, gamma, vega, theta, rho?

Delta, gamma, and theta can be determined from a single binomial tree. Vega is determined by making a small change to the volatility and recomputing the option price using a new tree. Rho is calculated by making a small change to the interest rate and recomputing the option price using a new tree.

Problem 20.2.
Calculate the price of a three-month American put option on a non-dividend-paying stock when the stock price is $60, the strike price is $60, the risk-free interest rate is 10% per annum, and the volatility is 45% per annum. Use a binomial tree with a time interval of one month.

In this case, $S_0 = 60$, $K = 60$, $r = 0.1$, $\sigma = 0.45$, $T = 0.25$, and $\Delta t = 0.0833$. Also

$$u = e^{\sigma\sqrt{\Delta t}} = e^{0.45\sqrt{0.0833}} = 1.1387$$

$$d = \frac{1}{u} = 0.8782$$

$$a = e^{r\Delta t} = e^{0.1\times0.0833} = 1.0084$$

$$p = \frac{a-d}{u-d} = 0.4998$$

$$1 - p = 0.5002$$

The output from DerivaGem for this example is shown in the Figure S20.1. The calculated price of the option is $5.16.

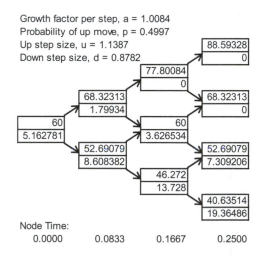

Growth factor per step, a = 1.0084
Probability of up move, p = 0.4997
Up step size, u = 1.1387
Down step size, d = 0.8782

			88.59328
			0
		77.80084	
		0	
	68.32313		68.32313
	1.79934		0
60		60	
5.162781		3.626534	
	52.69079		52.69079
	8.608382		7.309206
		46.272	
		13.728	
			40.63514
			19.36486

Node Time:
0.0000   0.0833   0.1667   0.2500

Figure S20.1   Tree for Problem 20.2

Problem 20.3.
Explain how the control variate technique is implemented when a tree is used to value American options.

The control variate technique is implemented by
(a) Valuing an American option using a binomial tree in the usual way $(= f_A)$.
(b) Valuing the European option with the same parameters as the American option using the same tree $(= f_E)$.
(c) Valuing the European option using Black-Scholes-Merton $(= f_{BS})$.
The price of the American option is estimated as $f_A + f_{BS} - f_E$.

Problem 20.4.
Calculate the price of a nine-month American call option on corn futures when the current futures price is 198 cents, the strike price is 200 cents, the risk-free interest rate is 8% per annum, and the volatility is 30% per annum. Use a binomial tree with a time interval of three months.

In this case $F_0 = 198$, $K = 200$, $r = 0.08$, $\sigma = 0.3$, $T = 0.75$, and $\Delta t = 0.25$. Also

$$u = e^{0.3\sqrt{0.25}} = 1.1618$$

$$d = \frac{1}{u} = 0.8607$$

$$a = 1$$

$$p = \frac{a-d}{u-d} = 0.4626$$

$$1 - p = 0.5373$$

The output from DerivaGem for this example is shown in the Figure S20.2. The calculated price of the option is 20.34 cents.

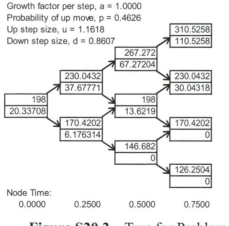

Growth factor per step, a = 1.0000
Probability of up move, p = 0.4626
Up step size, u = 1.1618
Down step size, d = 0.8607

			310.5258
			110.5258
		267.272	
		67.27204	
	230.0432		230.0432
	37.67771		30.04318
198		198	
20.33708		13.6219	
	170.4202		170.4202
	6.176314		0
		146.682	
		0	
			126.2504
			0

Node Time:
0.0000   0.2500   0.5000   0.7500

Figure S20.2   Tree for Problem 20.4

Problem 20.5.
Consider an option that pays off the amount by which the final stock price exceeds the average stock price achieved during the life of the option. Can this be valued using the

binomial tree approach? Explain your answer.

A binomial tree cannot be used in the way described in this chapter. This is an example of what is known as a history-dependent option. The payoff depends on the path followed by the stock price as well as its final value. The option cannot be valued by starting at the end of the tree and working backward since the payoff at the final branches is not known unambiguously. Chapter 26 describes an extension of the binomial tree approach that can be used to handle options where the payoff depends on the average value of the stock price.

Problem 20.6.
"For a dividend-paying stock, the tree for the stock price does not recombine; but the tree for the stock price less the present value of future dividends does recombine." Explain this statement.

Suppose a dividend equal to D is paid during a certain time interval. If S is the stock price at the beginning of the time interval, it will be either $Su - D$ or $Sd - D$ at the end of the time interval. At the end of the next time interval, it will be one of $(Su - D)u$, $(Su - D)d$, $(Sd - D)u$ and $(Sd - D)d$. Since $(Su - D)d$ does not equal $(Sd - D)u$ the tree does not recombine. If S is equal to the stock price less the present value of future dividends, this problem is avoided.

Problem 20.7.
Show that the probabilities in a Cox, Ross, and Rubinstein binomial tree are negative when the condition in footnote 9 holds.

With the usual notation

$$p = \frac{a - d}{u - d}$$

$$1 - p = \frac{u - a}{u - d}$$

If $a < d$ or $a > u$, one of the two probabilities is negative. This happens when

$$e^{(r-q)\Delta t} < e^{-\sigma\sqrt{\Delta t}}$$

or

$$e^{(r-q)\Delta t} > e^{\sigma\sqrt{\Delta t}}$$

This in turn happens when $(q - r)\sqrt{\Delta t} > \sigma$ or $(r - q)\sqrt{\Delta t} > \sigma$ Hence negative probabilities occur when

$$\sigma < |(r - q)\sqrt{\Delta t}|$$

This is the condition in footnote 9.

Problem 20.8.
Use stratified sampling with 100 trials to improve the estimate of π in Business Snapshot 20.1 and Table 20.1.

In Table 20.1 cells A1, A2, A3,..., A100 are random numbers between 0 and 1 defining how far to the right in the square the dart lands. Cells B1, B2, B3,...,B100 are random numbers between 0 and 1 defining how high up in the square the dart lands. For stratified sampling we could choose equally spaced values for the A's and the B's and consider every possible combination. To generate 100 samples we need ten equally spaced values for the A's and the

B's so that there are $10 \times 10 = 100$ combinations. The equally spaced values should be 0.05, 0.15, 0.25,..., 0.95. We could therefore set the A's and B's as follows:

$$A1 = A2 = A3 = ... = A10 = 0.05$$

$$A11 = A12 = A13 = ... = A20 = 0.15$$

...

...

$$A91 = A92 = A93 = ... = A100 = 0.95$$

and

$$B1 = B11 = B21 = ... = B91 = 0.05$$

$$B2 = B12 = B22 = ... = B92 = 0.15$$

...

...

$$B10 = B20 = B30 = ... = B100 = 0.95$$

We get a value for π equal to 3.2, which is closer to the true value than the value of 3.04 obtained with random sampling in Table 20.1. Because samples are not random we cannot easily calculate a standard error of the estimate.

Problem 20.9.
Explain why the Monte Carlo simulation approach cannot easily be used for American-style derivatives.

In Monte Carlo simulation sample values for the derivative security in a risk-neutral world are obtained by simulating paths for the underlying variables. On each simulation run, values for the underlying variables are first determined at time Δt, then at time $2\Delta t$, then at time $3\Delta t$, etc. At time $i\Delta t (i = 0,1,2...)$ it is not possible to determine whether early exercise is optimal since the range of paths which might occur after time $i\Delta t$ have not been investigated. In short, Monte Carlo simulation works by moving forward from time t to time T. Other numerical procedures which accommodate early exercise work by moving backwards from time T to time t.

Problem 20.10
A nine-month American put option on a non-dividend-paying stock has a strike price of $49. The stock price is $50, the risk-free rate is 5% per annum, and the volatility is 30% per annum. Use a three-step binomial tree to calculate the option price.

In this case, $S_0 = 50$, $K = 49$, $r = 0.05$, $\sigma = 0.30$, $T = 0.75$, and $\Delta t = 0.25$. Also

$$u = e^{\sigma\sqrt{\Delta t}} = e^{0.30\sqrt{0.25}} = 1.1618$$

$$d = \frac{1}{u} = 0.8607$$

$$a = e^{r\Delta t} = e^{0.05\times0.25} = 1.0126$$

$$p = \frac{a-d}{u-d} = 0.5043$$

$$1 - p = 0.4957$$

The output from DerivaGem for this example is shown in the Figure S20.3. The calculated price of the option is $4.29. Using 100 steps the price obtained is $3.91

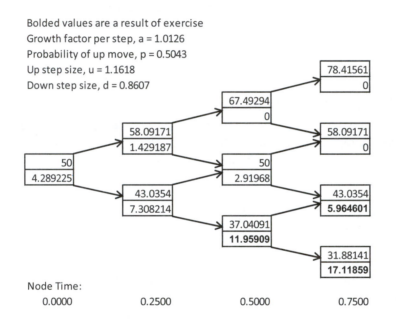

Bolded values are a result of exercise
Growth factor per step, a = 1.0126
Probability of up move, p = 0.5043
Up step size, u = 1.1618
Down step size, d = 0.8607

Node Time:
0.0000   0.2500   0.5000   0.7500

Figure S20.3   Tree for Problem 20.10

Problem 20.11.

Use a three-time-step tree to value a nine-month American call option on wheat futures. The current futures price is 400 cents, the strike price is 420 cents, the risk-free rate is 6%, and the volatility is 35% per annum. Estimate the delta of the option from your tree.

In this case $F_0 = 400$, $K = 420$, $r = 0.06$, $\sigma = 0.35$, $T = 0.75$, and $\Delta t = 0.25$. Also

$$u = e^{0.35\sqrt{0.25}} = 1.1912$$

$$d = \frac{1}{u} = 0.8395$$

$$a = 1$$

$$p = \frac{a-d}{u-d} = 0.4564$$

$$1 - p = 0.5436$$

The output from DerivaGem for this example is shown in the Figure S20.4. The calculated price of the option is 42.07 cents. Using 100 time steps the price obtained is 38.64. The option's delta is calculated from the tree is

$$(79.971 - 11.419)/(476.498 - 335.783) = 0.487$$

When 100 steps are used the estimate of the option's delta is 0.483.

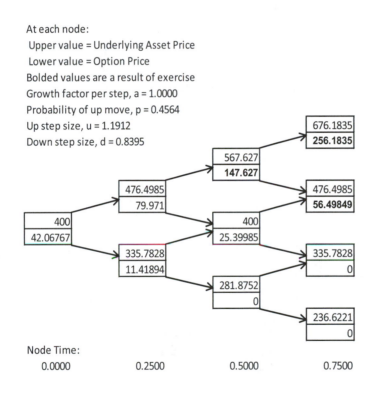

At each node:
Upper value = Underlying Asset Price
Lower value = Option Price
Bolded values are a result of exercise
Growth factor per step, a = 1.0000
Probability of up move, p = 0.4564
Up step size, u = 1.1912
Down step size, d = 0.8395

Figure S20.4   Tree for Problem 20.11

Problem 20.12
A three-month American call option on a stock has a strike price of $20. The stock price is $20, the risk-free rate is 3% per annum, and the volatility is 25% per annum. A dividend of $2 is expected in 1.5 months. Use a three-step binomial tree to calculate the option price.

In this case the present value of the dividend is $2e^{-0.03 \times 0.125} = 1.9925$. We first build a tree for $S_0 = 20 - 1.9925 = 18.0075$, $K = 20$, $r = 0.03$, $\sigma = 0.25$, and $T = 0.25$ with $\Delta t = 0.08333$.

This gives Figure S20.5. For nodes between times0 and 1.5 months we then add the present value of the dividend to the stock price. The result is the tree in Figure S20.6. The price of the option calculated from the tree is 0.674. When 100 steps are used the price obtained is 0.690.

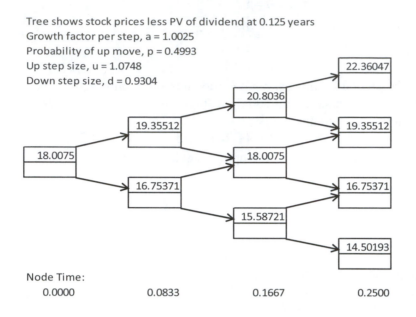

Tree shows stock prices less PV of dividend at 0.125 years
Growth factor per step, a = 1.0025
Probability of up move, p = 0.4993
Up step size, u = 1.0748
Down step size, d = 0.9304

Node Time:
0.0000   0.0833   0.1667   0.2500

Figure S20.5   First tree for Problem 20.12

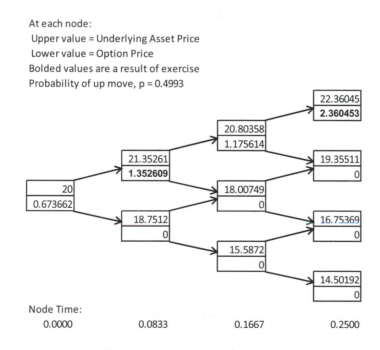

At each node:
Upper value = Underlying Asset Price
Lower value = Option Price
Bolded values are a result of exercise
Probability of up move, p = 0.4993

Node Time:
0.0000   0.0833   0.1667   0.2500

Figure S20.6   Final Tree for Problem 20.12

Problem 20.13

A one-year American put option on a non-dividend-paying stock has an exercise price of $18. The current stock price is $20, the risk-free interest rate is 15% per annum, and the volatility of the stock is 40% per annum. Use the DerivaGem software with four three-month time steps to estimate the value of the option. Display the tree and verify that the option prices at the final and penultimate nodes are correct. Use DerivaGem to value the European version of the option. Use the control variate technique to improve your estimate of the price of the American option.

In this case $S_0 = 20$, $K = 18$, $r = 0.15$, $\sigma = 0.40$, $T = 1$, and $\Delta t = 0.25$. The parameters for the tree are

$$u = e^{\sigma\sqrt{\Delta t}} = e^{0.4\sqrt{0.25}} = 1.2214$$

$$d = 1/u = 0.8187$$

$$a = e^{r\Delta t} = 1.0382$$

$$p = \frac{a-d}{u-d} = \frac{1.0382 - 0.8187}{1.2214 - 0.8187} = 0.545$$

The tree produced by DerivaGem for the American option is shown in Figure S20.7. The estimated value of the American option is $1.29.

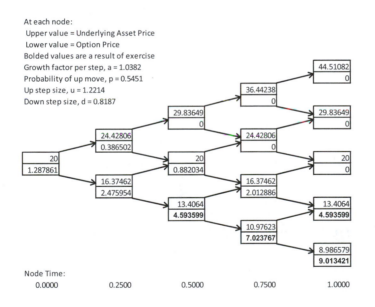

Figure S20.7   Tree to evaluate American option for Problem 20.13

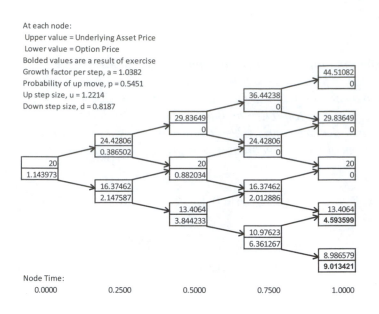

At each node:
 Upper value = Underlying Asset Price
 Lower value = Option Price
Bolded values are a result of exercise
Growth factor per step, a = 1.0382
Probability of up move, p = 0.5451
Up step size, u = 1.2214
Down step size, d = 0.8187

Node Time:
0.0000   0.2500   0.5000   0.7500   1.0000

Figure S20.8   Tree to evaluate European option in Problem 20.13

As shown in Figure S20.8, the same tree can be used to value a European put option with the same parameters. The estimated value of the European option is $1.14. The option parameters are $S_0 = 20$, $K = 18$, $r = 0.15$, $\sigma = 0.40$ and $T = 1$

$$d_1 = \frac{\ln(20/18) + 0.15 + 0.40^2/2}{0.40} = 0.8384$$

$$d_2 = d_1 - 0.40 = 0.4384$$

$$N(-d_1) = 0.2009; \quad N(-d_2) = 0.3306$$

The true European put price is therefore

$$18e^{-0.15} \times 0.3306 - 20 \times 0.2009 = 1.10$$

This can also be obtained from DerivaGem. The control variate estimate of the American put price is therefore $1.29 + 1.10 - 1.14 = \$1.25$.

Problem 20.14

A two-month American put option on a stock index has an exercise price of 480. The current level of the index is 484, the risk-free interest rate is 10% per annum, the dividend yield on the index is 3% per annum, and the volatility of the index is 25% per annum. Divide the life of the option into four half-month periods and use the binomial tree approach to estimate the value of the option.

In this case $S_0 = 484$, $K = 480$, $r = 0.10$, $\sigma = 0.25$ $q = 0.03$, $T = 0.1667$, and $\Delta t = 0.04167$

$$u = e^{\sigma\sqrt{\Delta t}} = e^{0.25\sqrt{0.04167}} = 1.0524$$

$$d = \frac{1}{u} = 0.9502$$

$$a = e^{(r-q)\Delta t} = 1.00292$$

$$p = \frac{a-d}{u-d} = \frac{1.0029 - 0.9502}{1.0524 - 0.9502} = 0.516$$

The tree produced by DerivaGem is shown in the Figure S20.9. The estimated price of the option is $14.93.

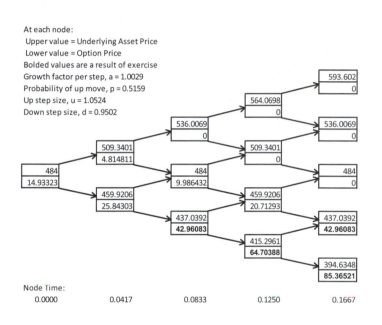

At each node:
Upper value = Underlying Asset Price
Lower value = Option Price
Bolded values are a result of exercise
Growth factor per step, a = 1.0029
Probability of up move, p = 0.5159
Up step size, u = 1.0524
Down step size, d = 0.9502

Node Time:
0.0000   0.0417   0.0833   0.1250   0.1667

Figure S20.9   Tree to evaluate option in Problem 20.14

Problem 20.15
How can the control variate approach to improve the estimate of the delta of an American option when the binomial tree approach is used?

First the delta of the American option is estimated in the usual way from the tree. Denote this by Δ_A^*. Then the delta of a European option which has the same parameters as the American option is calculated in the same way using the same tree. Denote this by Δ_B^*. Finally the true European delta, Δ_B, is calculated using the formulas in Chapter 18. The control variate estimate of delta is then:

$$\Delta_A^* - \Delta_B^* + \Delta_B$$

Problem 20.16.
Suppose that Monte Carlo simulation is being used to evaluate a European call option on a non-dividend-paying stock when the volatility is stochastic. How could the control variate

and antithetic variable technique be used to improve numerical efficiency? Explain why it is necessary to calculate six values of the option in each simulation trial when both the control variate and the antithetic variable technique are used.

In this case a simulation requires two sets of samples from standardized normal distributions. The first is to generate the volatility movements. The second is to generate the stock price movements once the volatility movements are known. The control variate technique involves carrying out a second simulation on the assumption that the volatility is constant. The same random number stream is used to generate stock price movements as in the first simulation. An improved estimate of the option price is

$$f_A^* - f_B^* + f_B$$

where f_A^* is the option value from the first simulation (when the volatility is stochastic), f_B^* is the option value from the second simulation (when the volatility is constant) and f_B is the true Black-Scholes-Merton value when the volatility is constant.

To use the antithetic variable technique, two sets of samples from standardized normal distributions must be used for each of volatility and stock price. Denote the volatility samples by $\{V_1\}$ and $\{V_2\}$ and the stock price samples by $\{S_1\}$ and $\{S_2\}$. $\{V_1\}$ is antithetic to $\{V_2\}$ and $\{S_1\}$ is antithetic to $\{S_2\}$. Thus if

$$\{V_1\} = +0.83, +0.41, -0.21...$$

then

$$\{V_2\} = -0.83, -0.41, +0.21...$$

Similarly for $\{S_1\}$ and $\{S_2\}$.

An efficient way of proceeding is to carry out six simulations in parallel:

      Simulation 1: Use $\{S_1\}$ with volatility constant

      Simulation 2: Use $\{S_2\}$ with volatility constant

      Simulation 3: Use $\{S_1\}$ and $\{V_1\}$

      Simulation 4: Use $\{S_1\}$ and $\{V_2\}$

      Simulation 5: Use $\{S_2\}$ and $\{V_1\}$

      Simulation 6: Use $\{S_2\}$ and $\{V_2\}$

If f_i is the option price from simulation i, simulations 3 and 4 provide an estimate $0.5(f_3 + f_4)$ for the option price. When the control variate technique is used we combine this estimate with the result of simulation 1 to obtain $0.5(f_3 + f_4) - f_1 + f_B$ as an estimate of the price where f_B is, as above, the Black-Scholes-Merton option price. Similarly simulations 2, 5 and 6 provide an estimate $0.5(f_5 + f_6) - f_2 + f_B$. Overall the best estimate is:

$$0.5[0.5(f_3 + f_4) - f_1 + f_B + 0.5(f_5 + f_6) - f_2 + f_B]$$

Problem 20.17.
Explain how equations (20.27) to (20.30) change when the implicit finite difference method is being used to evaluate an American call option on a currency.

For an American call option on a currency

$$\frac{\partial f}{\partial t} + (r - r_f)S\frac{\partial f}{\partial S} + \frac{1}{2}\sigma^2 S^2 \frac{\partial^2 f}{\partial S^2} = rf$$

With the notation in the text this becomes

$$\frac{f_{i+1,j} - f_{ij}}{\Delta t} + (r - r_f)j\Delta S \frac{f_{i,j+1} - f_{i,j-1}}{2\Delta S} + \frac{1}{2}\sigma^2 j^2 \Delta S^2 \frac{f_{i,j+1} - 2f_{i,j} + f_{i,j-1}}{\Delta S^2} = rf_{ij}$$

for $j = 1, 2 \ldots M - 1$ and $i = 0, 1 \ldots N - 1$. Rearranging terms we obtain

$$a_j f_{i,j-1} + b_j f_{ij} + c_j f_{i,j+1} = f_{i+1,j}$$

where

$$a_j = \frac{1}{2}(r - r_f)j\Delta t - \frac{1}{2}\sigma^2 j^2 \Delta t$$

$$b_j = 1 + \sigma^2 j^2 \Delta t + r\Delta t$$

$$c_j = -\frac{1}{2}(r - r_f)j\Delta t - \frac{1}{2}\sigma^2 j^2 \Delta t$$

Equations (20.28), (20.29) and (20.30) become

$$f_{Nj} = \max[j\Delta S - K, 0] \quad j = 0, 1 \ldots M$$

$$f_{i0} = 0 \quad i = 0, 1 \ldots N$$

$$f_{iM} = M\Delta S - K \quad i = 0, 1 \ldots N$$

Problem 20.18.

An American put option on a non-dividend-paying stock has four months to maturity. The exercise price is $21, the stock price is $20, the risk-free rate of interest is 10% per annum, and the volatility is 30% per annum. Use the explicit version of the finite difference approach to value the option. Use stock price intervals of $4 and time intervals of one month.

We consider stock prices of $0, $4, $8, $12, $16, $20, $24, $28, $32, $36 and $40. Using equation (20.34) with $r = 0.10$, $\Delta t = 0.0833$, $\Delta S = 4$, $\sigma = 0.30$, $K = 21$, $T = 0.3333$ we obtain the grid shown below. The option price is $1.56.

Stock Price	Time to Maturity (Months)				
($)	4	3	2	1	0
40	0.00	0.00	0.00	0.00	0.00
36	0.00	0.00	0.00	0.00	0.00
32	0.01	0.00	0.00	0.00	0.00
28	0.07	0.04	0.02	0.00	0.00
24	0.38	0.30	0.21	0.11	0.00
20	1.56	1.44	1.31	1.17	1.00
16	5.00	5.00	5.00	5.00	5.00
12	9.00	9.00	9.00	9.00	9.00
8	13.00	13.00	13.00	13.00	13.00
4	17.00	17.00	17.00	17.00	17.00
0	21.00	21.00	21.00	21.00	21.00

Problem 20.19.

The spot price of copper is $0.60 per pound. Suppose that the futures prices (dollars per pound) are as follows:
3 months   0.59
6 months   0.57
9 months   0.54
12 months   0.50

The volatility of the price of copper is 40% per annum and the risk-free rate is 6% per annum. Use a binomial tree to value an American call option on copper with an exercise price of $0.60 and a time to maturity of one year. Divide the life of the option into four 3-month periods for the purposes of constructing the tree. (Hint: As explained in Chapter 17, the futures price of a variable is its expected future price in a risk-neutral world.)

In this case $\Delta t = 0.25$ and $\sigma = 0.4$ so that

$$u = e^{0.4\sqrt{0.25}} = 1.2214$$

$$d = \frac{1}{u} = 0.8187$$

The futures prices provide estimates of the growth rate in copper in a risk-neutral world. During the first three months this growth rate (with continuous compounding) is

$$4\ln\frac{0.59}{0.60} = -6.72\% \text{ per annum}$$

The parameter p for the first three months is therefore

$$\frac{e^{-0.0672\times0.25} - 0.8187}{1.2214 - 0.8187} = 0.4088$$

The growth rate in copper is equal to -13.79%, -21.63% and -30.78% in the following three quarters. Therefore, the parameter p for the second three months is

$$\frac{e^{-0.1379\times0.25} - 0.8187}{1.2214 - 0.8187} = 0.3660$$

For the third quarter it is

$$\frac{e^{-0.2163\times0.25} - 0.8187}{1.2214 - 0.8187} = 0.3195$$

For the final quarter, it is

$$\frac{e^{-0.3078\times0.25} - 0.8187}{1.2214 - 0.8187} = 0.2663$$

The tree for the movements in copper prices in a risk-neutral world is shown in Figure S20.10. The value of the option is $0.062.

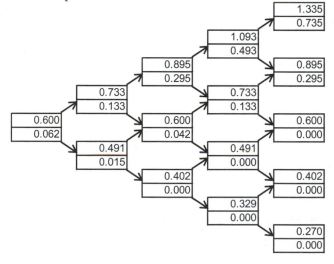

Figure S20.10   Tree to value option in Problem 20.19: At each node, upper number is price of copper and lower number is option price

Problem 20.20.

Use the binomial tree in Problem 20.19 to value a security that pays off x^2 in one year where x is the price of copper.

In this problem we use exactly the same tree for copper prices as in Problem 20.19. However, the values of the derivative are different. On the final nodes the values of the derivative equal the square of the price of copper. On other nodes they are calculated in the usual way. The current value of the security is $0.275 (see Figure S20.11).

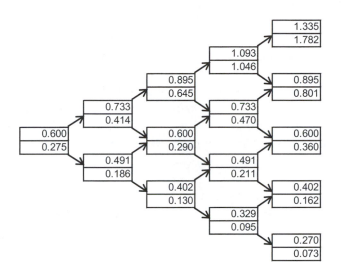

Figure S20.11   Tree to value derivative in Problem 20.20. At each node, upper number is price of copper and lower number is derivative security price.

Problem 20.21.

When do the boundary conditions for $S = 0$ and $S \longrightarrow \infty$ affect the estimates of derivative prices in the explicit finite difference method?

Define S_t as the current asset price, S_{max} as the highest asset price considered and S_{min} as the lowest asset price considered. (In the example in the text $S_{min} = 0$). Let

$$Q_1 = \frac{S_{max} - S_t}{\Delta S} \quad \text{and} \quad Q_2 = \frac{S_t - S_{min}}{\Delta S}$$

and let N be the number of time intervals considered. From the triangular structure of the calculations in the explicit version of the finite difference method, we can see that the values assumed for the derivative security at $S = S_{min}$ and $S = S_{max}$ affect the derivative's value if

$$N \geq \max(Q_1, Q_2)$$

Problem 20.22.

How would you use the antithetic variable method to improve the estimate of the European option in Business Snapshot 20.2 and Table 20.2?

The following changes could be made. Set LI as
= NORMSINV(RAND())
A1 as
=C*EXP(($E$2-$F$2*$F$2/2)*$G$2+$F$2*L2*SQRT($G$2))
H1 as
=C*EXP(($E$2-$F$2*$F$2/2)*$G$2-$F$2*L2*SQRT($G$2)).
I1 as
= EXP(-$E$2*$G$2)*MAX(H1-$D$2,0)
and J1 as
=0.5*(B1+J1)
Other entries in columns L, A, H, and I are defined similarly. The estimate of the value of the option is the average of the values in the J column

Problem 20.23.

A company has issued a three-year convertible bond that has a face value of $25 and can be exchanged for two of the company's shares at any time. The company can call the issue, forcing conversion, when the share price is greater than or equal to $18. Assuming that the company will force conversion at the earliest opportunity, what are the boundary conditions for the price of the convertible? Describe how you would use finite difference methods to value the convertible assuming constant interest rates. Assume there is no risk of the company defaulting.

The basic approach is similar to that described in Section 20.8. The only difference is the boundary conditions. For a sufficiently small value of the stock price, S_{min}, it can be assumed that conversion will never take place and the convertible can be valued as a straight bond. The highest stock price which needs to be considered, S_{max}, is $18. When this is reached the value of the convertible bond is $36. At maturity the convertible is worth the greater of $2S_T$ and $25 where S_T is the stock price.

The convertible can be valued by working backwards through the grid using either the explicit or the implicit finite difference method in conjunction with the boundary conditions. In formulas (20.25) and (20.32) the present value of the income on the convertible between time $t+i\Delta t$ and $t+(i+1)\Delta t$ discounted to time $t+i\Delta t$ must be added to the right-hand side. Chapter 26 considers the pricing of convertibles in more detail.

Problem 20.24.

Provide formulas that can be used for obtaining three random samples from standard normal distributions when the correlation between sample i and sample j is $\rho_{i,j}$.

Suppose x_1, x_2, and x_3 are random samples from three independent normal distributions. Random samples with the required correlation structure are ε_1, ε_2, ε_3 where

$$\varepsilon_1 = x_1$$

$$\varepsilon_2 = \rho_{12}x_1 + x_2\sqrt{1-\rho_{12}^2}$$

and

$$\varepsilon_3 = \alpha_1 x_1 + \alpha_2 x_2 + \alpha_3 x_3$$

where

$$\alpha_1 = \rho_{13}$$

$$\alpha_1 \rho_{12} + \alpha_2 \sqrt{1 - \rho_{12}^2} = \rho_{23}$$

and

$$\alpha_1^2 + \alpha_2^2 + \alpha_3^2 = 1$$

This means that

$$\alpha_1 = \rho_{13}$$

$$\alpha_2 = \frac{\rho_{23} - \rho_{13}\rho_{12}}{\sqrt{1 - \rho_{12}^2}}$$

$$\alpha_3 = \sqrt{1 - \alpha_1^2 - \alpha_2^2}$$

CHAPTER 21
Value at Risk

Problem 21.1.
Consider a position consisting of a $100,000 investment in asset A and a $100,000 investment in asset B. Assume that the daily volatilities of both assets are 1% and that the coefficient of correlation between their returns is 0.3. What is the 5-day 99% VaR for the portfolio?

The standard deviation of the daily change in the investment in each asset is $1,000. The variance of the portfolio's daily change is
$$1,000^2 + 1,000^2 + 2 \times 0.3 \times 1,000 \times 1,000 = 2,600,000$$
The standard deviation of the portfolio's daily change is the square root of this or $1,612.45. The standard deviation of the 5-day change is
$$1,612.45 \times \sqrt{5} = \$3,605.55$$
From the tables of $N(x)$ we see that $N(-2.33) = 0.01$. This means that 1% of a normal distribution lies more than 2.33 standard deviations below the mean. The 5-day 99 percent value at risk is therefore $2.33 \times 3,605.55 = \$8,401$.

Problem 21.2.
Describe three ways of handling interest-rate-dependent instruments when the model building approach is used to calculate VaR. How would you handle interest-rate-dependent instruments when historical simulation is used to calculate VaR?

The three alternative procedures mentioned in the chapter for handling interest rates when the model building approach is used to calculate VaR involve (a) the use of the duration model, (b) the use of cash flow mapping, and (c) the use of principal components analysis. When historical simulation is used we need to assume that the change in the zero-coupon yield curve between Day m and Day $m+1$ is the same as that between Day i and Day $i+1$ for different values of i. In the case of a LIBOR, the zero curve is usually calculated from deposit rates, Eurodollar futures quotes, and swap rates. We can assume that the percentage change in each of these between Day m and Day $m+1$ is the same as that between Day i and Day $i+1$. In the case of a Treasury curve it is usually calculated from the yields on Treasury instruments. Again we can assume that the percentage change in each of these between Day m and Day $m+1$ is the same as that between Day i and Day $i+1$.

Problem 21.3.
A financial institution owns a portfolio of options on the U.S. dollar–sterling exchange rate. The delta of the portfolio is 56.0. The current exchange rate is 1.5000. Derive an approximate linear relationship between the change in the portfolio value and the percentage change in the exchange rate. If the daily volatility of the exchange rate is 0.7%, estimate the 10-day 99% VaR.

The approximate relationship between the daily change in the portfolio value, ΔP, and the daily change in the exchange rate, ΔS, is
$$\Delta P = 56 \Delta S$$
The percentage daily change in the exchange rate, Δx, equals $\Delta S / 1.5$. It follows that

$$\Delta P = 56 \times 1.5 \Delta x$$

or

$$\Delta P = 84 \Delta x$$

The standard deviation of Δx equals the daily volatility of the exchange rate, or 0.7 percent. The standard deviation of ΔP is therefore $84 \times 0.007 = 0.588$. It follows that the 10-day 99 percent VaR for the portfolio is

$$0.588 \times 2.33 \times \sqrt{10} = 4.33$$

Problem 21.4.

Suppose you know that the gamma of the portfolio in the previous question is 16.2. How does this change your estimate of the relationship between the change in the portfolio value and the percentage change in the exchange rate?

The relationship is

$$\Delta P = 56 \times 1.5 \Delta x + \frac{1}{2} \times 1.5^2 \times 16.2 \times \Delta x^2$$

or

$$\Delta P = 84 \Delta x + 18.225 \Delta x^2$$

Problem 21.5.

Suppose that the daily change in the value of a portfolio is, to a good approximation, linearly dependent on two factors, calculated from a principal components analysis. The delta of a portfolio with respect to the first factor is 6 and the delta with respect to the second factor is −4. The standard deviations of the factor are 20 and 8, respectively. What is the 5-day 90% VaR?

The factors calculated from a principal components analysis are uncorrelated. The daily variance of the portfolio is

$$6^2 \times 20^2 + 4^2 \times 8^2 = 15,424$$

and the daily standard deviation is $\sqrt{15,424} = \$124.19$. Since $N(-1.282) = 0.9$, the 5-day 90% value at risk is

$$124.19 \times \sqrt{5} \times 1.282 = \$356.01$$

Problem 21.6.

Suppose a company has a portfolio consisting of positions in stocks, bonds, foreign exchange, and commodities. Assume there are no derivatives. Explain the assumptions underlying (a) the linear model and (b) the historical simulation model for calculating VaR.

The linear model assumes that the percentage daily change in each market variable has a normal probability distribution. The historical simulation model assumes that the probability distribution observed for the percentage daily changes in the market variables in the past is the probability distribution that will apply over the next day.

Problem 21.7.

Explain how an interest rate swap is mapped into a portfolio of zero-coupon bonds with standard maturities for the purposes of a VaR calculation.

When a final exchange of principal is added in, the floating side is equivalent a zero coupon bond with a maturity date equal to the date of the next payment. The fixed side is a coupon-bearing bond, which is equivalent to a portfolio of zero-coupon bonds. The swap can therefore be mapped into a portfolio of zero-coupon bonds with maturity dates corresponding to the payment dates. Each of the zero-coupon bonds can then be mapped into positions in the adjacent standard-maturity zero-coupon bonds.

Problem 21.8.
Explain the difference between Value at Risk and Expected Shortfall.

Value at risk is the loss that is expected to be exceeded $(100 - X)\%$ of the time in N days for specified parameter values, X and N. Expected shortfall is the expected loss conditional that the loss is greater than the Value at Risk.

Problem 21.9.
Explain why the linear model can provide only approximate estimates of VaR for a portfolio containing options.

The change in the value of an option is not linearly related to the change in the value of the underlying variables. When the change in the values of underlying variables is normal, the change in the value of the option is non-normal. The linear model assumes that it is normal and is, therefore, only an approximation.

Problem 21.10.
Some time ago a company has entered into a forward contract to buy £1 million for $1.5 million. The contract now has six months to maturity. The daily volatility of a six-month zero-coupon sterling bond (when its price is translated to dollars) is 0.06% and the daily volatility of a six-month zero-coupon dollar bond is 0.05%. The correlation between returns from the two bonds is 0.8. The current exchange rate is 1.53. Calculate the standard deviation of the change in the dollar value of the forward contract in one day. What is the 10-day 99% VaR? Assume that the six-month interest rate in both sterling and dollars is 5% per annum with continuous compounding.

The contract is a long position in a sterling bond combined with a short position in a dollar bond. The value of the sterling bond is $1.53e^{-0.05 \times 0.5}$ or $1.492 million. The value of the dollar bond is $1.5e^{-0.05 \times 0.5}$ or $1.463 million. The variance of the change in the value of the contract in one day is

$$1.492^2 \times 0.0006^2 + 1.463^2 \times 0.0005^2 - 2 \times 0.8 \times 1.492 \times 0.0006 \times 1.463 \times 0.0005$$
$$= 0.000000288$$

The standard deviation is therefore $0.000537 million. The 10-day 99% VaR is $0.000537 \times \sqrt{10} \times 2.33 = \$0.00396$ million.

Problem 21.11.
The text calculates a VaR estimate for the example in Table 21.9 assuming two factors. How does the estimate change if you assume (a) one factor and (b) three factors.

If we assume only one factor, the model is

$$\Delta P = -0.08 f_1$$

The standard deviation of f_1 is 17.49. The standard deviation of ΔP is therefore

$0.08 \times 17.49 = 1.40$ and the 1-day 99 percent value at risk is $1.40 \times 2.33 = 3.26$. If we assume three factors, our exposure to the third factor is
$$10 \times (-0.37) + 4 \times (-0.38) - 8 \times (-0.30) - 7 \times (-0.12) + 2 \times (-0.04) = -2.06$$
The model is therefore
$$\Delta P = -0.08 f_1 - 4.40 f_2 - 2.06 f_3$$
The variance of ΔP is
$$0.08^2 \times 17.49^2 + 4.40^2 \times 6.05^2 + 2.06^2 \times 3.10^2 = 751.36$$
The standard deviation of ΔP is $\sqrt{751.36} = 27.41$ and the 1-day 99% value at risk is $27.41 \times 2.33 = \$63.87$.
The example illustrates that the relative importance of different factors depends on the portfolio being considered. Normally the second factor is less important than the first, but in this case it is much more important.

Problem 21.12.
A bank has a portfolio of options on an asset. The delta of the options is –30 and the gamma is –5. Explain how these numbers can be interpreted. The asset price is 20 and its volatility per day is 1%. Adapt Sample Application E in the DerivaGem Application Builder software to calculate VaR.

The delta of the options is the rate if change of the value of the options with respect to the price of the asset. When the asset price increases by a small amount the value of the options decrease by 30 times this amount. The gamma of the options is the rate of change of their delta with respect to the price of the asset. When the asset price increases by a small amount, the delta of the portfolio decreases by five times this amount.
By entering 20 for S, 1% for the volatility per day, -30 for delta, -5 for gamma, and recomputing we see that $E(\Delta P) = -0.10$, $E(\Delta P^2) = 36.03$, and $E(\Delta P^3) = -32.415$. The 1-day, 99% VaR given by the software for the quadratic approximation is 14.5. This is a 99% 1-day VaR. The VaR is calculated using the formulas in footnote 9 and the results in Technical Note 10.

Problem 21.13.
Suppose that in Problem 21.12 the vega of the portfolio is -2 per 1% change in the annual volatility. Derive a model relating the change in the portfolio value in one day to delta, gamma, and vega. Explain without doing detailed calculations how you would use the model to calculate a VaR estimate.

Define σ as the volatility per year, $\Delta \sigma$ as the change in σ in one day, and Δw and the proportional change in σ in one day. We measure in σ as a multiple of 1% so that the current value of σ is $1 \times \sqrt{252} = 15.87$. The delta-gamma-vega model is
$$\Delta P = -30 \Delta S - .5 \times 5 \times (\Delta S)^2 - 2 \Delta \sigma$$
or
$$\Delta P = -30 \times 20 \Delta x - 0.5 \times 5 \times 20^2 (\Delta x)^2 - 2 \times 15.87 \Delta w$$
which simplifies to
$$\Delta P = -600 \Delta x - 1,000 (\Delta x)^2 - 31.74 \Delta w$$
The change in the portfolio value now depends on two market variables. Once the daily volatility of σ and the correlation between σ and S have been estimated we can estimate moments of ΔP and use a Cornish–Fisher expansion.

Problem 21.14.
The one-day 99% VaR is calculated for the four-index example in Section 21.2 as $253,385. Look at the underlying spreadsheets on the author's website and calculate the a) the 95% one-day VaR and b) the 97% one-day VaR.

The 95% one-day VaR is the 25th worst loss. This is $156,511. The 97% one-day VaR is the 15th worst loss. This is $172,224.

Problem 21.15.
Use the spreadsheets on the author's web site to calculate the one-day 99% VaR, using the basic methodology in Section 21.2 if the four-index portfolio considered in Section 21.2 is equally divided between the four indices.

In the "Scenarios" worksheet the portfolio investments are changed to 2500 in cells L2:O2. The losses are then sorted from the largest to the smallest. The fifth worst loss is $238,526. This is the one-day 99% VaR.

CHAPTER 22
Estimating Volatilities and Correlations

Problem 22.1.
Explain the exponentially weighted moving average (EWMA) model for estimating volatility from historical data.

Define u_i as $(S_i - S_{i-1})/S_{i-1}$, where S_i is value of a market variable on day i. In the EWMA model, the variance rate of the market variable (i.e., the square of its volatility) calculated for day n is a weighted average of the u_{n-i}^2's ($i = 1, 2, 3, ...$). For some constant λ ($0 < \lambda < 1$) the weight given to u_{n-i-1}^2 is λ times the weight given to u_{n-i}^2. The volatility estimated for day n, σ_n, is related to the volatility estimated for day $n-1$, σ_{n-1}, by

$$\sigma_n^2 = \lambda \sigma_{n-1}^2 + (1-\lambda)u_{n-1}^2$$

This formula shows that the EWMA model has one very attractive property. To calculate the volatility estimate for day n, it is sufficient to know the volatility estimate for day $n-1$ and u_{n-1}.

Problem 22.2.
What is the difference between the exponentially weighted moving average model and the GARCH(1,1) model for updating volatilities?

The EWMA model produces a forecast of the daily variance rate for day n which is a weighted average of (i) the forecast for day $n-1$, and (ii) the square of the proportional change on day $n-1$. The GARCH (1,1) model produces a forecast of the daily variance for day n which is a weighted average of (i) the forecast for day $n-1$, (ii) the square of the proportional change on day $n-1$. and (iii) a long run average variance rate. GARCH (1,1) adapts the EWMA model by giving some weight to a long run average variance rate. Whereas the EWMA has no mean reversion, GARCH (1,1) is consistent with a mean-reverting variance rate model.

Problem 22.3.
The most recent estimate of the daily volatility of an asset is 1.5% and the price of the asset at the close of trading yesterday was $30.00. The parameter λ in the EWMA model is 0.94. Suppose that the price of the asset at the close of trading today is $30.50. How will this cause the volatility to be updated by the EWMA model?

In this case $\sigma_{n-1} = 0.015$ and $u_n = 0.5/30 = 0.01667$, so that equation (22.7) gives

$$\sigma_n^2 = 0.94 \times 0.015^2 + 0.06 \times 0.01667^2 = 0.0002281$$

The volatility estimate on day n is therefore $\sqrt{0.0002281} = 0.015103$ or 1.5103%.

Problem 22.4.
A company uses an EWMA model for forecasting volatility. It decides to change the parameter λ from 0.95 to 0.85. Explain the likely impact on the forecasts.

Reducing λ from 0.95 to 0.85 means that more weight is put on recent observations of u_i^2 and less weight is given to older observations. Volatilities calculated with $\lambda = 0.85$ will react more quickly to new information and will "bounce around" much more than volatilities calculated with $\lambda = 0.95$.

Problem 22.5.
The volatility of a certain market variable is 30% per annum. Calculate a 99% confidence interval for the size of the percentage daily change in the variable.

The volatility per day is $30/\sqrt{252} = 1.89\%$. There is a 99% chance that a normally distributed variable will be within 2.57 standard deviations. We are therefore 99% confident that the daily change will be less than $2.57 \times 1.89 = 4.86\%$.

Problem 22.6.
A company uses the GARCH(1,1) model for updating volatility. The three parameters are ω, α, and β. Describe the impact of making a small increase in each of the parameters while keeping the others fixed.

The weight given to the long-run average variance rate is $1 - \alpha - \beta$ and the long-run average variance rate is $\omega/(1 - \alpha - \beta)$. Increasing ω increases the long-run average variance rate; increasing α increases the weight given to the most recent data item, reduces the weight given to the long-run average variance rate, and increases the level of the long-run average variance rate. Increasing β increases the weight given to the previous variance estimate, reduces the weight given to the long-run average variance rate, and increases the level of the long-run average variance rate.

Problem 22.7.
The most recent estimate of the daily volatility of the US dollar–sterling exchange rate is 0.6% and the exchange rate at 4 p.m. yesterday was 1.5000. The parameter λ in the EWMA model is 0.9. Suppose that the exchange rate at 4 p.m. today proves to be 1.4950. How would the estimate of the daily volatility be updated?

The proportional daily change is $-0.005/1.5000 = -0.003333$. The current daily variance estimate is $0.006^2 = 0.000036$. The new daily variance estimate is
$$0.9 \times 0.000036 + 0.1 \times 0.003333^2 = 0.000033511$$
The new volatility is the square root of this. It is 0.00579 or 0.579%.

Problem 22.8.
Assume that S&P 500 at close of trading yesterday was 1,040 and the daily volatility of the index was estimated as 1% per day at that time. The parameters in a GARCH(1,1) model are $\omega = 0.000002$, $\alpha = 0.06$, and $\beta = 0.92$. If the level of the index at close of trading today is 1,060, what is the new volatility estimate?

With the usual notation $u_{n-1} = 20/1040 = 0.01923$ so that
$$\sigma_n^2 = 0.000002 + 0.06 \times 0.01923^2 + 0.92 \times 0.01^2 = 0.0001162$$
so that $\sigma_n = 0.01078$. The new volatility estimate is therefore 1.078% per day.

Problem 22.9.

Suppose that the daily volatilities of asset A and asset B calculated at the close of trading yesterday are 1.6% and 2.5%, respectively. The prices of the assets at close of trading yesterday were $20 and $40 and the estimate of the coefficient of correlation between the returns on the two assets was 0.25. The parameter λ used in the EWMA model is 0.95.
(a) Calculate the current estimate of the covariance between the assets.
(b) On the assumption that the prices of the assets at close of trading today are $20.5 and $40.5, update the correlation estimate.

(a) The volatilities and correlation imply that the current estimate of the covariance is $0.25 \times 0.016 \times 0.025 = 0.0001$.

(b) If the prices of the assets at close of trading are $20.5 and $40.5, the proportional changes are $0.5/20 = 0.025$ and $0.5/40 = 0.0125$. The new covariance estimate is
$$0.95 \times 0.0001 + 0.05 \times 0.025 \times 0.0125 = 0.0001106$$
The new variance estimate for asset A is
$$0.95 \times 0.016^2 + 0.05 \times 0.025^2 = 0.00027445$$
so that the new volatility is 0.0166. The new variance estimate for asset B is
$$0.95 \times 0.025^2 + 0.05 \times 0.0125^2 = 0.000601562$$
so that the new volatility is 0.0245. The new correlation estimate is
$$\frac{0.0001106}{0.0166 \times 0.0245} = 0.272$$

Problem 22.10.

The parameters of a GARCH(1,1) model are estimated as $\omega = 0.000004$, $\alpha = 0.05$, and $\beta = 0.92$. What is the long-run average volatility and what is the equation describing the way that the variance rate reverts to its long-run average? If the current volatility is 20% per year, what is the expected volatility in 20 days?

The long-run average variance rate is $\omega/(1-\alpha-\beta)$ or $0.000004/0.03 = 0.0001333$. The long-run average volatility is $\sqrt{0.0001333}$ or 1.155%. The equation describing the way the variance rate reverts to its long-run average is equation (22.13)
$$E[\sigma_{n+k}^2] = V_L + (\alpha+\beta)^k (\sigma_n^2 - V_L)$$
In this case
$$E[\sigma_{n+k}^2] = 0.0001333 + 0.97^k (\sigma_n^2 - 0.0001333)$$
If the current volatility is 20% per year, $\sigma_n = 0.2/\sqrt{252} = 0.0126$. The expected variance rate in 20 days is
$$0.0001333 + 0.97^{20}(0.0126^2 - 0.0001333) = 0.0001471$$
The expected volatility in 20 days is therefore $\sqrt{0.0001471} = 0.0121$ or 1.21% per day.

Problem 22.11.

Suppose that the current daily volatilities of asset X and asset Y are 1.0% and 1.2%, respectively. The prices of the assets at close of trading yesterday were $30 and $50 and the estimate of the coefficient of correlation between the returns on the two assets made at this time was 0.50. Correlations and volatilities are updated using a GARCH(1,1) model. The estimates of the model's parameters are $\alpha = 0.04$ and $\beta = 0.94$. For the correlation $\omega = 0.000001$ and for the volatilities $\omega = 0.000003$. If the prices of the two assets at close of *trading today are $31 and $51, how is the correlation estimate updated?*

Using the notation in the text $\sigma_{u,n-1} = 0.01$ and $\sigma_{v,n-1} = 0.012$ and the most recent estimate of the covariance between the asset returns is $\text{cov}_{n-1} = 0.01 \times 0.012 \times 0.50 = 0.00006$. The variable $u_{n-1} = 1/30 = 0.03333$ and the variable $v_{n-1} = 1/50 = 0.02$. The new estimate of the covariance, cov_n, is

$$0.000001 + 0.04 \times 0.03333 \times 0.02 + 0.94 \times 0.00006 = 0.0000841$$

The new estimate of the variance of the first asset, $\sigma_{u,n}^2$ is

$$0.000003 + 0.04 \times 0.03333^2 + 0.94 \times 0.01^2 = 0.0001414$$

so that $\sigma_{u,n} = \sqrt{0.0001414} = 0.01189$ or 1.189%. The new estimate of the variance of the second asset, $\sigma_{v,n}^2$ is

$$0.000003 + 0.04 \times 0.02^2 + 0.94 \times 0.012^2 = 0.0001544$$

so that $\sigma_{v,n} = \sqrt{0.0001544} = 0.01242$ or 1.242%. The new estimate of the correlation between the assets is therefore $0.0000841 / (0.01189 \times 0.01242) = 0.569$.

Problem 22.12.
Suppose that the daily volatility of the FTSE 100 stock index (measured in pounds sterling) is 1.8% and the daily volatility of the dollar/sterling exchange rate is 0.9%. Suppose further that the correlation between the FTSE 100 and the dollar/sterling exchange rate is 0.4. What is the volatility of the FTSE 100 when it is translated to U.S. dollars? Assume that the dollar/sterling exchange rate is expressed as the number of U.S. dollars per pound sterling. (Hint: When $Z = XY$, the percentage daily change in Z is approximately equal to the percentage daily change in X plus the percentage daily change in Y .)

The FTSE expressed in dollars is XY where X is the FTSE expressed in sterling and Y is the exchange rate (value of one pound in dollars). Define x_i as the proportional change in X on day i and y_i as the proportional change in Y on day i. The proportional change in XY is approximately $x_i + y_i$. The standard deviation of x_i is 0.018 and the standard deviation of y_i is 0.009. The correlation between the two is 0.4. The variance of $x_i + y_i$ is therefore

$$0.018^2 + 0.009^2 + 2 \times 0.018 \times 0.009 \times 0.4 = 0.0005346$$

so that the volatility of $x_i + y_i$ is 0.0231 or 2.31%. This is the volatility of the FTSE expressed in dollars. Note that it is greater than the volatility of the FTSE expressed in sterling. This is the impact of the positive correlation. When the FTSE increases the value of sterling measured in dollars also tends to increase. This creates an even bigger increase in the value of FTSE measured in dollars. Similarly for a decrease in the FTSE.

Problem 22.13.
Suppose that in Problem 22.12 the correlation between the S&P 500 Index (measured in dollars) and the FT-SE 100 Index (measured in sterling) is 0.7, the correlation between the S&P 500 index (measured in dollars) and the dollar-sterling exchange rate is 0.3, and the daily volatility of the S&P 500 Index is 1.6%. What is the correlation between the S&P 500 Index (measured in dollars) and the FT-SE 100 Index when it is translated to dollars? (Hint: For three variables X , Y , and Z , the covariance between $X + Y$ and Z equals the covariance between X and Z plus the covariance between Y and Z .)

Continuing with the notation in Problem 22.12, define z_i as the proportional change in the value of the S&P 500 on day i. The covariance between x_i and z_i is $0.7 \times 0.018 \times 0.016 = 0.0002016$. The covariance between y_i and z_i is $0.3 \times 0.009 \times 0.016 = 0.0000432$. The covariance between $x_i + y_i$ and z_i equals the covariance between x_i and z_i plus the covariance between y_i and z_i. It is

$$0.0002016 + 0.0000432 = 0.0002448$$

The correlation between $x_i + y_i$ and z_i is

$$\frac{0.0002448}{0.016 \times 0.0231} = 0.662$$

Note that the volatility of the S&P 500 drops out in this calculation.

Problem 22.14.
Show that the GARCH (1,1) model

$$\sigma_n^2 = \omega + \alpha u_{n-1}^2 + \beta \sigma_{n-1}^2$$

in equation (22.9) is equivalent to the stochastic volatility model

$$dV = a(V_L - V)\,dt + \xi V\,dz$$

where time is measured in days and V is the square of the volatility of the asset price and

$$a = 1 - \alpha - \beta$$

$$V_L = \frac{\omega}{1 - \alpha - \beta}$$

$$\xi = \alpha\sqrt{2}$$

What is the stochastic volatility model when time is measure in years?
(Hint: The variable u_{n-1} is the return on the asset price in time Δt. It can be assumed to be normally distributed with mean zero and standard deviation σ_{n-1}. It follows that the mean of u_{n-1}^2 and u_{n-1}^4 are σ_{n-1}^2 and $3\sigma_{n-1}^4$, respectively.)

$$\sigma_n^2 = \omega + \alpha u_{n-1}^2 + \beta \sigma_{n-1}^2$$

so that

$$\sigma_n^2 - \sigma_{n-1}^2 = \omega + (\beta - 1)\sigma_{n-1}^2 + \alpha u_{n-1}^2$$

The variable u_{n-1}^2 has a mean of σ_{n-1}^2 and a variance of

$$E(u_{n-1})^4 - [E(u_{n-1}^2)]^2 = 2\sigma_{n-1}^4$$

The standard deviation of u_{n-1}^2 is $\sqrt{2}\sigma_{n-1}^2$. Assuming the u_i are generated by a Wiener process, dz, we can therefore write

$$u_{n-1}^2 = \sigma_{n-1}^2 + \sqrt{2}\sigma_{n-1}^2 \varepsilon$$

where ε is a random sample from a standard normal distribution. Substituting this into the equation for $\sigma_n^2 - \sigma_{n-1}^2$ we get

$$\sigma_n^2 - \sigma_{n-1}^2 = \omega + (\alpha + \beta - 1)\sigma_{n-1}^2 + \alpha\sqrt{2}\sigma_{n-1}^2 \varepsilon$$

We can write $\Delta V = \sigma_n^2 - \sigma_{n-1}^2$ and $V = \sigma_{n-1}^2$. Also $a = 1 - \alpha - \beta$, $aV_L = \omega$, and $\xi = \alpha\sqrt{2}$ so that

$$\Delta V = a(V_L - V) + \xi \varepsilon V$$

Because time is measured in days, $\Delta t = 1$ and

$$\Delta V = a(V_L - V)\Delta t + \xi V \varepsilon \sqrt{\Delta t}$$

The result follows.

When time is measured in years $\Delta t = 1/252$ so that

$$\Delta V = a(V_L - V)252\Delta t + \xi V \varepsilon \sqrt{252}\sqrt{\Delta t}$$

and the process for V is

$$dV = 252a(V_L - V)dt + \xi V \sqrt{252}\, dz$$

Problem 22.15

At the end of Section 22.8, the VaR for the four-index example was calculated using the model-building approach. How does the VaR calculated change if the investment is $2.5 million in each index? Carry out calculations when a) volatilities and correlations are estimated using the equally weighted model and b) when they are estimated using the EWMA model with $\lambda = 0.94$. Use the spreadsheets on the author's web site.

The alphas (row 21 for equal weights and row 7 for EWMA) should be changed to 2,500. This changes the one-day 99% VaR to $226,836 when volatilities and correlations are estimated using the equally weighted model and to $487,737 when EWMA with $\lambda = 0.94$ is used.

Problem 22.16.

What is the effect of changing λ from 0.94 to 0.97 in the EWMA calculations in the four-index example at the end of Section 22.8? Use the spreadsheets on the author's website.

The parameter λ is in cell N3 of the EWMA worksheet. Changing it to 0.97 reduces the one-day 99% VaR from $471,025 to $389,290. This is because less weight is given to recent observations.

CHAPTER 23
Credit Risk

Problem 23.1.

The spread between the yield on a three-year corporate bond and the yield on a similar risk-free bond is 50 basis points. The recovery rate is 30%. Estimate the average hazard rate per year over the three-year period.

From equation (23.2) the average hazard rate over the three years is $0.0050/(1-0.3) = 0.0071$ or 0.71% per year.

Problem 23.2.

Suppose that in Problem 23.1 the spread between the yield on a five-year bond issued by the same company and the yield on a similar risk-free bond is 60 basis points. Assume the same recovery rate of 30%. Estimate the average hazard rate per year over the five-year period. What do your results indicate about the average hazard rate in years 4 and 5?

From equation (23.2) the average hazard rate over the five years is $0.0060/(1-0.3) = 0.0086$ or 0.86% per year. Using the results in the previous question, the hazard rate is 0.71% per year for the first three years and

$$\frac{0.0086 \times 5 - 0.0071 \times 3}{2} = 0.0107$$

or 1.07% per year in years 4 and 5.

Problem 23.3.

Should researchers use real-world or risk-neutral default probabilities for a) calculating credit value at risk and b) adjusting the price of a derivative for defaults?

Real-world probabilities of default should be used for calculating credit value at risk. Risk-neutral probabilities of default should be used for adjusting the price of a derivative for default.

Problem 23.4.

How are recovery rates usually defined?

The recovery rate for a bond is the value of the bond immediately after the issuer defaults as a percent of its face value.

Problem 23.5.

Explain the difference between an unconditional default probability density and a hazard rate.

The hazard rate, $h(t)$ at time t is defined so that $h(t)\Delta t$ is the probability of default between times t and $t+\Delta t$ conditional on no default prior to time t. The unconditional default probability density $q(t)$ is defined so that $q(t)\Delta t$ is the probability of default between times t and $t+\Delta t$ as seen at time zero.

Problem 23.6.

Verify a) that the numbers in the second column of Table 23.4 are consistent with the numbers in Table 23.1 and b) that the numbers in the fourth column of Table 23.5 are consistent with the numbers in Table 23.4 and a recovery rate of 40%.

The first number in the second column of Table 23.4 is calculated as

$$-\frac{1}{7}\ln(1 - 0.00245) = 0.0003504$$

or 0.04% per year when rounded. Other numbers in the column are calculated similarly. The numbers in the fourth column of Table 23.5 are the numbers in the second column of Table 23.4 multiplied by one minus the expected recovery rate. In this case the expected recovery rate is 0.4.

Problem 23.7.

Describe how netting works. A bank already has one transaction with a counterparty on its books. Explain why a new transaction by a bank with a counterparty can have the effect of increasing or reducing the bank's credit exposure to the counterparty.

Suppose company A goes bankrupt when it has a number of outstanding contracts with company B. Netting means that the contracts with a positive value to A are netted against those with a negative value in order to determine how much, if anything, company A owes company B. Company A is not allowed to "cherry pick" by keeping the positive-value contracts and defaulting on the negative-value contracts.

The new transaction will increase the bank's exposure to the counterparty if the contract tends to have a positive value whenever the existing contract has a positive value and a negative value whenever the existing contract has a negative value. However, if the new transaction tends to offset the existing transaction, it is likely to have the incremental effect of reducing credit risk.

Problem 23.8.

What is meant by a haircut in a collateralization agreement? A company offers to post its own equity as collateral. How would you respond?

When securities are pledged as collateral the haircut is the discount applied to their market value for margin calculations. A company's own equity would not be good collateral. When the company defaults on its contracts its equity is likely to be worth very little.

Problem 23.9.

Explain the difference between the Gaussian copula model for the time to default and CreditMetrics as far as the following are concerned: a) the definition of a credit loss and b) the way in which default correlation is modeled.

(a)   In the Gaussian copula model for time to default a credit loss is recognized only when a default occurs. In CreditMetrics it is recognized when there is a credit downgrade as well as when there is a default.

(b)   In the Gaussian copula model of time to default, the default correlation arises because the value of the factor M. This defines the default environment or average default rate in the economy. In CreditMetrics a copula model is applied to credit ratings migration and this determines the joint probability of particular changes in the credit ratings of two companies.

Problem 23.10.

Suppose that the LIBOR/swap curve is flat at 6% with continuous compounding and a five-year bond with a coupon of 5% (paid semiannually) sells for 90.00. How would an asset swap on the bond be structured? What is the asset swap spread that would be calculated in this situation?

Suppose that the principal is $100. The asset swap is structured so that the $10 is paid initially. After that $2.50 is paid every six months. In return LIBOR plus a spread is received on the principal of $100. The present value of the fixed payments is

$$10 + 2.5e^{-0.06 \times 0.5} + 2.5e^{-0.06 \times 1} + \ldots + 2.5e^{-0.06 \times 5} + 100e^{-0.06 \times 5} = 105.3579$$

The spread over LIBOR must therefore have a present value of 5.3579. The present value of $1 received every six months for five years is 8.5105. The spread received every six months must therefore be $5.3579 / 8.5105 = \$0.6296$. The asset swap spread is therefore $2 \times 0.6296 = 1.2592\%$ per annum.

Problem 23.11.

Show that the value of a coupon-bearing corporate bond is the sum of the values of its constituent zero-coupon bonds when the amount claimed in the event of default is the no-default value of the bond, but that this is not so when the claim amount is the face value of the bond plus accrued interest.

When the claim amount is the no-default value, the loss for a corporate bond arising from a default at time t is

$$v(t)(1 - \hat{R})B^*$$

where $v(t)$ is the discount factor for time t and B^* is the no-default value of the bond at time t. Suppose that the zero-coupon bonds comprising the corporate bond have no-default values at time t of Z_1, Z_2, ..., Z_n, respectively. The loss from the ith zero-coupon bond arising from a default at time t is

$$v(t)(1 - \hat{R})Z_i$$

The total loss from all the zero-coupon bonds is

$$v(t)(1 - \hat{R})\sum_i^n Z_i = v(t)(1 - \hat{R})B^*$$

This shows that the loss arising from a default at time t is the same for the corporate bond as for the portfolio of its constituent zero-coupon bonds. It follows that the value of the corporate bond is the same as the value of its constituent zero-coupon bonds.

When the claim amount is the face value plus accrued interest, the loss for a corporate bond arising from a default at time t is

$$v(t)B^* - v(t)\hat{R}[L + a(t)]$$

where L is the face value and $a(t)$ is the accrued interest at time t. In general this is not the same as the loss from the sum of the losses on the constituent zero-coupon bonds.

Problem 23.12.

A four-year corporate bond provides a coupon of 4% per year payable semiannually and has a yield of 5% expressed with continuous compounding. The risk-free yield curve is flat at 3% with continuous compounding. Assume that defaults can take place at the end of each year (immediately before a coupon or principal payment and the recovery rate is 30%. Estimate the risk-neutral default probability on the assumption that it is the same each year.

Define Q as the risk-free rate. The calculations are as follows

Time (yrs)	Def. Prob.	Recovery Amount ($)	Risk-free Value ($)	Loss Given Default ($)	Discount Factor	PV of Expected Loss ($)
1.0	Q	30	104.78	74.78	0.9704	72.57Q
2.0	Q	30	103.88	73.88	0.9418	69.58Q
3.0	Q	30	102.96	72.96	0.9139	66.68Q
4.0	Q	30	102.00	72.00	0.8869	63.86Q
Total						272.69Q

The bond pays a coupon of 2 every six months and has a continuously compounded yield of 5% per year. Its market price is 96.19. The risk-free value of the bond is obtained by discounting the promised cash flows at 3%. It is 103.66. The total loss from defaults should therefore be equated to $103.66 - 96.19 = 7.46$. The value of Q implied by the bond price is therefore given by $272.69Q = 7.46$. or $Q = 0.0274$. The implied probability of default is 2.74% per year.

Problem 23.13.

A company has issued 3- and 5-year bonds with a coupon of 4% per annum payable annually. The yields on the bonds (expressed with continuous compounding) are 4.5% and 4.75%, respectively. Risk-free rates are 3.5% with continuous compounding for all maturities. The recovery rate is 40%. Defaults can take place half way through each year. The risk-neutral default rates per year are Q_1 for years 1 to 3 and Q_2 for years 4 and 5. Estimate Q_1 and Q_2.

The table for the first bond is

Time (yrs)	Def. Prob.	Recovery Amount ($)	Risk-free Value ($)	Loss Given Default ($)	Discount Factor	PV of Expected Loss ($)
0.5	Q_1	40	103.01	63.01	0.9827	$61.92Q_1$
1.5	Q_1	40	102.61	62.61	0.9489	$59.41Q_1$
2.5	Q_1	40	102.20	62.20	0.9162	$56.98Q_1$
Total						$178.31Q_1$

The market price of the bond is 98.35 and the risk-free value is 101.23. It follows that Q_1 is given by

$$178.31Q_1 = 101.23 - 98.35$$

so that $Q_1 = 0.0161$.

The table for the second bond is

Time (yrs)	Def. Prob.	Recovery Amount ($)	Risk-free Value ($)	Loss Given Default ($)	Discount Factor	PV of Expected Loss ($)
0.5	Q_1	40	103.77	63.77	0.9827	$62.67Q_1$
1.5	Q_1	40	103.40	63.40	0.9489	$60.16Q_1$
2.5	Q_1	40	103.01	63.01	0.9162	$57.73Q_1$
3.5	Q_2	40	102.61	62.61	0.8847	$55.39Q_2$
4.5	Q_2	40	102.20	62.20	0.8543	$53.13Q_2$
Total						$180.56Q_1 + 108.53Q_2$

The market price of the bond is 96.24 is and the risk-free value is 101.97. It follows that

$$180.56Q_1 + 108.53Q_2 = 101.97 - 96.24$$

From which we get $Q_2 = 0.0260$ The bond prices therefore imply a probability of default of 1.61% per year for the first three years and 2.60% for the next two years.

Problem 23.14.

 Suppose that a financial institution has entered into a swap dependent on the sterling interest rate with counterparty X and an exactly offsetting swap with counterparty Y. Which of the following statements are true and which are false.

 (a) *The total present value of the cost of defaults is the sum of the present value of the cost of defaults on the contract with X plus the present value of the cost of defaults on the contract with Y.*
 (b) *The expected exposure in one year on both contracts is the sum of the expected exposure on the contract with X and the expected exposure on the contract with Y.*
 (c) *The 95% upper confidence limit for the exposure in one year on both contracts is the sum of the 95% upper confidence limit for the exposure in one year on the contract with X and the 95% upper confidence limit for the exposure in one year on the contract with Y.*

Explain your answers.

The statements in (a) and (b) are true. The statement in (c) is not. Suppose that v_X and v_Y are the exposures to X and Y. The expected value of $v_X + v_Y$ is the expected value of v_X plus the expected value of v_Y. The same is not true of 95% confidence limits.

Problem 23.15.

 A company enters into a one-year forward contract to sell $100 for AUD150. The contract is initially at the money. In other words, the forward exchange rate is 1.50. The one-year dollar risk-free rate of interest is 5% per annum. The one-year dollar rate of interest at which the counterparty can borrow is 6% per annum. The exchange rate volatility is 12% per annum. Estimate the present value of the cost of defaults on the contract Assume that defaults are recognized only at the end of the life of the contract.

The cost of defaults is uv where u is percentage loss from defaults during the life of the contract and v is the value of an option that pays off $\max(150S_T - 100, 0)$ in one year and S_T is the value in dollars of one AUD. The value of u is

$$u = 1 - e^{-(0.06-0.05)\times 1} = 0.009950$$

The variable v is 150 times a call option to buy one AUD for 0.6667. The formula for the call option in terms of forward prices is

$$[FN(d_1) - KN(d_2)]e^{-rT}$$

where

$$d_1 = \frac{\log(F/K) + \sigma^2 T/2}{\sigma\sqrt{T}}$$

$$d_2 = d_1 - \sigma\sqrt{T}$$

In this case, $F = 0.6667$, $K = 0.6667$, $\sigma = 0.12$, $T = 1$, and $r = 0.05$ so that $d_1 = 0.06$, $d_2 = -0.06$ and the value of the call option is 0.0303. It follows that $v = 150 \times 0.0303 = 4.545$

so that the cost of defaults is

$$4.545 \times 0.009950 = 0.04522$$

Problem 23.16.

Suppose that in Problem 23.15, the six-month forward rate is also 1.50 and the six-month dollar risk-free interest rate is 5% per annum. Suppose further that the six-month dollar rate of interest at which the counterparty can borrow is 5.5% per annum. Estimate the present value of the cost of defaults assuming that defaults can occur either at the six-month point or at the one-year point? (If a default occurs at the six-month point, the company's potential loss is the market value of the contract.)

In this case the costs of defaults is $u_1 v_1 + u_2 v_2$ where

$$u_1 = 1 - e^{-(0.055 - 0.05) \times 0.5} = 0.002497$$

$$u_2 = e^{-(0.055 - 0.05) \times 0.5} - e^{-(0.06 - 0.05) \times 1} = 0.007453$$

v_1 is the value of an option that pays off $\max(150 S_T - 100, 0)$ in six months and v_2 is the value of an option that pays off $\max(150 S_T - 100, 0)$ in one year. The calculations in Problem 23.17 show that v_2 is 4.545. Similarly $v_1 = 3.300$ so that the cost of defaults is

$$0.002497 \times 3.300 + 0.007453 \times 4.545 = 0.04211$$

Problem 23.17.

"A long forward contract subject to credit risk is a combination of a short position in a no-default put and a long position in a call subject to credit risk." Explain this statement.

Assume that defaults happen only at the end of the life of the forward contract. In a default-free world the forward contract is the combination of a long European call and a short European put where the strike price of the options equals the delivery price and the maturity of the options equals the maturity of the forward contract. If the no-default value of the contract is positive at maturity, the call has a positive value and the put is worth zero. The impact of defaults on the forward contract is the same as that on the call. If the no-default value of the contract is negative at maturity, the call has a zero value and the put has a positive value. In this case defaults have no effect. Again the impact of defaults on the forward contract is the same as that on the call. It follows that the contract has a value equal to a long position in a call that is subject to default risk and short position in a default-free put.

Problem 23.18.

Explain why the credit exposure on a matched pair of forward contracts resembles a straddle.

Suppose that the forward contract provides a payoff at time T. With our usual notation, the value of a long forward contract is $S_T - Ke^{-rT}$. The credit exposure on a long forward contract is therefore $\max(S_T - Ke^{-rT}, 0)$; that is, it is a call on the asset price with

©2012 Pearson Education, Inc. Publishing as Prentice Hall.

strike price Ke^{-rT}. Similarly the credit exposure on a short forward contract is $\max(Ke^{-rT} - S_T, 0)$; that is, it is a put on the asset price with strike price Ke^{-rT}. The total credit exposure is, therefore, a straddle with strike price Ke^{-rT}.

Problem 23.19.
Explain why the impact of credit risk on a matched pair of interest rate swaps tends to be less than that on a matched pair of currency swaps.

The credit risk on a matched pair of interest rate swaps is $|B_{\text{fixed}} - B_{\text{floating}}|$. As maturity is approached all bond prices tend to par and this tends to zero. The credit risk on a matched pair of currency swaps is $|SB_{\text{foreign}} - B_{\text{fixed}}|$ where S is the exchange rate. The expected value of this tends to increase as the swap maturity is approached because of the uncertainty in S.

Problem 23.20.
"When a bank is negotiating currency swaps, it should try to ensure that it is receiving the lower interest rate currency from a company with a low credit risk." Explain.

As time passes there is a tendency for the currency which has the lower interest rate to strengthen. This means that a swap where we are receiving this currency will tend to move in the money (i.e., have a positive value). Similarly a swap where we are paying the currency will tend to move out of the money (i.e., have a negative value). From this it follows that our expected exposure on the swap where we are receiving the low-interest currency is much greater than our expected exposure on the swap where we are receiving the high-interest currency. We should therefore look for counterparties with a low credit risk on the side of the swap where we are receiving the low-interest currency. On the other side of the swap we are far less concerned about the creditworthiness of the counterparty.

Problem 23.21.
Does put–call parity hold when there is default risk? Explain your answer.

No, put–call parity does not hold when there is default risk. Suppose c^* and p^* are the no-default prices of a European call and put with strike price K and maturity T on a non-dividend-paying stock whose price is S, and that c and p are the corresponding values when there is default risk. The text shows that when we make the independence assumption (that is, we assume that the variables determining the no-default value of the option are independent of the variables determining default probabilities and recovery rates),
$c = c^* e^{-[y(T)-y^*(T)]T}$ and $p = p^* e^{-[y(T)-y^*(T)]T}$. The relationship

$$c^* + Ke^{-y^*(T)T} = p^* + S$$

which holds in a no-default world therefore becomes

$$c + Ke^{-y(T)T} = p + Se^{-[y(T)-y^*(T)]T}$$

when there is default risk. This is not the same as regular put–call parity. What is more, the relationship depends on the independence assumption and cannot be deduced from the same sort of simple no-arbitrage arguments that we used in Chapter 10 for the put–call parity relationship in a no-default world.

Problem 23.22.

Suppose that in an asset swap B is the market price of the bond per dollar of principal, B^* is the default-free value of the bond per dollar of principal, and V is the present value of the asset swap spread per dollar of principal. Show that $V = B^* - B$.

We can assume that the principal is paid and received at the end of the life of the swap without changing the swap's value. If the spread were zero the present value of the floating payments per dollar of principal would be 1. The payment of LIBOR plus the spread therefore has a present value of $1+V$. The payment of the bond cash flows has a present value per dollar of principal of B^*. The initial payment required from the payer of the bond cash flows per dollar of principal is $1-B$. (This may be negative; an initial amount of $B-1$ is then paid by the payer of the floating rate). Because the asset swap is initially worth zero we have

$$1+V = B^* + 1 - B$$

so that

$$V = B^* - B$$

Problem 23.23.

Show that under Merton's model in Section 23.6 the credit spread on a T-year zero-coupon bond is $-\ln[N(d_2) + N(-d_1)/L]/T$ where $L = De^{-rT}/V_0$.

The value of the debt in Merton's model is $V_0 - E_0$ or
$$De^{-rT}N(d_2) - V_0N(d_1) + V_0 = De^{-rT}N(d_2) + V_0N(-d_1)$$
If the credit spread is s this should equal $De^{-(r+s)T}$ so that
$$De^{-(r+s)T} = De^{-rT}N(d_2) + V_0N(-d_1)$$
Substituting $De^{-rT} = LV_0$
$$LV_0e^{-sT} = LV_0N(d_2) + V_0N(-d_1)$$
or
$$Le^{-sT} = LN(d_2) + N(-d_1)$$
so that
$$s = -\ln[N(d_2) + N(-d_1)/L]/T$$

Problem 23.24.

Suppose that the spread between the yield on a 3-year zero-coupon riskless bond and a 3-year zero-coupon bond issued by a corporation is 1%. By how much does Black-Scholes-Merton overstate the value of a 3-year European option sold by the corporation.

When the default risk of the seller of the option is taken into account the option value is the Black-Scholes-Merton price multiplied by $e^{-0.01 \times 3} = 0.9704$. Black-Scholes-Merton overprices the option by about 3%.

Problem 23.25.

Give an example of a) right-way risk and b) wrong-way risk.

(a) Right way risk describes the situation when a default by the counterparty is most likely to occur when the contract has a positive value to the counterparty. An example of right way risk would be when a counterparty's future depends on the price of a commodity and it enters into a contract to partially hedging that exposure.

(b) Wrong way risk describes the situation when a default by the counterparty is most likely to occur when the contract has a negative value to the counterparty. An example of right way risk would be when a counterparty is a speculator and the contract has the same exposure as the rest of the counterparty's portfolio.

CHAPTER 24
Credit Derivatives

Problem 24.1.
Explain the difference between a regular credit default swap and a binary credit default swap.

Both provide insurance against a particular company defaulting during a period of time. In a credit default swap the payoff is the notional principal amount multiplied by one minus the recovery rate. In a binary swap the payoff is the notional principal.

Problem 24.2.
A credit default swap requires a semiannual payment at the rate of 60 basis points per year. The principal is $300 million and the credit default swap is settled in cash. A default occurs after four years and two months, and the calculation agent estimates that the price of the cheapest deliverable bond is 40% of its face value shortly after the default. List the cash flows and their timing for the seller of the credit default swap.

The seller receives
$$300,000,000 \times 0.0060 \times 0.5 = \$900,000$$
at times 0.5, 1.0, 1.5, 2.0, 2.5, 3.0, 3.5, and 4.0 years. The seller also receives a final accrual payment of about $300,000 ($= \$300,000,000 \times 0.060 \times 2/12$) at the time of the default (4 years and two months). The seller pays
$$300,000,000 \times 0.6 = \$180,000,000$$
at the time of the default.

Problem 24.3.
Explain the two ways a credit default swap can be settled.

Sometimes there is physical settlement and sometimes there is cash settlement. In the event of a default when there is physical settlement the buyer of protection sells bonds issued by the reference entity for their face value. Bonds with a total face value equal to the notional principal can be sold. Cash settlement is now more usual. A calculation agent, often using an auction process, estimates the value of the cheapest-to-deliver bonds issued by the reference entity a specified number of days after the default event. The cash payoff is then based on the excess of the face value of these bonds over the estimated value.

Problem 24.4.
Explain how a cash CDO and a synthetic CDO are created.

A cash CDO is created by forming a portfolio of credit sensitive instruments such as bonds. The returns from the bond portfolio flow to a number of tranches (i.e., different categories of investors). A waterfall defines the way interest and principal payments flow to tranches. The more senior a tranche the more likely it is receive promised payments. In a synthetic CDO n portfolio is created. Instead a portfolio of credit default swaps is sold and the resulting credit risks are allocated to tranches.

Problem 24.5.

Explain what a first-to-default credit default swap is. Does its value increase or decrease as the default correlation between the companies in the basket increases? Explain.

In a first-to-default basket CDS there are a number of reference entities. When the first one defaults there is a payoff (calculated in the usual way for a CDS) and basket CDS terminates. The value of a first-to-default basket CDS decreases as the correlation between the reference entities in the basket increases. This is because the probability of a default is high when the correlation is zero and decreases as the correlation increases. In the limit when the correlation is one there is in effect only one company and the probability of a default is quite low.

Problem 24.6.

Explain the difference between risk-neutral and real-world default probabilities.

Risk-neutral default probabilities are backed out from credit default swaps or bond prices. Real-world default probabilities are calculated from historical data.

Problem 24.7.

Explain why a total return swap can be useful as a financing tool.

Suppose a company wants to buy some assets. If a total return swap is used, a financial institution buys the assets and enters into a swap with the company where it pays the company the return on the assets and receives from the company LIBOR plus a spread. The financial institution has less risk than it would have if it lent the company money and used the assets as collateral. This is because, in the event of a default by the company, it owns the assets.

Problem 24.8.

Suppose that the risk-free zero curve is flat at 7% per annum with continuous compounding and that defaults can occur half way through each year in a new five-year credit default swap. Suppose that the recovery rate is 30% and the default probabilities each year conditional on no earlier default are 3%. Estimate the credit default swap spread. Assume payments are made annually.

The table corresponding to Tables 24.1, giving unconditional default probabilities, is

Time (years)	Default Probability	Survival Probability
1	0.0300	0.9700
2	0.0291	0.9409
3	0.0282	0.9127
4	0.0274	0.8853
5	0.0266	0.8587

The table corresponding to Table 24.2, giving the present value of the expected regular payments (payment rate is s per year), is

Time (yrs)	Probability of survival	Expected Payment	Discount Factor	PV of Expected Payment
1	0.9700	0.9700s	0.9324	0.9044s
2	0.9409	0.9409s	0.8694	0.8180s
3	0.9127	0.9127s	0.8106	0.7398s
4	0.8853	0.8853s	0.7558	0.6691s
5	0.8587	0.8587s	0.7047	0.6051s
Total				3.7364s

The table corresponding to Table 24.3, giving the present value of the expected payoffs (notional principal =$1), is

Time (yrs)	Probability of default	Recovery Rate	Expected Payoff	Discount Factor	PV of Expected Payment
0.5	0.0300	0.3	0.0210	0.9656	0.0203
1.5	0.0291	0.3	0.0204	0.9003	0.0183
2.5	0.0282	0.3	0.0198	0.8395	0.0166
3.5	0.0274	0.3	0.0192	0.7827	0.0150
4.5	0.0266	0.3	0.0186	0.7298	0.0136
Total					0.0838

The table corresponding to Table 24.4, giving the present value of accrual payments, is

Time (yrs)	Probability of default	Expected Accrual Payment	Discount Factor	PV of Expected Accrual Payment
0.5	0.0300	0.0150s	0.9656	0.0145s
1.5	0.0291	0.0146s	0.9003	0.0131s
2.5	0.0282	0.0141s	0.8395	0.0118s
3.5	0.0274	0.0137s	0.7827	0.0107s
4.5	0.0266	0.0133s	0.7298	0.0097s
Total				0.0598s

The credit default swap spread s is given by:
$$3.7364s + 0.0598s = 0.0838$$
It is 0.0221 or 221 basis points.

Problem 24.9.

What is the value of the swap in Problem 24.8 per dollar of notional principal to the protection buyer if the credit default swap spread is 150 basis points?

If the credit default swap spread is 150 basis points, the value of the swap to the buyer of protection is:
$$0.0838 - (3.7364 + 0.0598) \times 0.0150 = 0.0269$$
per dollar of notional principal.

Problem 24.10.

What is the credit default swap spread in Problem 24.8 if it is a binary CDS?

If the swap is a binary CDS, the present value of expected payoffs is calculated as follows

Time (years)	Probability of Default	Expected Payoff	Discount Factor	PV of expected Payoff
0.5	0.0300	0.0300	0.9656	0.0290
1.5	0.0291	0.0291	0.9003	0.0262
2.5	0.0282	0.0282	0.8395	0.0237
3.5	0.0274	0.0274	0.7827	0.0214
4.5	0.0266	0.0266	0.7298	0.0194
				0.1197

The credit default swap spread s is given by:
$$3.7364s + 0.0598s = 0.1197$$
It is 0.0315 or 315 basis points.

Problem 24.11.
How does a five-year nth-to-default credit default swap work? Consider a basket of 100 reference entities where each reference entity has a probability of defaulting in each year of 1%. As the default correlation between the reference entities increases what would you expect to happen to the value of the swap when a) $n=1$ and b) $n=25$. Explain your answer.

A five-year nth to default credit default swap works in the same way as a regular credit default swap except that there is a basket of companies. The payoff occurs when the nth default from the companies in the basket occurs. After the nth default has occurred the swap ceases to exist. When $n=1$ (so that the swap is a "first to default") an increase in the default correlation lowers the value of the swap. When the default correlation is zero there are 100 independent events that can lead to a payoff. As the correlation increases the probability of a payoff decreases. In the limit when the correlation is perfect there is in effect only one company and therefore only one event that can lead to a payoff.
When $n=25$ (so that the swap is a 25th to default) an increase in the default correlation increases the value of the swap. When the default correlation is zero there is virtually no chance that there will be 25 defaults and the value of the swap is very close to zero. As the correlation increases the probability of multiple defaults increases. In the limit when the correlation is perfect there is in effect only one company and the value of a 25th-to-default credit default swap is the same as the value of a first-to-default swap.

Problem 24.12.
What is the formula relating the payoff on a CDS to the notional principal and the recovery rate?

The payoff is $L(1-R)$ where L is the notional principal and R is the recovery rate.

Problem 24.13.
Show that the spread for a new plain vanilla CDS should be $(1-R)$ times the spread for a similar new binary CDS where R is the recovery rate.

The payoff from a plain vanilla CDS is $1-R$ times the payoff from a binary CDS with the same principal. The payoff always occurs at the same time on the two instruments. It follows that the regular payments on a new plain vanilla CDS must be $1 - R$ times the payments on a new binary CDS. Otherwise there would be an arbitrage opportunity.

Problem 24.14.
Verify that if the CDS spread for the example in Tables 24.1 to 24.4 is 100 basis points and the probability of default in a year (conditional on no earlier default) must be 1.61%. How does the probability of default change when the recovery rate is 20% instead of 40%? Verify that your answer is consistent with the implied probability of default being approximately proportional to $1/(1-R)$ where R is the recovery rate.

The 1.61% implied default probability can be calculated by setting up a worksheet in Excel and using Solver. To verify that 1.61% is correct we note that, with a conditional default probability of 1.61%, the unconditional probabilities are:

Time (years)	Default Probability	Survival Probability
1	0.0161	0.9839
2	0.0158	0.9681
3	0.0156	0.9525
4	0.0153	0.9371
5	0.0151	0.9221

The present value of the regular payments becomes $4.1170s$, the present value of the expected payoffs becomes 0.0415, and the present value of the expected accrual payments becomes $0.0346s$ .When $s = 0.01$ the present value of the expected payments equals the present value of the expected payoffs.

When the recovery rate is 20% the implied default probability (calculated using Solver) is 1.21% per year. Note that $1.21/1.61$ is approximately equal to $(1-0.4)/(1-0.2)$ showing that the implied default probability is approximately proportional to $1/(1-R)$.

In passing we note that if the CDS spread is used to imply an unconditional default probability (assumed to be the same each year) then this implied unconditional default probability is exactly proportional to $1/(1-R)$. When we use the CDS spread to imply a conditional default probability (assumed to be the same each year) it is only approximately proportional to $1/(1-R)$.

Problem 24.15.
A company enters into a total return swap where it receives the return on a corporate bond paying a coupon of 5% and pays LIBOR. Explain the difference between this and a regular swap where 5% is exchanged for LIBOR.

In the case of a total return swap a company receives (pays) the increase (decrease) in the value of the bond. In the regular swap this does not happen.

Problem 24.16.
Explain how forward contracts and options on credit default swaps are structured.

When a company enters into a long (short) forward contract it is obligated to buy (sell) the protection given by a specified credit default swap with a specified spread at a specified future time. When a company buys a call (put) option contract it has the option to buy (sell) the protection given by a specified credit default swap with a specified spread at a specified future time. Both contracts are normally structured so that they cease to exist if a default occurs during the life of the contract.

Problem 24.17.
"The position of a buyer of a credit default swap is similar to the position of someone who is long a risk-free bond and short a corporate bond." Explain this statement.

A credit default swap insures a corporate bond issued by the reference entity against default. Its approximate effect is to convert the corporate bond into a risk-free bond. The buyer of a credit default swap has therefore chosen to exchange a corporate bond for a risk-free bond. This means that the buyer is long a risk-free bond and short a similar corporate bond.

Problem 24.18.
Why is there a potential asymmetric information problem in credit default swaps?

Payoffs from credit default swaps depend on whether a particular company defaults. Arguably some market participants have more information about this than other market participants. (See Business Snapshot 24.3.)

Problem 24.19.
Does valuing a CDS using real-world default probabilities rather than risk-neutral default probabilities overstate or understate its value? Explain your answer.

Real world default probabilities are less than risk-neutral default probabilities. It follows that the use of real world (historical) default probabilities will tend to understate the value of a CDS.

Problem 24.20.
What is the difference between a total return swap and an asset swap?

In an asset swap the bond's promised payments are swapped for LIBOR plus a spread. In a total return swap the bond's actual payments are swapped for LIBOR plus a spread.

Problem 24.21.
Suppose that in a one-factor Gaussian copula model the five-year probability of default for each of 125 names is 3% and the pair wise copula correlation is 0.2. Calculate, for factor values of −2, −1, 0, 1, and 2, a) the default probability conditional on the factor value and b) the probability of more than 10 defaults conditional on the factor value.

Using equation (24.2) the probability of default conditional on a factor value of M is

$$N\left(\frac{N^{-1}(0.03) - \sqrt{0.2}M}{\sqrt{1-0.2}} \right)$$

For M equal to −2, −1, 0, 1, and 2 the probabilities of default are 0.135, 0.054, 0.018, 0.005, and 0.001 respectively. To six decimal places the probability of more than 10 defaults for these values of M can be calculated using the BINOMDIST function in Excel. They are 0.959284, 0.79851, 0.000016, 0, and 0, respectively.

Problem 24.22.
Explain the difference between base correlation and compound correlation

Compound correlation for a tranche is the correlation which when substituted into the one-factor Gaussian copula model produces the market quote for the tranche. Base correlation is the correlation which is consistent with the one-factor Gaussian copula and market quotes for the 0 to X% tranche where X% is a detachment point. It ensures that the expected loss on the 0 to X% tranche equals the sum of the expected losses on the underlying traded tranches.

Problem 24.23.
In Example 24.2, what is the tranche spread for the 9% to 12% tranche?

In this case $a_L = 0.09$ and $a_H = 0.12$. Proceeding similarly to Example 24.2 the tranche spread is calculated as 30 basis points.

CHAPTER 25
Exotic Options

Problem 25.1.
Explain the difference between a forward start option and a chooser option.

A forward start option is an option that is paid for now but will start at some time in the future. The strike price is usually equal to the price of the asset at the time the option starts. A chooser option is an option where, at some time in the future, the holder chooses whether the option is a call or a put.

Problem 25.2.
Describe the payoff from a portfolio consisting of a floating lookback call and a floating lookback put with the same maturity.

A floating lookback call provides a payoff of $S_T - S_{min}$. A floating lookback put provides a payoff of $S_{max} - S_T$. A combination of a floating lookback call and a floating lookback put therefore provides a payoff of $S_{max} - S_{min}$.

Problem 25.3.
Consider a chooser option where the holder has the right to choose between a European call and a European put at any time during a two-year period. The maturity dates and strike prices for the calls and puts are the same regardless of when the choice is made. Is it ever optimal to make the choice before the end of the two-year period? Explain your answer.

No, it is never optimal to choose early. The resulting cash flows are the same regardless of when the choice is made. There is no point in the holder making a commitment earlier than necessary. This argument applies when the holder chooses between two American options providing the options cannot be exercised before the 2-year point. If the early exercise period starts as soon as the choice is made, the argument does not hold. For example, if the stock price fell to almost nothing in the first six months, the holder would choose a put option at this time and exercise it immediately.

Problem 25.4.
Suppose that c_1 and p_1 are the prices of a European average price call and a European average price put with strike price K and maturity T, c_2 and p_2 are the prices of a European average strike call and European average strike put with maturity T, and c_3 and p_3 are the prices of a regular European call and a regular European put with strike price K and maturity T. Show that

$$c_1 + c_2 - c_3 = p_1 + p_2 - p_3$$

The payoffs from $c_1, c_2, c_3, p_1, p_2, p_3$ are, respectively, as follows:

$$\max(\bar{S} - K, 0)$$
$$\max(S_T - \bar{S}, 0)$$
$$\max(S_T - K, 0)$$

$$\max(K - \overline{S}, 0)$$
$$\max(\overline{S} - S_T, 0)$$
$$\max(K - S_T, 0)$$

The payoff from $c_1 - p_1$ is always $\overline{S} - K$; The payoff from $c_2 - p_2$ is always $S_T - \overline{S}$; The payoff from $c_3 - p_3$ is always $S_T - K$; It follows that

$$c_1 - p_1 + c_2 - p_2 = c_3 - p_3$$

or

$$c_1 + c_2 - c_3 = p_1 + p_2 - p_3$$

Problem 25.5.

The text derives a decomposition of a particular type of chooser option into a call maturing at time T_2 and a put maturing at time T_1. Derive an alternative decomposition into a call maturing at time T_1 and a put maturing at time T_2.

Substituting for c, put-call parity gives

$$\max(c, p) = \max\left[p, p + S_1 e^{-q(T_2 - T_1)} - K e^{-r(T_2 - T_1)} \right]$$

$$= p + \max\left[0, S_1 e^{-q(T_2 - T_1)} - K e^{-r(T_2 - T_1)} \right]$$

This shows that the chooser option can be decomposed into:
    A put option with strike price K and maturity T_2; and
$e^{-q(T_2 - T_1)}$ call options with strike price $K e^{-(r-q)(T_2 - T_1)}$ and maturity T_1.

Problem 25.6.

Section 25.8 gives two formulas for a down-and-out call. The first applies to the situation where the barrier, H, is less than or equal to the strike price, K. The second applies to the situation where $H \geq K$. Show that the two formulas are the same when $H = K$.

Consider the formula for c_{do} when $H \geq K$

$$c_{do} = S_0 N(x_1) e^{-qT} - K e^{-rT} N(x_1 - \sigma\sqrt{T}) - S_0 e^{-qT} (H / S_0)^{2\lambda} N(y_1)$$

$$+ K e^{-rT} (H / S_0)^{2\lambda - 2} N(y_1 - \sigma\sqrt{T})$$

Substituting $H = K$ and noting that

$$\lambda = \frac{r - q + \sigma^2 / 2}{\sigma^2}$$

we obtain $x_1 = d_1$ so that

$$c_{do} = c - S_0 e^{-qT} (H / S_0)^{2\lambda} N(y_1) + K e^{-rT} (H / S_0)^{2\lambda - 2} N(y_1 - \sigma\sqrt{T})$$

The formula for c_{di} when $H \leq K$ is

$$c_{di} = S_0 e^{-qT} (H / S_0)^{2\lambda} N(y) - K e^{-rT} (H / S_0)^{2\lambda - 2} N(y - \sigma\sqrt{T})$$

Since $c_{do} = c - c_{di}$

$$c_{do} = c - S_0 e^{-qT} (H / S_0)^{2\lambda} N(y) + K e^{-rT} (H / S_0)^{2\lambda - 2} N(y - \sigma\sqrt{T})$$

From the formulas in the text $y_1 = y$ when $H = K$. The two expression for c_{do} are therefore equivalent when $H = K$

Problem 25.7.
Explain why a down-and-out put is worth zero when the barrier is greater than the strike price.

The option is in the money only when the asset price is less than the strike price. However, in these circumstances the barrier has been hit and the option has ceased to exist.

Problem 25.8.
Suppose that the strike price of an American call option on a non-dividend-paying stock grows at rate g. Show that if g is less than the risk-free rate, r, it is never optimal to exercise the call early.

The argument is similar to that given in Chapter 10 for a regular option on a non-dividend-paying stock. Consider a portfolio consisting of the option and cash equal to the present value of the terminal strike price. The initial cash position is
$$Ke^{gT-rT}$$
By time τ ($0 \le \tau \le T$), the cash grows to
$$Ke^{-r(T-\tau)+gT} = Ke^{g\tau}e^{-(r-g)(T-\tau)}$$
Since $r > g$, this is less than $Ke^{g\tau}$ and therefore is less than the amount required to exercise the option. It follows that, if the option is exercised early, the terminal value of the portfolio is less than S_T. At time T the cash balance is Ke^{gT}. This is exactly what is required to exercise the option. If the early exercise decision is delayed until time T, the terminal value of the portfolio is therefore
$$\max[S_T, Ke^{gT}]$$
This is at least as great as S_T. It follows that early exercise cannot be optimal.

Problem 25.9.
How can the value of a forward start put option on a non-dividend-paying stock be calculated if it is agreed that the strike price will be 10% greater than the stock price at the time the option starts?

When the strike price of an option on a non-dividend-paying stock is defined as 10% greater that the stock price, the value of the option is proportional to the stock price. The same argument as that given in the text for forward start options shows that if t_1 is the time when the option starts and t_2 is the time when it finishes, the option has the same value as an option starting today with a life of $t_2 - t_1$ and a strike price of 1.1 times the current stock price.

Problem 25.10.
If a stock price follows geometric Brownian motion, what process does $A(t)$ follow where $A(t)$ is the arithmetic average stock price between time zero and time t?

Assume that we start calculating averages from time zero. The relationship between $A(t + \Delta t)$ and $A(t)$ is
$$A(t + \Delta t) \times (t + \Delta t) = A(t) \times t + S(t) \times \Delta t$$

where $S(t)$ is the stock price at time t and terms of higher order than Δt are ignored. If we continue to ignore terms of higher order than Δt, it follows that

$$A(t + \Delta t) = A(t)\left[1 - \frac{\Delta t}{t}\right] + S(t)\frac{\Delta t}{t}$$

Taking limits as Δt tends to zero

$$dA(t) = \frac{S(t) - A(t)}{t} dt$$

The process for $A(t)$ has a stochastic drift and no dz term. The process makes sense intuitively. Once some time has passed, the change in S in the next small portion of time has only a second order effect on the average. If S equals A the average has no drift; if $S > A$ the average is drifting up; if $S < A$ the average is drifting down.

Problem 25.11.
Explain why delta hedging is easier for Asian options than for regular options.

In an Asian option the payoff becomes more certain as time passes and the delta always approaches zero as the maturity date is approached. This makes delta hedging easy. Barrier options cause problems for delta hedgers when the asset price is close to the barrier because delta is discontinuous.

Problem 25.12.
Calculate the price of a one-year European option to give up 100 ounces of silver in exchange for one ounce of gold. The current prices of gold and silver are $380 and $4, respectively; the risk-free interest rate is 10% per annum; the volatility of each commodity price is 20%; and the correlation between the two prices is 0.7. Ignore storage costs.

The value of the option is given by the formula in the text
$$V_0 e^{-q_2 T} N(d_1) - U_0 e^{-q_1 T} N(d_2)$$
where

$$d_1 = \frac{\ln(V_0 / U_0) + (q_1 - q_2 + \sigma^2 / 2)T}{\sigma\sqrt{T}}$$

$$d_2 = d_1 - \sigma\sqrt{T}$$

and

$$\sigma = \sqrt{\sigma_1^2 + \sigma_2^2 - 2\rho\sigma_1\sigma_2}$$

In this case, $V_0 = 380$, $U_0 = 400$, $q_1 = 0$, $q_2 = 0$, $T = 1$, and

$$\sigma = \sqrt{0.2^2 + 0.2^2 - 2 \times 0.7 \times 0.2 \times 0.2} = 0.1549$$

Because $d_1 = -0.2537$ and $d_2 = -0.4086$, the option price is
$$380N(-0.2537) - 400N(-0.4086) = 15.38$$

or $15.38.

Problem 25.13.
Is a European down-and-out option on an asset worth the same as a European down-and-out option on the asset's futures price for a futures contract maturing at the same time as the option?

No. If the future's price is above the spot price during the life of the option, it is possible that the spot price will hit the barrier when the futures price does not.

Problem 25.14.
Answer the following questions about compound options

(a) *What put–call parity relationship exists between the price of a European call on a call and a European put on a call? Show that the formulas given in the text satisfy the relationship.*

(b) *What put–call parity relationship exists between the price of a European call on a put and a European put on a put? Show that the formulas given in the text satisfy the relationship.*

(a) The put–call relationship is

$$cc + K_1 e^{-rT_1} = pc + c$$

where cc is the price of the call on the call, pc is the price of the put on the call, c is the price today of the call into which the options can be exercised at time T_1, and K_1 is the exercise price for cc and pc. The proof is similar to that in Chapter 10 for the usual put–call parity relationship. Both sides of the equation represent the values of portfolios that will be worth $\max(c, K_1)$ at time T_1. Because

$$M(a,b;\rho) = N(a) - M(a,-b;-\rho) = N(b) - M(-a,b,;-\rho)$$

and

$$N(x) = 1 - N(-x)$$

we obtain

$$cc - pc = Se^{-qT_2} N(b_1) - K_2 e^{-rT_2} N(b_2) - K_1 e^{-rT_1}$$

Since

$$c = Se^{-qT_2} N(b_1) - K_2 e^{-rT_2} N(b_2)$$

put–call parity is consistent with the formulas

(b) The put–call relationship is

$$cp + K_1 e^{-rT_1} = pp + p$$

where cp is the price of the call on the put, pp is the price of the put on the put, p is the price today of the put into which the options can be exercised at time T_1, and K_1 is the exercise price for cp and pp. The proof is similar to that in Chapter 10 for the usual put–call parity relationship. Both sides of the equation represent the values of portfolios that will be worth $\max(p, K_1)$ at time T_1. Because

$$M(a,b;\rho) = N(a) - M(a,-b;-\rho) = N(b) - M(-a,b,;-\rho)$$

and

$$N(x) = 1 - N(-x)$$

it follows that

$$cp - pp = -Se^{-qT_2} N(-b_1) + K_2 e^{-rT_2} N(-b_2) - K_1 e^{-rT_1}$$

Because

$$p = -Se^{-qT_2} N(-b_1) + K_2 e^{-rT_2} N(-b_2)$$

put–call parity is consistent with the formulas.

Problem 25.15.
Does a floating lookback call become more valuable or less valuable as we increase the

frequency with which we observe the asset price in calculating the minimum?

As we increase the frequency we observe a more extreme minimum which increases the value of a floating lookback call.

Problem 25.16.
Does a down-and-out call become more valuable or less valuable as we increase the frequency with which we observe the asset price in determining whether the barrier has been crossed? What is the answer to the same question for a down-and-in call?

As we increase the frequency with which the asset price is observed, the asset price becomes more likely to hit the barrier and the value of a down-and-out call goes down. For a similar reason the value of a down-and-in call goes up. The adjustment mentioned in the text, suggested by Broadie, Glasserman, and Kou, moves the barrier further out as the asset price is observed less frequently. This increases the price of a down-and-out option and reduces the price of a down-and-in option.

Problem 25.17.
Explain why a regular European call option is the sum of a down-and-out European call and a down-and-in European call. Is the same true for American call options?

If the barrier is reached the down-and-out option is worth nothing while the down-and-in option has the same value as a regular option. If the barrier is not reached the down-and-in option is worth nothing while the down-and-out option has the same value as a regular option. This is why a down-and-out call option plus a down-and-in call option is worth the same as a regular option. A similar argument cannot be used for American options.

Problem 25.18.
What is the value of a derivative that pays off $100 in six months if the S&P 500 index is greater than 1,000 and zero otherwise? Assume that the current level of the index is 960, the risk-free rate is 8% per annum, the dividend yield on the index is 3% per annum, and the volatility of the index is 20%.

This is a cash-or-nothing call. The value is $100N(d_2)e^{-0.08 \times 0.5}$ where

$$d_2 = \frac{\ln(960/1000) + (0.08 - 0.03 - 0.2^2 / 2) \times 0.5}{0.2 \times \sqrt{0.5}} = -0.1826$$

Since $N(d_2) = 0.4276$ the value of the derivative is $41.08.

Problem 25.19.
In a three-month down-and-out call option on silver futures the strike price is $20 per ounce and the barrier is $18. The current futures price is $19, the risk-free interest rate is 5%, and the volatility of silver futures is 40% per annum. Explain how the option works and calculate its value. What is the value of a regular call option on silver futures with the same terms? What is the value of a down-and-in call option on silver futures with the same terms?

This is a regular call with a strike price of $20 that ceases to exist if the futures price hits $18. With the notation in the text $H = 18$, $K = 20$, $S = 19$, $r = 0.05$, $\sigma = 0.4$, $q = 0.05$, $T = 0.25$ From this $\lambda = 0.5$ and

$$y = \frac{\ln[18^2 / (19 \times 20)]}{0.4\sqrt{0.25}} + 0.5 \times 0.4\sqrt{0.25} = -0.69714$$

The value of a down-and-out call plus a down-and-in call equals the value of a regular call. Substituting into the formula given when $H < K$ we get $c_{di} = 0.4638$. The regular Black-Scholes-Merton formula gives $c = 1.0902$. Hence $c_{do} = 0.6264$. (These answers can be checked with DerivaGem.)

Problem 25.20.
A new European-style floating lookback call option on a stock index has a maturity of nine months. The current level of the index is 400, the risk-free rate is 6% per annum, the dividend yield on the index is 4% per annum, and the volatility of the index is 20%. Use DerivaGem to value the option.

DerivaGem shows that the value is 53.38. Note that the Minimum to date and Maximum to date should be set equal to the current value of the index for a new deal. (See material on DerivaGem at the end of the book.)

Problem 25.21.
Estimate the value of a new six-month European-style average price call option on a non-dividend-paying stock. The initial stock price is $30, the strike price is $30, the risk-free interest rate is 5%, and the stock price volatility is 30%.

We can use the analytic approximation given in the text.
$$M_1 = \frac{(e^{0.05 \times 0.5} - 1) \times 30}{0.05 \times 0.5} = 30.378$$

Also $M_2 = 936.9$ so that $\sigma = 17.41\%$. The option can be valued as a futures option with $F_0 = 30.378$, $K = 30$, $r = 5\%$, $\sigma = 17.41\%$, and $t = 0.5$. The price is 1.637.

Problem 25.22.
Use DerivaGem to calculate the value of:
(a) *A regular European call option on a non-dividend-paying stock where the stock price is $50, the strike price is $50, the risk-free rate is 5% per annum, the volatility is 30%, and the time to maturity is one year.*
(b) *A down-and-out European call which is as in (a) with the barrier at $45.*
(c) *A down-and-in European call which is as in (a) with the barrier at $45.*
Show that the option in (a) is worth the sum of the values of the options in (b) and (c).

The price of a regular European call option is 7.116. The price of the down-and-out call option is 4.696. The price of the down-and-in call option is 2.419.
The price of a regular European call is the sum of the prices of down-and-out and down-and-in options.

Problem 25.23.
Explain adjustments that have to be made when $r = q$ for a) the valuation formulas for lookback call options in Section 25.10 and b) the formulas for M_1 and M_2 in Section 25.12.

When $r = q$ in the expression for a floating lookback call in Section 25.10 $a_1 = a_3$ and

$Y_1 = \ln(S_0 / S_{min})$ so that the expression for a floating lookback call becomes

$$S_0 e^{-qT} N(a_1) - S_{min} e^{-rT} N(a_2)$$

As q approaches r in Section 25.12 we get

$$M_1 = S_0$$

$$M_2 = \frac{2e^{\sigma^2 T} S_0^2}{\sigma^4 T^2} - \frac{2S_0^2}{T^2} \frac{1 + \sigma^2 T}{\sigma^4}$$

Problem 25.24.
Value the variance swap in Example 25.4 of Section 25.15 assuming that the implied volatilities for options with strike prices 800, 850, 900, 950, 1,000, 1,050, 1,100, 1,150, 1,200 are 20%, 20.5%, 21%, 21.5%, 22%, 22.5%, 23%, 23.5%, 24%, respectively.

In this case, DerivaGem shows that $Q(K_1) = 0.1772$, $Q(K_2) = 1.1857$, $Q(K_3) = 4.9123$, $Q(K_4) = 14.2374$, $Q(K_5) = 45.3738$, $Q(K_6) = 35.9243$, $Q(K_7) = 20.6883$, $Q(K_8) = 11.4135$, $Q(K_9) = 6.1043$. $\hat{E}(\overline{V}) = 0.0502$. The value of the variance swap is $0.51 million.

CHAPTER 26
More on Models and Numerical Procedures

Problem 26.1.

Confirm that the CEV model formulas satisfy put–call parity.

It follows immediately from the equations in Section 26.1 that

$$p - c = Ke^{-rT} - S_0 e^{-qT}$$

in all cases.

Problem 26.2.

Use Monte Carlo simulation to show that Merton's value for a European option is correct when r=0.05, q=0, λ=0.3, k=0.5, σ =0.25, and S₀ =30

In this case $\lambda' = 0.3 \times 1.5 = 0.45$. The variable f_n is the Black-Scholes-Merton price when the volatility is $0.25^2 + ns^2/T$ and the risk-free rate is $-0.1 + n \times \ln(1.5)/T$. A spreadsheet can be constructed to

a) Value the option using the first (say) 20 terms in the Merton expansion.

$$\sum_{n=0}^{\infty} \frac{e^{-\lambda'T}(\lambda'T)^n}{n!} f_n$$

It is convenient to use the DerivaGem functions to do this.:

b) Value the option using Monte Carlo simulation. There are a number of alternative approaches. One is as follows. Sample to determine the number of jumps in time T as described in the text. The probability of N jumps is

$$\frac{e^{-\lambda T}(\lambda T)^N}{N!}$$

The proportional increase in the stock price arising from jumps is the product of N random samples from lognormal distributions. Each random sample is $\exp(X)$ where X is a random sample from a normal distribution with mean $\ln(1.5) - s^2/2$ and standard deviation s. (Note that it is one plus the percentage jump that is lognormal.) The proportional increase in the stock price arising from the diffusion component of the process is

$$\exp((0.05 - 0.3 \times 0.5 - 0.25^2/2)T + 0.25\varepsilon\sqrt{T})$$

where ε is a random sample from a standard normal distribution. The final stock price is 30 times the product of the increase arising from jumps and the increase from the diffusion component. The payoff from the option can be calculated from this and the present value of the average payoff over many simulations is the estimate of the value of the option.

I find that the two approaches give similar answers. For example, for a call option with $T = 1$, $s=0.5$, and $K=30$, the option value given by both methods is about 5.47.

Problem 26.3.

Confirm that Merton's jump diffusion model satisfies put–call parity when the jump size is lognormal.

With the notation in the text the value of a call option, c is

$$\sum_{n=0}^{\infty} \frac{e^{-\lambda'T}(\lambda'T)^n}{n!} c_n$$

where c_n is the Black-Scholes-Merton price of a call option where the variance rate is

$$\sigma^2 + \frac{ns^2}{T}$$

and the risk-free rate is

$$r - \lambda k + \frac{n\gamma}{T}$$

where $\gamma = \ln(1+k)$. Similarly the value of a put option p is

$$\sum_{n=0}^{\infty} \frac{e^{-\lambda'T}(\lambda'T)^n}{n!} p_n$$

where p_n is the Black-Scholes-Merton price of a put option with this variance rate and risk-free rate. It follows that

$$p - c = \sum_{n=0}^{\infty} \frac{e^{-\lambda'T}(\lambda'T)^n}{n!}(p_n - c_n)$$

From put–call parity

$$p_n - c_n = Ke^{(-r+\lambda k)T} e^{-n\gamma} - S_0 e^{-qT}$$

Because

$$e^{-n\gamma} = (1+k)^{-n}$$

it follows that

$$p - c = \sum_{n=0}^{\infty} \frac{e^{-\lambda'T+\lambda kT}(\lambda'T/(1+k))^n}{n!} Ke^{-rT} - \sum_{n=0}^{\infty} \frac{e^{-\lambda'T}(\lambda'T)^n}{n!} S_0 e^{-qT}$$

Using $\lambda' = \lambda(1+k)$ this becomes

$$\frac{1}{e^{\lambda T}} \sum_{n=0}^{\infty} \frac{(\lambda T)^n}{n!} Ke^{-rT} - \frac{1}{e^{\lambda'T}} \sum_{n=0}^{\infty} \frac{(\lambda'T)^n}{n!} S_0 e^{-qT}$$

From the expansion of the exponential function we get

$$e^{\lambda T} = \sum_{n=0}^{\infty} \frac{(\lambda T)^n}{n!}$$

$$e^{\lambda'T} = \sum_{n=0}^{\infty} \frac{(\lambda'T)^n}{n!}$$

Hence

$$p - c = Ke^{-rT} - S_0 e^{-qT}$$

showing that put–call parity holds.

Problem 26.4.

Suppose that the volatility of an asset will be 20% from month 0 to month 6, 22% from month 6 to month 12, and 24% from month 12 to month 24. What volatility should be used in Black-Scholes-Merton to value a two-year option?

199

The average variance rate is

$$\frac{6 \times 0.2^2 + 6 \times 0.22^2 + 12 \times 0.24^2}{24} = 0.0509$$

The volatility used should be $\sqrt{0.0509} = 0.2256$ or 22.56%.

Problem 26.5.

Consider the case of Merton's jump diffusion model where jumps always reduce the asset price to zero. Assume that the average number of jumps per year is λ. Show that the price of a European call option is the same as in a world with no jumps except that the risk-free rate is $r + \lambda$ rather than r. Does the possibility of jumps increase or reduce the value of the call option in this case? (Hint: Value the option assuming no jumps and assuming one or more jumps. The probability of no jumps in time T is $e^{-\lambda T}$).

In a risk-neutral world the process for the asset price exclusive of jumps is

$$\frac{dS}{S} = (r - q - \lambda k)\, dt + \sigma\, dz$$

In this case $k = -1$ so that the process is

$$\frac{dS}{S} = (r - q + \lambda)\, dt + \sigma\, dz$$

The asset behaves like a stock paying a dividend yield of $q - \lambda$. This shows that, conditional on no jumps, call price

$$S_0 e^{-(q-\lambda)T} N(d_1) - K e^{-rT}$$

where

$$d_1 = \frac{\ln(S_0 / K) + (r - q + \lambda + \sigma^2 / 2)T}{\sigma \sqrt{T}}$$

$$d_2 = d_1 - \sigma \sqrt{T}$$

There is a probability of $e^{-\lambda T}$ that there will be no jumps and a probability of $1 - e^{-\lambda T}$ that there will be one or more jumps so that the final asset price is zero. It follows that there is a probability of $e^{-\lambda T}$ that the value of the call is given by the above equation and $1 - e^{-\lambda T}$ that it will be zero. Because jumps have no systematic risk it follows that the value of the call option is

$$e^{-\lambda T} [S_0 e^{-(q-\lambda)T} N(d_1) - K e^{-rT}]$$

or

$$S_0 e^{-qT} N(d_1) - K e^{-(r+\lambda)T}$$

This is the required result. The value of a call option is an increasing function of the risk-free interest rate (see Chapter 10). It follows that the possibility of jumps increases the value of the call option in this case.

Problem 26.6.

At time zero the price of a non-dividend-paying stock is S_0. Suppose that the time interval between 0 and T is divided into two subintervals of length t_1 and t_2. During the first *subinterval, the risk-free interest rate and volatility are r_1 and σ_1, respectively. During the second subinterval, they are r_2 and σ_2, respectively. Assume that the world is risk neutral.*

(a) *Use the results in Chapter 14 to determine the stock price distribution at time T in terms of r_1, r_2, σ_1, σ_2, t_1, t_2, and S_0.*

(b) *Suppose that $\bar{r}$ is the average interest rate between time zero and T and that $\bar{V}$ is the average variance rate between times zero and T. What is the stock price distribution as a function of T in terms of $\bar{r}$, $\bar{V}$, T, and S_0?*

(c) *What are the results corresponding to (a) and (b) when there are three subintervals with different interest rates and volatilities?*

(d) *Show that if the risk-free rate, r, and the volatility, σ, are known functions of time, the stock price distribution at time T in a risk-neutral world is*

$$\ln S_T \sim \varphi\left[\ln S_0 + \left(\bar{r} - \frac{\bar{V}}{2}\right)T, \bar{V}T\right]$$

where $\bar{r}$ is the average value of r, $\bar{V}$ is equal to the average value of σ^2, and S_0 is the stock price today.

(a) Suppose that S_1 is the stock price at time t_1 and S_T is the stock price at time T. From equation (14.3), it follows that in a risk- neutral world:

$$\ln S_1 - \ln S_0 \sim \varphi\left[\left(r_1 - \frac{\sigma_1^2}{2}\right)t_1, \sigma_1^2 t_1\right]$$

$$\ln S_T - \ln S_1 \sim \varphi\left[\left(r_2 - \frac{\sigma_2^2}{2}\right)t_2, \sigma_2^2 t_2\right]$$

Since the sum of two independent normal distributions is normal with mean equal to the sum of the means and variance equal to the sum of the variances

$$\ln S_T - \ln S_0 = (\ln S_T - \ln S_1) + (\ln S_1 - \ln S_0)$$
$$\sim \varphi\left[r_1 t_1 + r_2 t_2 - \frac{\sigma_1^2 t_1}{2} - \frac{\sigma_2^2 t_2}{2}, \sigma_1^2 t_1 + \sigma_2^2 t_2\right]$$

(b) Because

$$r_1 t_1 + r_2 t_2 = \bar{r}T$$

and

$$\sigma_1^2 t_1 + \sigma_2^2 t_2 = \bar{V}T$$

it follows that:

$$\ln S_T - \ln S_0 \sim \varphi\left[\left(\bar{r} - \frac{\bar{V}}{2}\right)T, \bar{V}T\right]$$

(c) If σ_i and r_i are the volatility and risk-free interest rate during the ith subinterval

$(i = 1, 2, 3)$, an argument similar to that in (a) shows that:

$$\ln S_T - \ln S_0 \sim \varphi\left[r_1 t_1 + r_2 t_2 + r_3 t_3 - \frac{\sigma_1^2 t_1}{2} - \frac{\sigma_2^2 t_2}{2} - \frac{\sigma_3^2 t_3}{2}, \sigma_1^2 t_1 + \sigma_2^2 t_2 + \sigma_3^2 t_3\right]$$

where t_1, t_2 and t_3 are the lengths of the three subintervals. It follows that the result in (b) is still true.

(d) The result in (b) remains true as the time between time zero and time T is divided into more subintervals, each having its own risk-free interest rate and volatility. In the limit, it follows that, if r and σ are known functions of time, the stock price distribution at time T is the same as that for a stock with a constant interest rate and variance rate with the constant interest rate equal to the average interest rate and the constant variance rate equal to the average variance rate.

Problem 26.7.
Write down the equations for simulating the path followed by the asset price in the stochastic volatility model in equation (26.2) and (26.3).

The equations are:

$$S(t + \Delta t) = S(t)\exp[(r - q - V(t)/2)\Delta t + \varepsilon_1 \sqrt{V(t)\Delta t}]$$

$$V(t + \Delta t) - V(t) = a[V_L - V(t)]\Delta t + \xi\varepsilon_2 V(t)^\alpha \sqrt{\Delta t}$$

Problem 26.8.
"The IVF model does not necessarily get the evolution of the volatility surface correct." Explain this statement.

The IVF model is designed to match the volatility surface today. There is no guarantee that the volatility surface given by the model at future times will reflect the true evolution of the volatility surface.

Problem 26.9.
"When interest rates are constant the IVF model correctly values any derivative whose payoff depends on the value of the underlying asset at only one time." Explain why.

The IVF model ensures that the risk-neutral probability distribution of the asset price at any future time conditional on its value today is correct (or at least consistent with the market prices of options). When a derivative's payoff depends on the value of the asset at only one time the IVF model therefore calculates the expected payoff from the asset correctly. The value of the derivative is the present value of the expected payoff. When interest rates are constant the IVF model calculates this present value correctly.

Problem 26.10.
Use a three-time-step tree to value an American floating lookback call option on a currency when the initial exchange rate is 1.6, the domestic risk-free rate is 5% per annum, the foreign risk-free interest rate is 8% per annum, the exchange rate volatility is 15%, and the time to maturity is 18 months. Use the approach in Section 26.5.

In this case $S_0 = 1.6$, $r = 0.05$, $r_f = 0.08$, $\sigma = 0.15$, $T = 1.5$, $\Delta t = 0.5$. This means that

$$u = e^{0.15\sqrt{0.5}} = 1.1119$$

$$d = \frac{1}{u} = 0.8994$$

$$a = e^{(0.05-0.08)\times0.5} = 0.9851$$

$$p = \frac{a-d}{u-d} = 0.4033$$

$$1 - p = 0.5967$$

The option pays off

$$S_T - S_{\min}$$

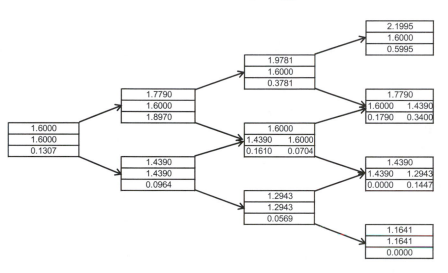

Figure S26.1 Binomial tree for Problem 26.10.

The tree is shown in Figure S26.1. At each node, the upper number is the exchange rate, the middle number(s) are the minimum exchange rate(s) so far, and the lower number(s) are the value(s) of the option. The tree shows that the value of the option today is 0.131.

Problem 26.11.

What happens to the variance-gamma model as the parameter v tends to zero?

As v tends to zero the value of g becomes T with certainty. This can be demonstrated using the GAMMADIST function in Excel. By using a series expansion for the ln function we see that ω becomes $-\theta T$. In the limit the distribution of $\ln S_T$ therefore has a mean of $\ln S_0 + (r-q)T$ and a standard deviation of $\sigma\sqrt{T}$ so that the model becomes geometric Brownian motion.

Problem 26.12.

Use a three-time-step tree to value an American put option on the geometric average of the price of a non-dividend-paying stock when the stock price is $40, the strike price is $40, the risk-free interest rate is 10% per annum, the volatility is 35% per annum, and the time to maturity is three months. The geometric average is measured from today until the option matures.

In this case $S_0 = 40$, $K = 40$, $r = 0.1$, $\sigma = 0.35$, $T = 0.25$, $\Delta t = 0.08333$. This means that

$$u = e^{0.35\sqrt{0.08333}} = 1.1063$$

$$d = \frac{1}{u} = 0.9039$$

$$a = e^{0.1 \times 0.08333} = 1.008368$$

$$p = \frac{a-d}{u-d} = 0.5161$$

$$1 - p = 0.4839$$

The option pays off

$$40 - \overline{S}$$

where $\overline{S}$ denotes the geometric average. The tree is shown in Figure S26.2. At each node, the upper number is the stock price, the middle number(s) are the geometric average(s), and the lower number(s) are the value(s) of the option. The geometric averages are calculated using the first, the last and all intermediate stock prices on the path. The tree shows that the value of the option today is $1.40.

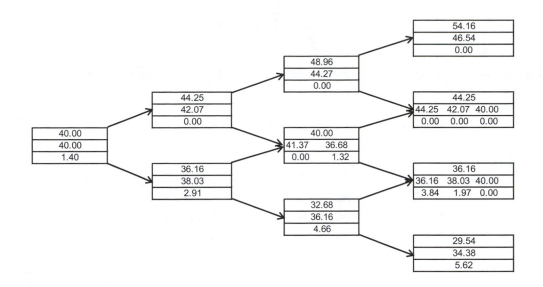

Figure S26.2   Binomial tree for Problem 26.12.

Problem 26.13.

Can the approach for valuing path dependent options in Section 26.5 be used for a two-year American-style option that provides a payoff equal to $\max(S_{ave} - K, 0)$ *where* S_{ave} *is the average asset price over the three months preceding exercise? Explain your answer.*

As mentioned in Section 26.5, for the procedure to work it must be possible to calculate the value of the path function at time $\tau + \Delta t$ from the value of the path function at time τ and the value of the underlying asset at time $\tau + \Delta t$. When S_{ave} is calculated from time zero until the end of the life of the option (as in the example considered in Section 26.5) this condition is satisfied. When it is calculated over the last three months it is not satisfied. This is because, in order to update the average with a new observation on S, it is necessary to know the observation on S from three months ago that is now no longer part of the average calculation.

Problem 26.14.
Verify that the 6.492 number in Figure 26.4 is correct.

We consider the situation where the average at node X is 53.83. If there is an up movement to node Y the new average becomes:

$$\frac{53.83 \times 5 + 54.68}{6} = 53.97$$

Interpolating, the value of the option at node Y when the average is 53.97 is

$$\frac{(53.97 - 51.12) \times 8.635 + (54.26 - 53.97) \times 8.101}{54.26 - 51.12} = 8.586$$

Similarly if there is a down movement the new average will be

$$\frac{53.83 \times 5 + 45.72}{6} = 52.48$$

In this case the option price is 4.416. The option price at node X when the average is 53.83 is therefore:

$$8.586 \times 0.5056 + 4.416 \times 0.4944)e^{-0.1 \times 0.05} = 6.492$$

Problem 26.15.

Examine the early exercise policy for the eight paths considered in the example in Section 26.8. What is the difference between the early exercise policy given by the least squares approach and the exercise boundary parameterization approach? Which gives a higher option price for the paths sampled?

Under the least squares approach we exercise at time $t = 1$ in paths 4, 6, 7, and 8. We exercise at time $t = 2$ for none of the paths. We exercise at time $t = 3$ for path 3. Under the exercise boundary parameterization approach we exercise at time $t = 1$ for paths 6 and 8. We exercise at time $t = 2$ for path 7. We exercise at time $t = 3$ for paths 3 and 4. For the paths sampled the exercise boundary parameterization approach gives a higher value for the option. However, it may be biased upward. As mentioned in the text, once the early exercise boundary has been determined in the exercise boundary parameterization approach a new Monte Carlo simulation should be carried out.

Problem 26.16.

Consider a European put option on a non-dividend paying stock when the stock price is $100, the strike price is $110, the risk-free rate is 5% per annum, and the time to maturity is one year. Suppose that the average variance rate during the life of an option has a 0.20 probability of being 0.06, a 0.5 probability of being 0.09, and a 0.3 probability of being 0.12. The volatility is uncorrelated with the stock price. Estimate the value of the option. Use DerivaGem.

If the average variance rate is 0.06, the value of the option is given by Black-Scholes with a volatility of $\sqrt{0.06} = 24.495\%$; it is 12.460. If the average variance rate is 0.09, the value of the option is given by Black-Scholes with a volatility of $\sqrt{0.09} = 30.000\%$; it is 14.655. If the average variance rate is 0.12, the value of the option is given by Black-Scholes-Merton with a volatility of $\sqrt{0.12} = 34.641\%$; it is 16.506. The value of the option is the Black-Scholes-Merton price integrated over the probability distribution of the average variance rate. It is

$$0.2 \times 12.460 + 0.5 \times 14.655 + 0.3 \times 16.506 = 14.77$$

Problem 26.17.

When there are two barriers how can a tree be designed so that nodes lie on both barriers?

Suppose that there are two horizontal barriers, H_1 and H_2, with $H_1 < H_2$ and that the underlying stock price follows geometric Brownian motion. In a trinomial tree, there are three possible movements in the asset's price at each node: up by a proportional amount u;

stay the same; and down by a proportional amount d where $d = 1/u$. We can always choose u so that nodes lie on both barriers. The condition that must be satisfied by u is

$$H_2 = H_1 u^N$$

or

$$\ln H_2 = \ln H_1 + N \ln u$$

for some integer N.

When discussing trinomial trees in Section 20.4, the value suggested for u was $e^{\sigma\sqrt{3\Delta t}}$ so that $\ln u = \sigma\sqrt{3\Delta t}$. In the situation considered here, a good rule is to choose $\ln u$ as close as possible to this value, consistent with the condition given above. This means that we set

$$\ln u = \frac{\ln H_2 - \ln H_1}{N}$$

where

$$N = \text{int}\left[\frac{\ln H_2 - \ln H_1}{\sigma\sqrt{3\Delta t}} + 0.5\right]$$

and $\text{int}(x)$ is the integral part of x. This means that nodes are at values of the stock price equal to H_1, $H_1 u$, $H_1 u^2$, ..., $H_1 u^N = H_2$.

Normally the trinomial stock price tree is constructed so that the central node is the initial stock price. In this case, it is unlikely that the current stock price happens to be $H_1 u^i$ for some i. To deal with this, the first trinomial movement should be from the initial stock price to $H_1 u^{i-1}$, $H_1 u^i$ and $H_1 u^{i+1}$ where i is chosen so that $H_1 u^i$ is closest to the current stock price. The probabilities on all branches of the tree are chosen, as usual, to match the first two moments of the stochastic process followed by the asset price. The approach works well except when the initial asset price is close to a barrier.

Problem 26.18.

Consider an 18-month zero-coupon bond with a face value of $100 that can be converted into five shares of the company's stock at any time during its life. Suppose that the current share price is $20, no dividends are paid on the stock, the risk-free rate for all maturities is 6% per annum with continuous compounding, and the share price volatility is 25% per annum. Assume that the default intensity is 3% per year and the recovery rate is 35%. The bond is callable at $110. Use a three-time-step tree to calculate the value of the bond. What is the value of the conversion option (net of the issuer's call option)?

In this case $\Delta t = 0.5$, $\lambda = 0.03$, $\sigma = 0.25$, $r = 0.06$ and $q = 0$ so that $u = 1.1360$, $d = 0.8803$, $a = 1.0305$, $p_u = 0.6386$, $p_d = 0.3465$, and the probability on default branches is 0.0149. This leads to the tree shown in Figure S26.3. The bond is called at nodes B and D and this forces exercise. Without the call the value at node D would be 129.55, the value at node B would be 115.94, and the value at node A would be 105.18. The value of the call option to the bond issuer is therefore $105.18 - 103.72 = 1.46$.

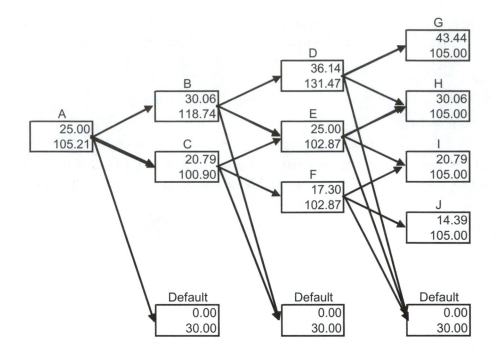

Figure S26.3   Tree for Problem 26.18

CHAPTER 27
Martingales and Measures

Problem 27.1.
How is the market price of risk defined for a variable that is not the price of an investment asset?

The market price of risk for a variable that is not the price of an investment asset is the market price of risk of an investment asset whose price is instantaneously perfectly positively correlated with the variable.

Problem 27.2.
Suppose that the market price of risk for gold is zero. If the storage costs are 1% per annum and the risk-free rate of interest is 6% per annum, what is the expected growth rate in the price of gold? Assume that gold provides no income.

If its market price of risk is zero, gold must, after storage costs have been paid, provide an expected return equal to the risk-free rate of interest. In this case, the expected return after storage costs must be 6% per annum. It follows that the expected growth rate in the price of gold must be 7% per annum.

Problem 27.3.
Consider two securities both of which are dependent on the same market variable. The expected returns from the securities are 8% and 12%. The volatility of the first security is 15%. The instantaneous risk-free rate is 4%. What is the volatility of the second security?

The market price of risk is
$$\frac{\mu - r}{\sigma}$$
This is the same for both securities. From the first security we know it must be
$$\frac{0.08 - 0.04}{0.15} = 0.26667$$
The volatility, σ for the second security is given by
$$\frac{0.12 - 0.04}{\sigma} = 0.26667$$
The volatility is 30%.

Problem 27.4.
An oil company is set up solely for the purpose of exploring for oil in a certain small area of Texas. Its value depends primarily on two stochastic variables: the price of oil and the quantity of proven oil reserves. Discuss whether the market price of risk for the second of these two variables is likely to be positive, negative, or zero.

It can be argued that the market price of risk for the second variable is zero. This is because the risk is unsystematic, i.e., it is totally unrelated to other risks in the economy. To put this another way, there is no reason why investors should demand a higher return for bearing the risk since the risk can be totally diversified away.

Problem 27.5.

> *Deduce the differential equation for a derivative dependent on the prices of two non-dividend-paying traded securities by forming a riskless portfolio consisting of the derivative and the two traded securities.*

Suppose that the price, f, of the derivative depends on the prices, S_1 and S_2, of two traded securities. Suppose further that:

$$dS_1 = \mu_1 S_1 dt + \sigma_1 S_1 dz_1$$

$$dS_2 = \mu_2 S_2 dt + \sigma_2 S_2 dz_2$$

where dz_1 and dz_2 are Wiener processes with correlation ρ. From Ito's lemma

$$df = \left(\mu_1 S_1 \frac{\partial f}{\partial S_1} + \mu_2 S_2 \frac{\partial f}{\partial S_2} + \frac{\partial f}{\partial t} + \frac{1}{2} \sigma_1^2 S_1^2 \frac{\partial^2 f}{\partial S_1^2} + \frac{1}{2} \sigma_2^2 S_2^2 \frac{\partial^2 f}{\partial S_2^2} \right.$$
$$\left. + \rho \sigma_1 \sigma_2 S_1 S_2 \frac{\partial^2 f}{\partial S_1 \partial S_2} \right) dt + \sigma_1 S_1 \frac{\partial f}{\partial S_1} dz_1 + \sigma_2 S_2 \frac{\partial f}{\partial S_2} dz_2$$

To eliminate the dz_1 and dz_2 we choose a portfolio, Π, consisting of

$$-1: \qquad \text{derivative}$$

$$+\frac{\partial f}{\partial S_1}: \qquad \text{first traded security}$$

$$+\frac{\partial f}{\partial S_2}: \qquad \text{second traded security}$$

$$\Pi = -f + \frac{\partial f}{\partial S_1} S_1 + \frac{\partial f}{\partial S_2} S_2$$

$$d\Pi = -df + \frac{\partial f}{\partial S_1} dS_1 + \frac{\partial f}{\partial S_2} dS_2$$

$$= -\left(\frac{\partial f}{\partial t} + \frac{1}{2} \sigma_1^2 S_1^2 \frac{\partial^2 f}{\partial S_1^2} + \frac{1}{2} \sigma_2^2 S_2^2 \frac{\partial^2 f}{\partial S_2^2} + \rho \sigma_1 \sigma_2 S_1 S_2 \frac{\partial^2 f}{\partial S_1 \partial S_2} \right) dt$$

Since the portfolio is instantaneously risk-free it must instantaneously earn the risk-free rate of interest. Hence

$$d\Pi = r\Pi dt$$

Combining the above equations

$$-\left[\frac{\partial f}{\partial t} + \frac{1}{2} \sigma_1^2 S_1^2 \frac{\partial^2 f}{\partial S_1^2} + \frac{1}{2} \sigma_2^2 S_2^2 \frac{\partial^2 f}{\partial S_2^2} + \rho \sigma_1 \sigma_2 S_1 S_2 \frac{\partial^2 f}{\partial S_1 \partial S_2} \right] dt$$

$$= r\left[-f + \frac{\partial f}{\partial S_1} S_1 + \frac{\partial f}{\partial S_2} S_2 \right] dt$$

so that:

$$\frac{\partial f}{\partial t} + r S_1 \frac{\partial f}{\partial S_1} + r S_2 \frac{\partial f}{\partial S_2} + \frac{1}{2}\sigma_1^2 S_1^2 \frac{\partial^2 f}{\partial S_1^2} + \frac{1}{2}\sigma_2^2 S_2^2 \frac{\partial^2 f}{\partial S_2^2} + \rho\sigma_1\sigma_2 S_1 S_2 \frac{\partial^2 f}{\partial S_1 \partial S_2} = rf$$

Problem 27.6.

Suppose that an interest rate, x, follows the process

$$dx = a(x_0 - x)\,dt + c\sqrt{x}\,dz$$

where a, x_0, and c are positive constants. Suppose further that the market price of risk for x is λ. What is the process for x in the traditional risk-neutral world

The process for x can be written

$$\frac{dx}{x} = \frac{a(x_0 - x)}{x}\,dt + \frac{c}{\sqrt{x}}\,dz$$

Hence the expected growth rate in x is:

$$\frac{a(x_0 - x)}{x}$$

and the volatility of x is

$$\frac{c}{\sqrt{x}}$$

In a risk neutral world the expected growth rate should be changed to

$$\frac{a(x_0 - x)}{x} - \lambda \frac{c}{\sqrt{x}}$$

so that the process is

$$\frac{dx}{x} = \left[\frac{a(x_0 - x)}{x} - \lambda \frac{c}{\sqrt{x}}\right]dt + \frac{c}{\sqrt{x}}\,dz$$

i.e.

$$dx = \left[a(x_0 - x) - \lambda c\sqrt{x}\right]dt + c\sqrt{x}\,dz$$

Hence the drift rate should be reduced by $\lambda c\sqrt{x}$.

Problem 27.7.

Prove that when the security f provides income at rate q equation (27.9) becomes $\mu + q - r = \lambda\sigma$. (Hint: Form a new security, f^* that provides no income by assuming that all the income from f is reinvested in f.)

As suggested in the hint we form a new security f^* which is the same as f except that all income produced by f is reinvested in f. Assuming we start doing this at time zero, the relationship between f and f^* is

$$f^* = fe^{qt}$$

If μ^* and σ^* are the expected return and volatility of f^*, Ito's lemma shows that

$$\mu^* = \mu + q$$

$$\sigma^* = \sigma$$

From equation (27.9)

$$\mu^* - r = \lambda\sigma^*$$

It follows that

$$\mu + q - r = \lambda\sigma$$

Problem 27.8.

Show that when f and g provide income at rates q_f and q_g respectively, equation (27.15) becomes

$$f_0 = g_0 e^{(q_f - q_g)T} E_g\left(\frac{f_T}{g_T}\right)$$

(Hint: Form new securities f^* and g^* that provide no income by assuming that all the income from f is reinvested in f and all the income in g is reinvested in g.)

As suggested in the hint, we form two new securities f^* and g^* which are the same as f and g at time zero, but are such that income from f is reinvested in f and income from g is reinvested in g. By construction f^* and g^* are non-income producing and their values at time t are related to f and g by

$$f^* = fe^{q_f t} \qquad g^* = ge^{q_g t}$$

From Ito's lemma, the securities g and g^* have the same volatility. We can apply the analysis given in Section 27.3 to f^* and g^* so that from equation (27.15)

$$f_0^* = g_0^* E_g\left(\frac{f_T^*}{g_T^*}\right)$$

or

$$f_0 = g_0 E_g\left(\frac{f_T e^{q_f T}}{g_T e^{q_g T}}\right)$$

or

$$f_0 = g_0 e^{(q_f - q_g)T} E_g\left(\frac{f_T}{g_T}\right)$$

Problem 27.9.

"The expected future value of an interest rate in a risk-neutral world is greater than it is in the real world." What does this statement imply about the market price of risk for (a) an interest rate and (b) a bond price. Do you think the statement is likely to be true? Give reasons.

This statement implies that the interest rate has a negative market price of risk. Since bond prices and interest rates are negatively correlated, the statement implies that the market price of risk for a bond price is positive. The statement is reasonable. When interest rates increase, there is a tendency for the stock market to decrease. This implies that interest rates have negative systematic risk, or equivalently that bond prices have positive systematic risk.

Problem 27.10.

The variable S is an investment asset providing income at rate q measured in currency A. It follows the process

$$dS = \mu_S S\, dt + \sigma_S S\, dz$$

in the real world. Defining new variables as necessary, give the process followed by S, and the corresponding market price of risk, in
(a) A world that is the traditional risk-neutral world for currency A.
(b) A world that is the traditional risk-neutral world for currency B.
(c) A world that is forward risk neutral with respect to a zero-coupon currency A bond maturing at time T.
(d) A world that is forward risk neutral with respect to a zero coupon currency B bond maturing at time T.

(a)   In the traditional risk-neutral world the process followed by S is

$$dS = (r - q)S\, dt + \sigma_S S\, dz$$

where r is the instantaneous risk-free rate. The market price of dz-risk is zero.

(b)   In the traditional risk-neutral world for currency B the process is

$$dS = (r - q + \rho_{QS}\sigma_S\sigma_Q)S\, dt + \sigma_S S\, dz$$

where Q is the exchange rate (units of A per unit of B), σ_Q is the volatility of Q and ρ_{QS} is the coefficient of correlation between Q and S. The market price of dz-risk is $\rho_{QS}\sigma_Q$.

(c)   In a world that is forward risk neutral with respect to a zero-coupon bond in currency A maturing at time T

$$dS = (r - q + \sigma_S\sigma_P)S\, dt + \sigma_S S\, dz$$

where σ_P is the bond price volatility. The market price of dz-risk is σ_P.

(d)   In a world that is forward risk neutral with respect to a zero-coupon bond in currency B maturing at time T

$$dS = (r - q + \sigma_S \sigma_P + \rho_{FS} \sigma_S \sigma_F)S\, dt + \sigma_S S\, dz$$

where F is the forward exchange rate, σ_F is the volatility of F (units of A per unit of B, and ρ_{FS} is the correlation between F and S. The market price of dz-risk is $\sigma_P + \rho_{FS}\sigma_F$.

Problem 27.11.

Explain the difference between the way a forward interest rate is defined and the way the forward values of other variables such as stock prices, commodity prices, and exchange rates are defined.

The forward value of a stock price, commodity price, or exchange rate is the delivery price in a forward contract that causes the value of the forward contract to be zero. A forward bond price is calculated in this way. However, a forward interest rate is the interest rate implied by the forward bond price.

Problem 27.12.

Prove the result in Section 27.5 that when

$$df = \left[r + \sum_{i=1}^{n} \lambda_i \sigma_{f,i} \right] f\, dt + \sum_{i=1}^{n} \sigma_{f,i} f\, dz_i$$

and

$$dg = \left[r + \sum_{i=1}^{n} \lambda_i \sigma_{g,i} \right] g\, dt + \sum_{i=1}^{n} \sigma_{g,i} g\, dz_i$$

with the dz_i uncorrelated, f/g is a martingale for $\lambda_i = \sigma_{g,i}$. (Hint: Start by using equation (13A.11) to get the processes for $\ln f$ and $\ln g$.)

$$d\ln f = \left[r + \sum_{i=1}^{n} (\lambda_i \sigma_{f,i} - \sigma_{f,i}^2 / 2) \right] dt + \sum_{i=1}^{n} \sigma_{f,i} dz_i$$

$$d\ln g = \left[r + \sum_{i=1}^{n} (\lambda_i \sigma_{g,i} - \sigma_{g,i}^2 / 2) \right] dt + \sum_{i=1}^{n} \sigma_{g,i} dz_i$$

so that

$$d\ln \frac{f}{g} = d(\ln f - \ln g) = \left[\sum_{i=1}^{n} (\lambda_i \sigma_{f,i} - \lambda_i \sigma_{g,i} - \sigma_{f,i}^2 / 2 + \sigma_{g,i}^2 / 2) \right] dt + \sum_{i=1}^{n} (\sigma_{f,i} - \sigma_{g,i}) dz_i$$

Applying Ito's lemma again

$$d\frac{f}{g} = \frac{f}{g} \left[\sum_{i=1}^{n} (\lambda_i \sigma_{f,i} - \lambda_i \sigma_{g,i} - \sigma_{f,i}^2 / 2 + \sigma_{g,i}^2 / 2) + (\sigma_{f,i} - \sigma_{g,i})^2 / 2 \right] dt + \frac{f}{g} \sum_{i=1}^{n} (\sigma_{f,i} - \sigma_{g,i}) dz_i$$

When $\lambda_i = \sigma_{g,i}$ the coefficient of dt is zero and f/g is a martingale.

Problem 27.13.

Show that when $w = h/g$ and h and g are each dependent on n Wiener processes, the ith component of the volatility of w is the ith component of the volatility of h minus the ith component of the volatility of g. Use this to prove the result that if σ_U is the volatility of U and σ_V is the volatility of V then the volatility of U/V is $\sqrt{\sigma_U^2 + \sigma_V^2 - 2\rho\sigma_U\sigma_V}$. (Hint: Start by using equation (13A.11) to get the processes for $\ln g$ and $\ln h$.)

$$d \ln h = ... + \sum_{i=1}^{n} \sigma_{h,i} dz_i$$

$$d \ln g = ... + \sum_{i=1}^{n} \sigma_{g,i} dz_i$$

so that

$$d \ln \frac{h}{g} = ... + \sum_{i=1}^{n} (\sigma_{h,i} - \sigma_{g,i}) dz_i$$

Applying Ito's lemma again

$$d \frac{h}{g} = ... + \frac{h}{g} \sum_{i=1}^{n} (\sigma_{h,i} - \sigma_{g,i}) dz_i$$

This proves the result.

CHAPTER 28
Interest Rate Derivatives: The Standard Market Models

Problem 28.1.
A company caps three-month LIBOR at 10% per annum. The principal amount is $20 million. On a reset date, three-month LIBOR is 12% per annum. What payment would this lead to under the cap? When would the payment be made?

An amount
$$\$20,000,000 \times 0.02 \times 0.25 = \$100,000$$
would be paid out 3 months later.

Problem 28.2.
Explain why a swap option can be regarded as a type of bond option.

A swap option (or swaption) is an option to enter into an interest rate swap at a certain time in the future with a certain fixed rate being used. An interest rate swap can be regarded as the exchange of a fixed-rate bond for a floating-rate bond. A swaption is therefore the option to exchange a fixed-rate bond for a floating-rate bond. The floating-rate bond will be worth its face value at the beginning of the life of the swap. The swaption is therefore an option on a fixed-rate bond with the strike price equal to the face value of the bond.

Problem 28.3.
Use the Black's model to value a one-year European put option on a 10-year bond. Assume that the current value of the bond is $125, the strike price is $110, the one-year interest rate is 10% per annum, the bond's forward price volatility is 8% per annum, and the present value of the coupons to be paid during the life of the option is $10.

In this case, $F_0 = (125-10)e^{0.1 \times 1} = 127.09$, $K = 110$, $P(0,T) = e^{-0.1 \times 1}$, $\sigma_B = 0.08$, and $T = 1.0$.
$$d_1 = \frac{\ln(127.09/110) + (0.08^2/2)}{0.08} = 1.8456$$
$$d_2 = d_1 - 0.08 = 1.7656$$
From equation (28.2) the value of the put option is
$$110e^{-0.1 \times 1} N(-1.7656) - 127.09e^{-0.1 \times 1} N(-1.8456) = 0.12$$
or $0.12.

Problem 28.4.
Explain carefully how you would use (a) spot volatilities and (b) flat volatilities to value a five-year cap.

When spot volatilities are used to value a cap, a different volatility is used to value each caplet. When flat volatilities are used, the same volatility is used to value each caplet within a given cap. Spot volatilities are a function of the maturity of the caplet. Flat volatilities are a function of the maturity of the cap.

Problem 28.5.

Calculate the price of an option that caps the three-month rate, starting in 15 month' time, at 13% (quoted with quarterly compounding) on a principal amount of $1,000. The forward interest rate for the period in question is 12% per annum (quoted with quarterly compounding), the 18-month risk-free interest rate (continuously compounded) is 11.5% per annum, and the volatility of the forward rate is 12% per annum.

In this case $L = 1000$, $\delta_k = 0.25$, $F_k = 0.12$, $R_K = 0.13$, $r = 0.115$, $\sigma_k = 0.12$, $t_k = 1.25$, $P(0, t_{k+1}) = 0.8416$.

$$L\delta_k = 250$$

$$d_1 = \frac{\ln(0.12/0.13) + 0.12^2 \times 1.25/2}{0.12\sqrt{1.25}} = -0.5295$$

$$d_2 = -0.5295 - 0.12\sqrt{1.25} = -0.6637$$

The value of the option is

$$250 \times 0.8416 \times [0.12 N(-0.5295) - 0.13 N(-0.6637)]$$

$$= 0.59$$

or $0.59.

Problem 28.6.

A bank uses Black's model to price European bond options. Suppose that an implied price volatility for a 5-year option on a bond maturing in 10 years is used to price a 9-year option on the bond. Would you expect the resultant price to be too high or too low? Explain.

The implied volatility measures the standard deviation of the logarithm of the bond price at the maturity of the option divided by the square root of the time to maturity. In the case of a five year option on a ten year bond, the bond has five years left at option maturity. In the case of a nine year option on a ten year bond it has one year left. The standard deviation of a one year bond price observed in nine years can be normally be expected to be considerably less than that of a five year bond price observed in five years. (See Figure 28.1.) We would therefore expect the price to be too high.

Problem 28.7.

Calculate the value of a four-year European call option on bond that will mature five years from today using Black's model. The five-year cash bond price is $105, the cash price of a four-year bond with the same coupon is $102, the strike price is $100, the four-year risk-free interest rate is 10% per annum with continuous compounding, and the volatility for the bond price in four years is 2% per annum.

The present value of the principal in the four year bond is $100e^{-4 \times 0.1} = 67.032$. The present value of the coupons is, therefore, $102 - 67.032 = 34.968$. This means that the forward price of the five-year bond is

$$(105 - 34.968)e^{4 \times 0.1} = 104.475$$

The parameters in Black's model are therefore $F_B = 104.475$, $K = 100$, $r = 0.1$, $T = 4$, and $\sigma_B = 0.02$.

$$d_1 = \frac{\ln 1.04475 + 0.5 \times 0.02^2 \times 4}{0.02\sqrt{4}} = 1.1144$$

$$d_2 = d_1 - 0.02\sqrt{4} = 1.0744$$

The price of the European call is

$$e^{-0.1\times 4}[104.475N(1.1144) - 100N(1.0744)] = 3.19$$

or \$3.19.

Problem 28.8.

If the yield volatility for a five-year put option on a bond maturing in 10 years time is specified as 22%, how should the option be valued? Assume that, based on today's interest rates the modified duration of the bond at the maturity of the option will be 4.2 years and the forward yield on the bond is 7%.

The option should be valued using Black's model in equation (28.2) with the bond price volatility being

$$4.2 \times 0.07 \times 0.22 = 0.0647$$

or 6.47%.

Problem 28.9.

What other instrument is the same as a five-year zero-cost collar where the strike price of the cap equals the strike price of the floor? What does the common strike price equal?

A 5-year zero-cost collar where the strike price of the cap equals the strike price of the floor is the same as an interest rate swap agreement to receive floating and pay a fixed rate equal to the strike price. The common strike price is the swap rate. Note that the swap is actually a forward swap that excludes the first exchange. (See Business Snapshot 28.1)

Problem 28.10.

Derive a put–call parity relationship for European bond options.

There are two way of expressing the put–call parity relationship for bond options. The first is in terms of bond prices:

$$c + I + Ke^{-RT} = p + B_0$$

where c is the price of a European call option, p is the price of the corresponding European put option, I is the present value of the bond coupon payments during the life of the option, K is the strike price, T is the time to maturity, B_0 is the bond price, and R is the risk-free interest rate for a maturity equal to the life of the options. To prove this we can consider two portfolios. The first consists of a European put option plus the bond; the second consists of the European call option, and an amount of cash equal to the present value of the coupons plus the present value of the strike price. Both can be seen to be worth the same at the maturity of the options.

The second way of expressing the put–call parity relationship is

$$c + Ke^{-RT} = p + F_B e^{-RT}$$

where F_B is the forward bond price. This can also be proved by considering two portfolios.

The first consists of a European put option plus a forward contract on the bond plus the present value of the forward price; the second consists of a European call option plus the present value of the strike price. Both can be seen to be worth the same at the maturity of the options.

Problem 28.11.
Derive a put–call parity relationship for European swap options.

The put–call parity relationship for European swap options is
$$c + V = p$$
where c is the value of a call option to pay a fixed rate of s_K and receive floating, p is the value of a put option to receive a fixed rate of s_K and pay floating, and V is the value of the forward swap underlying the swap option where s_K is received and floating is paid. This can be proved by considering two portfolios. The first consists of the put option; the second consists of the call option and the swap. Suppose that the actual swap rate at the maturity of the options is greater than s_K. The call will be exercised and the put will not be exercised. Both portfolios are then worth zero. Suppose next that the actual swap rate at the maturity of the options is less than s_K. The put option is exercised and the call option is not exercised. Both portfolios are equivalent to a swap where s_K is received and floating is paid. In all states of the world the two portfolios are worth the same at time T. They must therefore be worth the same today. This proves the result.

Problem 28.12.
Explain why there is an arbitrage opportunity if the implied Black (flat) volatility of a cap is different from that of a floor. Do the broker quotes in Table 28.1 present an arbitrage opportunity?

Suppose that the cap and floor have the same strike price and the same time to maturity. The following put–call parity relationship must hold:
$$cap + swap = floor$$
where the swap is an agreement to receive the cap rate and pay floating over the whole life of the cap/floor. If the implied Black volatilities for the cap equal those for the floor, the Black formulas show that this relationship holds. In other circumstances it does not hold and there is an arbitrage opportunity. The broker quotes in Table 28.1 do not present an arbitrage opportunity because the cap offer is always higher than the floor bid and the floor offer is always higher than the cap bid.

Problem 28.13.
When a bond's price is lognormal can the bond's yield be negative? Explain your answer.

Yes. If a zero-coupon bond price at some future time is lognormal, there is some chance that the price will be above par. This in turn implies that the yield to maturity on the bond is negative.

Problem 28.14.
What is the value of a European swap option that gives the holder the right to enter into a 3-year annual-pay swap in four years where a fixed rate of 5% is paid and LIBOR is received? The swap principal is $10 million. Assume that the yield curve is flat at 5% per annum with annual compounding and the volatility of the swap rate is 20%. Compare your answer to that given by DerivaGem.

In equation (28.10), $L = 10,000,000$, $s_K = 0.05$, $s_0 = 0.05$, $d_1 = 0.2\sqrt{4}/2 = 0.2$, $d_2 = -.2$, and

$$A = \frac{1}{1.05^5} + \frac{1}{1.05^6} + \frac{1}{1.05^7} = 2.2404$$

The value of the swap option (in millions of dollars) is
$$10 \times 2.2404[0.05N(0.2) - 0.05N(-0.2)] = 0.178$$

This is the same as the answer given by DerivaGem. (For the purposes of using the DerivaGem software, note that the interest rate is 4.879% with continuous compounding for all maturities.)

Problem 28.15.
Suppose that the yield, R, on a zero-coupon bond follows the process
$$dR = \mu\, dt + \sigma\, dz$$
where μ and σ are functions of R and t, and dz is a Wiener process. Use Ito's lemma to show that the volatility of the zero-coupon bond price declines to zero as it approaches maturity.

The price of the bond at time t is $e^{-R(T-t)}$ where T is the time when the bond matures. Using Itô's lemma the volatility of the bond price is

$$\sigma \frac{\partial}{\partial R} e^{-R(T-t)} = -\sigma(T-t)e^{-R(T-t)}$$

This tends to zero as t approaches T.

Problem 28.16.
Carry out a manual calculation to verify the option prices in Example 28.2.

The cash price of the bond is
$$4e^{-0.05\times0.50} + 4e^{-0.05\times1.00} + ... + 4e^{-0.05\times10} + 100e^{-0.05\times10} = 122.82$$
As there is no accrued interest this is also the quoted price of the bond. The interest paid during the life of the option has a present value of
$$4e^{-0.05\times0.5} + 4e^{-0.05\times1} + 4e^{-0.05\times1.5} + 4e^{-0.05\times2} = 15.04$$
The forward price of the bond is therefore
$$(122.82 - 15.04)e^{0.05\times2.25} = 120.61$$
The yield with semiannual compounding is 5.0630%.
The duration of the bond at option maturity is
$$\frac{0.25\times4e^{-0.05\times0.25} + ... + 7.75\times4e^{-0.05\times7.75} + 7.75\times100e^{-0.05\times7.75}}{4e^{-0.05\times0.25} + 4e^{-0.05\times0.75} + ... + 4e^{-0.05\times7.75} + 100e^{-0.05\times7.75}}$$
or 5.994. The modified duration is 5.994/1.025315=5.846. The bond price volatility is therefore $5.846 \times 0.050630 \times 0.2 = 0.0592$. We can therefore value the bond option using Black's model with $F_B = 120.61$, $P(0,2.25) = e^{-0.05\times2.25} = 0.8936$, $\sigma_B = 5.92\%$, and $T = 2.25$. When the strike price is the cash price $K = 115$ and the value of the option is 1.74. When the strike price is the quoted price $K = 117$ and the value of the option is 2.36. This is in agreement with DerivaGem.

Problem 28.17.
Suppose that the 1-year, 2-year, 3-year, 4-year and 5-year zero rates are 6%, 6.4%, 6.7%, 6.9%, and 7%. The price of a 5-year semiannual cap with a principal of $100 at a cap rate of

8% is $3. Use DerivaGem to determine
   (c)   The 5-year flat volatility for caps and floors
   (d)   The floor rate in a zero-cost 5-year collar when the cap rate is 8%

We choose the Caps and Swap Options worksheet of DerivaGem and choose Cap/Floor as the Underlying Type. We enter the 1-, 2-, 3-, 4-, 5-year zero rates as 6%, 6.4%, 6.7%, 6.9%, and 7.0% in the Term Structure table. We enter Semiannual for the Settlement Frequency, 100 for the Principal, 0 for the Start (Years), 5 for the End (Years), 8% for the Cap/Floor Rate, and $3 for the Price. We select Black-European as the Pricing Model and choose the Cap button. We check the Imply Volatility box and Calculate. The implied volatility is 24.90%. We then uncheck Implied Volatility, select Floor, check Imply Breakeven Rate. The floor rate that is calculated is 6.71%. This is the floor rate for which the floor is worth $3.A collar when the floor rate is 6.71% and the cap rate is 8% has zero cost.

Problem 28.18.
Show that $V_1 + f = V_2$ where V_1 is the value of a swaption to pay a fixed rate of s_K and receive LIBOR between times T_1 and T_2, f is the value of a forward swap to receive a fixed rate of s_K and pay LIBOR between times T_1 and T_2, and V_2 is the value of a swap option to receive a fixed rate of s_K between times T_1 and T_2. Deduce that $V_1 = V_2$ when s_K equals the current forward swap rate.

We prove this result by considering two portfolios. The first consists of the swap option to receive s_K; the second consists of the swap option to pay s_K and the forward swap. Suppose that the actual swap rate at the maturity of the options is greater than s_K. The swap option to pay s_K will be exercised and the swap option to receive s_K will not be exercised. Both portfolios are then worth zero since the swap option to pay s_K is neutralized by the forward swap. Suppose next that the actual swap rate at the maturity of the options is less than s_K. The swap option to receive s_K is exercised and the swap option to pay s_K is not exercised. Both portfolios are then equivalent to a swap where s_K is received and floating is paid. In all states of the world the two portfolios are worth the same at time T_1. They must therefore be worth the same today. This proves the result. When s_K equals the current forward swap rate $f = 0$ and $V_1 = V_2$. A swap option to pay fixed is therefore worth the same as a similar swap option to receive fixed when the fixed rate in the swap option is the forward swap rate.

Problem 28.19.
Suppose that zero rates are as in Problem 28.17. Use DerivaGem to determine the value of an option to pay a fixed rate of 6% and receive LIBOR on a five-year swap starting in one year. Assume that the principal is $100 million, payments are exchanged semiannually, and the swap rate volatility is 21%.

We choose the Caps and Swap Options worksheet of DerivaGem and choose Swap Option as the Underlying Type. We enter 100 as the Principal, 1 as the Start (Years), 6 as the End (Years), 6% as the Swap Rate, and Semiannual as the Settlement Frequency. We choose Black-European as the pricing model, enter 21% as the Volatility and check the Pay Fixed button. We do not check the Imply Breakeven Rate and Imply Volatility boxes. The value of the swap option is 5.63.

Problem 28.20.

Describe how you would (a) calculate cap flat volatilities from cap spot volatilities and (b) calculate cap spot volatilities from cap flat volatilities.

(a) To calculate flat volatilities from spot volatilities we choose a strike rate and use the spot volatilities to calculate caplet prices. We then sum the caplet prices to obtain cap prices and imply flat volatilities from Black's model. The answer is slightly dependent on the strike price chosen. This procedure ignores any volatility smile in cap pricing.

(b) To calculate spot volatilities from flat volatilities the first step is usually to interpolate between the flat volatilities so that we have a flat volatility for each caplet payment date. We choose a strike price and use the flat volatilities to calculate cap prices. By subtracting successive cap prices we obtain caplet prices from which we can imply spot volatilities. The answer is slightly dependent on the strike price chosen. This procedure also ignores any volatility smile in caplet pricing.

CHAPTER 29
Convexity, Timing, and Quanto Adjustments

Problem 29.1.
Explain how you would value a derivative that pays off $100R$ in five years where R is the one-year interest rate (annually compounded) observed in four years. What difference would it make if the payoff were in (a) 4 years and (b) 6 years?

The value of the derivative is $100R_{4,5}P(0,5)$ where $P(0,t)$ is the value of a t-year zero-coupon bond today and R_{t_1,t_2} is the forward rate for the period between t_1 and t_2, expressed with annual compounding. If the payoff is made in four years the value is $100(R_{4,5}+c)P(0,4)$ where c is the convexity adjustment given by equation (29.2). The formula for the convexity adjustment is:

$$c = \frac{4R_{4,5}^2\sigma_{4,5}^2}{(1+R_{4,5})}$$

where σ_{t_1,t_2} is the volatility of the forward rate between times t_1 and t_2.
The expression $100(R_{4,5}+c)$ is the expected payoff in a world that is forward risk neutral with respect to a zero-coupon bond maturing at time four years. If the payoff is made in six years, the value is from equation (29.4) given by

$$100(R_{4,5}+c)P(0,6)\exp\left[-\frac{4\rho\sigma_{4,5}\sigma_{4,6}R_{4,6}\times 2}{1+R_{4,6}}\right]$$

where ρ is the correlation between the (4,5) and (4,6) forward rates. As an approximation we can assume that $\rho=1$, $\sigma_{4,5}=\sigma_{4,6}$, and $R_{4,5}=R_{4,6}$. Approximating the exponential function we then get the value of the derivative as $100(R_{4,5}-c)P(0,6)$.

Problem 29.2.
Explain whether any convexity or timing adjustments are necessary when
  (a) *We wish to value a spread option that pays off every quarter the excess (if any) of the five-year swap rate over the three-month LIBOR rate applied to a principal of $100. The payoff occurs 90 days after the rates are observed.*
  (b) *We wish to value a derivative that pays off every quarter the three-month LIBOR rate minus the three-month Treasury bill rate. The payoff occurs 90 days after the rates are observed.*

(a) A convexity adjustment is necessary for the swap rate
(b) No convexity or timing adjustments are necessary.

Problem 29.3.
Suppose that in Example 28.3 of Section 28.2 the payoff occurs after one year (i.e., when the interest rate is observed) rather than in 15 months. What difference does this make to the inputs to Black's models?

There are two differences. The discounting is done over a 1.0-year period instead of over a 1.25-year period. Also a convexity adjustment to the forward rate is necessary. From equation

(29.2) the convexity adjustment is:
$$\frac{0.07^2 \times 0.2^2 \times 0.25 \times 1}{1+0.25\times 0.07} = 0.00005$$
or about half a basis point.

In the formula for the caplet we set $F_k = 0.07005$ instead of 0.07. This means that $d_1 = -0.5642$ and $d_2 = -0.7642$. With continuous compounding the 15-month rate is 6.5% and the forward rate between 12 and 15 months is 6.94%. The 12 month rate is therefore 6.39% The caplet price becomes
$$0.25 \times 10,000 e^{-0.069394 \times 1.0} [0.07005 N(-0.5642) - 0.08 N(-0.7642)] = 5.29$$
or $5.29.

Problem 29.4.

The yield curve is flat at 10% per annum with annual compounding. Calculate the value of an instrument where, in five years' time, the two-year swap rate (with annual compounding) is received and a fixed rate of 10% is paid. Both are applied to a notional principal of $100. Assume that the volatility of the swap rate is 20% per annum. Explain why the value of the instrument is different from zero.

The convexity adjustment discussed in Section 29.1 leads to the instrument being worth an amount slightly different from zero. Define $G(y)$ as the value as seen in five years of a two-year bond with a coupon of 10% as a function of its yield.

$$G(y) = \frac{0.1}{1+y} + \frac{1.1}{(1+y)^2}$$

$$G'(y) = -\frac{0.1}{(1+y)^2} - \frac{2.2}{(1+y)^3}$$

$$G''(y) = \frac{0.2}{(1+y)^3} + \frac{6.6}{(1+y)^4}$$

It follows that $G'(0.1) = -1.7355$ and $G''(0.1) = 4.6582$ and the convexity adjustment that must be made for the two-year swap- rate is
$$0.5 \times 0.1^2 \times 0.2^2 \times 5 \times \frac{4.6582}{1.7355} = 0.00268$$

We can therefore value the instrument on the assumption that the swap rate will be 10.268% in five years. The value of the instrument is
$$\frac{0.268}{1.1^5} = 0.167$$
or $0.167.

Problem 29.5.

What difference does it make in Problem 29.4 if the swap rate is observed in five years, but the exchange of payments takes place in (a) six years, and (b) seven years? Assume that the volatilities of all forward rates are 20%. Assume also that the forward swap rate for the period between years five and seven has a correlation of 0.8 with the forward interest rate between years five and six and a correlation of 0.95 with the forward interest rate between years five and seven.

In this case we have to make a timing adjustment as well as a convexity adjustment to the forward swap rate. For (a) equation (29.4) shows that the timing adjustment involves multiplying the swap rate by

$$\exp\left[-\frac{0.8\times0.20\times0.20\times0.1\times5}{1+0.1}\right] = 0.9856$$

so that it becomes $10.268\times0.9856 = 10.120$. The value of the instrument is

$$\frac{0.120}{1.1^6} = 0.068$$

or $0.068.

For (b) equation (29.4) shows that the timing adjustment involves multiplying the swap rate by

$$\exp\left[-\frac{0.95\times0.2\times0.2\times0.1\times2\times5}{1+0.1}\right] = 0.9660$$

so that it becomes $10.268\times0.966 = 9.919$. The value of the instrument is now

$$-\frac{0.081}{1.1^7} = -0.042$$

or –$0.042.

Problem 29.6.

The price of a bond at time T, measured in terms of its yield, is $G(y_T)$. Assume geometric Brownian motion for the forward bond yield, y, in a world that is forward risk neutral with respect to a bond maturing at time T. Suppose that the growth rate of the forward bond yield is α and its volatility σ_y.

  (a) *Use Ito's lemma to calculate the process for the forward bond price in terms of α, σ_y, y, and $G(y)$.*

  (b) *The forward bond price should follow a martingale in the world considered. Use this fact to calculate an expression for α.*

  (c) *Show that the expression for α is, to a first approximation, consistent with equation (29.1).*

(a) The process for y is

$$dy = \alpha y\, dt + \sigma_y y\, dz$$

The forward bond price is $G(y)$. From Itô's lemma, its process is

$$d[G(y)] = [G'(y)\alpha y + \frac{1}{2}G''(y)\sigma_y^2 y^2]dt + G'(y)\sigma_y y\, dz$$

(b) Since the expected growth rate of $G(y)$ is zero

$$G'(y)\alpha y + \frac{1}{2}G''(y)\sigma_y^2 y^2 = 0$$

or

$$\alpha = -\frac{1}{2}\frac{G''(y)}{G'(y)}\sigma_y^2 y$$

(c) Assuming as an approximation that y always equals its initial value of y_0, this shows that the growth rate of y is

$$-\frac{1}{2}\frac{G''(y_0)}{G'(y_0)}\sigma_y^2 y_0$$

The variable y starts at y_0 and ends as y_T. The convexity adjustment to y_0 when we are calculating the expected value of y_T in a world that is forward risk neutral with respect to a zero-coupon bond maturing at time T is approximately $y_0 T$ times this or

$$-\frac{1}{2}\frac{G''(y_0)}{G'(y_0)}\sigma_y^2 y_0^2 T$$

This is consistent with equation (29.1).

Problem 29.7.

The variable S is an investment asset providing income at rate q measured in currency A. It follows the process

$$dS = \mu_s S \, dt + \sigma_s S \, dz$$

in the real world. Defining new variables as necessary, give the process followed by S, and the corresponding market price of risk, in
(a) A world that is the traditional risk-neutral world for currency A.
(b) A world that is the traditional risk-neutral world for currency B.
(c) A world that is forward risk neutral with respect to a zero-coupon currency A bond maturing at time T.
(d) A world that is forward risk neutral with respect to a zero coupon currency B bond maturing at time T.

(a) In the traditional risk-neutral world the process followed by S is
$$dS = (r - q)S \, dt + \sigma_s S \, dz$$
where r is the instantaneous risk-free rate. The market price of dz-risk is zero.

(b) In the traditional risk-neutral world for currency B the process is
$$dS = (r - q + \rho_{QS}\sigma_s\sigma_Q)S \, dt + \sigma_s S \, dz$$
where Q is the exchange rate (units of A per unit of B), σ_Q is the volatility of Q and ρ_{QS} is the coefficient of correlation between Q and S. The market price of dz-risk is $\rho_{QS}\sigma_Q$

(c) In a world that is forward risk neutral with respect to a zero-coupon bond in currency A maturing at time T
$$dS = (r - q + \sigma_s\sigma_P)S \, dt + \sigma_s S \, dz$$
where σ_P is the bond price volatility. The market price of dz-risk is σ_P

(d) In a world that is forward risk neutral with respect to a zero-coupon bond in currency B maturing at time T
$$dS = (r - q + \sigma_s\sigma_P + \rho_{FS}\sigma_s\sigma_F)S \, dt + \sigma_s S \, dz$$
where F is the forward exchange rate, σ_F is the volatility of F (units of A per unit of B, and ρ_{FS} is the correlation between F and S. The market price of dz-risk is $\sigma_P + \rho_{FS}\sigma_F$.

Problem 29.8.

A call option provides a payoff at time T of $\max(S_T - K, 0)$ yen, where S_T is the dollar price of gold at time T and K is the strike price. Assuming that the storage costs of gold are zero and defining other variables as necessary, calculate the value of the contract.

Define

$P(t,T)$: Price in yen at time t of a bond paying 1 yen at time T

$E_T(.)$: Expectation in world that is forward risk neutral with respect to $P(t,T)$

F: Dollar forward price of gold for a contract maturing at time T

F_0: Value of F at time zero

σ_F: Volatility of F

G: Forward exchange rate (dollars per yen)

σ_G: Volatility of G

We assume that S_T is lognormal. We can work in a world that is forward risk neutral with respect to $P(t,T)$ to get the value of the call as

$$P(0,T)[E_T(S_T)N(d_1) - N(d_2)]$$

where

$$d_1 = \frac{\ln[E_T(S_T)/K] + \sigma_F^2 T/2}{\sigma_F \sqrt{T}}$$

$$d_2 = \frac{\ln[E_T(S_T)/K] - \sigma_F^2 T/2}{\sigma_F \sqrt{T}}$$

The expected gold price in a world that is forward risk-neutral with respect to a zero-coupon dollar bond maturing at time T is F_0. It follows from equation (29.6) that

$$E_T(S_T) = F_0(1 + \rho\sigma_F\sigma_G T)$$

Hence the option price, measured in yen, is

$$P(0,T)[F_0(1 + \rho\sigma_F\sigma_G T)N(d_1) - KN(d_2)]$$

where

$$d_1 = \frac{\ln[F_0(1 + \rho\sigma_F\sigma_G T)/K] + \sigma_F^2 T/2}{\sigma_F \sqrt{T}}$$

$$d_2 = \frac{\ln[F_0(1 + \rho\sigma_F\sigma_G T)/K] - \sigma_F^2 T/2}{\sigma_F \sqrt{T}}$$

Problem 29.9.

Suppose that an index of Canadian stocks currently stands at 400. The Canadian dollar is currently worth 0.70 U.S. dollars. The risk-free interest rates in Canada and the U.S. are constant at 6% and 4%, respectively. The dividend yield on the index is 3%. Define Q as the number of Canadian dollars per U.S dollar and S as the value of the index. The volatility of S is 20%, the volatility of Q is 6%, and the correlation between S and Q is 0.4. Use DerivaGem to determine the value of a two year American-style call option on the index if
(a) It pays off in Canadian dollars the amount by which the index exceeds 400.
(b) It pays off in U.S. dollars the amount by which the index exceeds 400.

(a)   The value of the option can be calculated by setting $S_0 = 400$, $K = 400$, $r = 0.06$, $q = 0.03$, $\sigma = 0.2$, and $T = 2$. With 100 time steps the value (in Canadian dollars) is 52.92.

(b)   The growth rate of the index using the CDN numeraire is $0.06 - 0.03$ or 3%. When we switch to the USD numeraire we increase the growth rate of the index by $0.4 \times 0.2 \times 0.06$ or 0.48% per year to 3.48%. The option can therefore be calculated using DerivaGem with $S_0 = 400$, $K = 400$, $r = 0.04$, $q = 0.04 - 0.0348 = 0.0052$, $\sigma = 0.2$, and $T = 2$. With 100 time steps DerivaGem gives the value as 57.51.

CHAPTER 30
Interest Rate Derivatives: Models of the Short Rate

Problem 30.1.
What is the difference between an equilibrium model and a no-arbitrage model?

Equilibrium models usually start with assumptions about economic variables and derive the behavior of interest rates. The initial term structure is an output from the model. In a no-arbitrage model the initial term structure is an input. The behavior of interest rates in a no-arbitrage model is designed to be consistent with the initial term structure.

Problem 30.2.
Suppose that the short rate is currently 4% and its standard deviation is 1% per annum. What happens to the standard deviation when the short rate increases to 8% in (a) Vasicek's model; (b) Rendleman and Bartter's model; and (c) the Cox, Ingersoll, and Ross model?

In Vasicek's model the standard deviation stays at 1%. In the Rendleman and Bartter model the standard deviation is proportional to the level of the short rate. When the short rate increases from 4% to 8% the standard deviation increases from 1% to 2%. In the Cox, Ingersoll, and Ross model the standard deviation of the short rate is proportional to the square root of the short rate. When the short rate increases from 4% to 8% the standard deviation increases from 1% to 1.414%.

Problem 30.3.
If a stock price were mean reverting or followed a path-dependent process there would be market inefficiency. Why is there not market inefficiency when the short-term interest rate does so?

If the price of a traded security followed a mean-reverting or path-dependent process there would be market inefficiency. The short-term interest rate is not the price of a traded security. In other words we cannot trade something whose price is always the short-term interest rate. There is therefore no market inefficiency when the short-term interest rate follows a mean-reverting or path-dependent process. We can trade bonds and other instruments whose prices do depend on the short rate. The prices of these instruments do not follow mean-reverting or path-dependent processes.

Problem 30.4.
Explain the difference between a one-factor and a two-factor interest rate model.

In a one-factor model there is one source of uncertainty driving all rates. This usually means that in any short period of time all rates move in the same direction (but not necessarily by the same amount). In a two-factor model, there are two sources of uncertainty driving all rates. The first source of uncertainty usually gives rise to a roughly parallel shift in rates. The second gives rise to a twist where long and short rates moves in opposite directions.

Problem 30.5.
Can the approach described in Section 30.4 for decomposing an option on a coupon-bearing bond into a portfolio of options on zero-coupon bonds be used in conjunction with a two-

factor model? Explain your answer.

No. The approach in Section 30.4 relies on the argument that, at any given time, all bond prices are moving in the same direction. This is not true when there is more than one factor.

Problem 30.6.
Suppose that $a = 0.1$ and $b = 0.1$ in both the Vasicek and the Cox, Ingersoll, Ross model. In both models, the initial short rate is 10% and the initial standard deviation of the short rate change in a short time Δt is $0.02\sqrt{\Delta t}$. Compare the prices given by the models for a zero-coupon bond that matures in year 10.

In Vasicek's model, $a = 0.1$, $b = 0.1$, and $\sigma = 0.02$ so that
$$B(t, t+10) = \frac{1}{0.1}(1 - e^{-0.1 \times 10}) = 6.32121$$

$$A(t, t+10) = \exp\left[\frac{(6.32121 - 10)(0.1^2 \times 0.1 - 0.0002)}{0.01} - \frac{0.0004 \times 6.32121^2}{0.4}\right]$$

$$= 0.71587$$

The bond price is therefore $0.71587e^{-6.32121 \times 0.1} = 0.38046$

In the Cox, Ingersoll, and Ross model, $a = 0.1$, $b = 0.1$ and $\sigma = 0.02/\sqrt{0.1} = 0.0632$. Also
$$\gamma = \sqrt{a^2 + 2\sigma^2} = 0.13416$$

Define
$$\beta = (\gamma + a)(e^{10\gamma} - 1) + 2\gamma = 0.92992$$

$$B(t, t+10) = \frac{2(e^{10\gamma} - 1)}{\beta} = 6.07650$$

$$A(t, t+10) = \left(\frac{2\gamma e^{5(a+\gamma)}}{\beta}\right)^{2ab/\sigma^2} = 0.69746$$

The bond price is therefore $0.69746e^{-6.07650 \times 0.1} = 0.37986$

Problem 30.7.
Suppose that $a = 0.1$, $b = 0.08$, and $\sigma = 0.015$ in Vasicek's model with the initial value of the short rate being 5%. Calculate the price of a one-year European call option on a zero-coupon bond with a principal of $100 that matures in three years when the strike price is $87.

Using the notation in the text, $s = 3$, $T = 1$, $L = 100$, $K = 87$, and
$$\sigma_P = \frac{0.015}{0.1}(1 - e^{-2 \times 0.1})\sqrt{\frac{1 - e^{-2 \times 0.1 \times 1}}{2 \times 0.1}} = 0.025886$$

From equation (30.6), $P(0,1) = 0.94988$, $P(0,3) = 0.85092$, and $h = 1.14277$ so that equation (30.20) gives the call price as call price is
$$100 \times 0.85092 \times N(1.14277) - 87 \times 0.94988 \times N(1.11688) = 2.59$$

or $2.59.

230

Problem 30.8.

Repeat Problem 30.7 valuing a European put option with a strike of $87. What is the put–call parity relationship between the prices of European call and put options? Show that the put and call option prices satisfy put–call parity in this case.

As mentioned in the text, equation (30.20) for a call option is essentially the same as Black's model. By analogy with Black's formulas corresponding expression for a put option is

$$KP(0,T)N(-h+\sigma_P)-LP(0,s)N(-h)$$

In this case the put price is

$$87 \times 0.94988 \times N(-1.11688) - 100 \times 0.85092 \times N(-1.14277) = 0.14$$

Since the underlying bond pays no coupon, put–call parity states that the put price plus the bond price should equal the call price plus the present value of the strike price. The bond price is 85.09 and the present value of the strike price is $87 \times 0.94988 = 82.64$. Put–call parity is therefore satisfied:

$$82.64 + 2.59 = 85.09 + 0.14$$

Problem 30.9.

Suppose that $a = 0.05$, $b = 0.08$, and $\sigma = 0.015$ in Vasicek's model with the initial short-term interest rate being 6%. Calculate the price of a 2.1-year European call option on a bond that will mature in three years. Suppose that the bond pays a coupon of 5% semiannually. The principal of the bond is 100 and the strike price of the option is 99. The strike price is the cash price (not the quoted price) that will be paid for the bond.

As explained in Section 30.4, the first stage is to calculate the value of r at time 2.1 years which is such that the value of the bond at that time is 99. Denoting this value of r by r^*, we must solve

$$2.5A(2.1,2.5)e^{-B(2.1,2.5)r^*} + 102.5A(2.1,3.0)e^{-B(2.1,3.0)r^*} = 99$$

where the A and B functions are given by equations (30.7) and (30.8). The solution to this is $r^* = 0.066$. Since

$$2.5A(2.1,2.5)e^{-B(2.1,2.5)\times0.066} = 2.43473$$

and

$$102.5A(2.1,3.0)e^{-B(2.1,3.0)\times0.063} = 96.56438$$

the call option on the coupon-bearing bond can be decomposed into a call option with a strike price of 2.43473 on a bond that pays off 2.5 at time 2.5 years and a call option with a strike price of 96.56438 on a bond that pays off 102.5 at time 3.0 years. Equation (30.20) shows that the value of the first option is 0.009085 and the value of the second option is 0.806143. The total value of the option is therefore 0.815238.

Problem 30.10.

Use the answer to Problem 30.9 and put–call parity arguments to calculate the price of a put option that has the same terms as the call option in Problem 30.9.

Put-call parity shows that:

$$c + I + PV(K) = p + B_0$$

or

$$p = c + PV(K) - (B_0 - I)$$

where c is the call price, K is the strike price, I is the present value of the coupons, and B_0 is the bond price. In this case $c = 0.8152$, $PV(K) = 99 \times P(0,2.1) = 87.1222$, $B_0 - I = 2.5 \times P(0,2.5) + 102.5 \times P(0,3) = 87.4730$ so that the put price is
$$0.8152 + 87.1222 - 87.4730 = 0.4644$$

Problem 30.11.

In the Hull–White model, $a = 0.08$ and $\sigma = 0.01$. Calculate the price of a one-year European call option on a zero-coupon bond that will mature in five years when the term structure is flat at 10%, the principal of the bond is \$100, and the strike price is \$68.

Using the notation in the text $P(0,T) = e^{-0.1 \times 1} = 0.9048$ and $P(0,s) = e^{-0.1 \times 5} = 0.6065$. Also
$$\sigma_P = \frac{0.01}{0.08}(1 - e^{-4 \times 0.08})\sqrt{\frac{1 - e^{-2 \times 0.08 \times 1}}{2 \times 0.08}} = 0.0329$$
and $h = -0.4192$ so that the call price is
$$100 \times 0.6065 N(h) - 68 \times 0.9048 N(h - \sigma_P) = 0.439$$

Problem 30.12.

Suppose that $a = 0.05$ and $\sigma = 0.015$ in the Hull–White model with the initial term structure being flat at 6% with semiannual compounding. Calculate the price of a 2.1-year European call option on a bond that will mature in three years. Suppose that the bond pays a coupon of 5% per annum semiannually. The principal of the bond is 100 and the strike price of the option is 99. The strike price is the cash price (not the quoted price) that will be paid for the bond.

The relevant parameters for the Hull–White model are $a = 0.05$ and $\sigma = 0.015$. Setting $\Delta t = 0.4$
$$\hat{B}(2.1,3) = \frac{B(2.1,3)}{B(2.1,2.5)} \times 0.4 = 0.88888$$
Also from equation (30.26), $\hat{A}(2.1,3) = 0.99925$ The first stage is to calculate the value of R at time 2.1 years which is such that the value of the bond at that time is 99. Denoting this value of R by R^*, we must solve
$$2.5e^{-R^* \times 0.4} + 102.5\hat{A}(2.1,3)e^{-\hat{B}(2.1,3)R^*} = 99$$
The solution to this for R^* turns out to be 6.626%. The option on the coupon bond is decomposed into an option with a strike price of 96.565 on a zero-coupon bond with a principal of 102.5 and an option with a strike price of 2.435 on a zero-coupon bond with a principal of 2.5. The first option is worth 0.0103 and the second option is worth 0.9343. The total value of the option is therefore 0.9446. (Note that the initial short rate with continuous compounding is 5.91%.)

Problem 30.13.

Use a change of numeraire argument to show that the relationship between the futures rate and forward rate for the Ho–Lee model is as shown in Section 6.3. Use the relationship to verify the expression for $\theta(t)$ given for the Ho–Lee model in equation (30.11). (Hint: The futures price is a martingale when the market price of risk is zero. The forward price is a martingale when the market price of risk is a zero-coupon bond maturing at the same time as the forward contract.)

We will consider instantaneous forward and futures rates. (A more general result involving the forward and futures rate applying to a period of time between T_1 and T_2 is proved in Technical Note 1 on the author's site.)

$$F(t,T) = -\frac{\partial}{\partial T}\left[\ln P(t,T)\right]$$

Because $P(t,T) = A(t,T)e^{-r(T-t)}$

$$F(t,T) = -\frac{\partial}{\partial T}\left[\ln A(t,T) - r(T-t)\right]$$

$$\frac{\partial F(t,T)}{\partial r} = -\frac{\partial}{\partial r}\frac{\partial}{\partial T}\left[\ln A(t,T) - r(T-t)\right]$$

$$= -\frac{\partial}{\partial T}\frac{\partial}{\partial r}\left[\ln A(t,T) - r(T-t)\right] = 1$$

From Itô's lemma

$$dF(0,T) = \ldots + \sigma\, dz$$

The instantaneous forward rate with maturity T has a drift of zero in a world that is forward risk neutral with respect to $P(t,T)$. This is a world where the market price of risk is $-\sigma(T-t)$. When we move to a world where the market price of risk is zero the drift of the forward rate increases to $\sigma^2(T-t)$. Integrating this between $t=0$ and $t=T$ we see that the forward rate grows by a total of $\sigma^2 T^2/2$ between time 0 and time T in a world where the market price of risk is zero. The futures rate has zero growth rate in this world. At time T the forward rate equals the futures rate. It follows that the futures rate must exceed the forward rate by $\sigma^2 T^2/2$ at time zero. This is consistent with the formula in Section 6.4. Define $G(0,t)$ as the instantaneous futures rate for maturity t so that

$$G(0,t) - F(0,t) = \sigma^2 t^2/2$$

and

$$G_t(0,t) - F_t(0,t) = \sigma^2 t$$

In the traditional risk-neutral world the expected value of r at time t is the futures rate, $G(0,t)$. This means that the expected growth in r at time t must be $G_t(0,t)$ so that $\theta(t) = G_t(0,t)$. It follows that

$$\theta(t) = F_t(0,t) + \sigma^2 t$$

This is equation (30.11).

Problem 30.14.

Use a similar approach to that in Problem 30.13 to derive the relationship between the futures rate and the forward rate for the Hull–White model. Use the relationship to verify the expression for $\theta(t)$ given for the Hull–White model in equation (30.14)

$$F(t,T) = -\frac{\partial}{\partial T}\left[\ln P(t,T)\right]$$

Because $P(t,T) = A(t,T)e^{-rB(t,T)}$

$$F(t,T) = -\frac{\partial}{\partial T}\left[\ln A(t,T) - rB(t,T)\right]$$

$$\frac{\partial F(t,T)}{\partial r} = -\frac{\partial}{\partial r}\frac{\partial}{\partial T}\left[\ln A(t,T) - rB(t,T)\right]$$

$$= -\frac{\partial}{\partial T}\frac{\partial}{\partial r}\left[\ln A(t,T) - rB(t,T)\right] = e^{-a(T-t)}$$

From Itô's lemma

$$dF(0,T) = \ldots + \sigma e^{-a(T-t)}\, dz$$

This has drift of zero in a world that is forward risk neutral with respect to $P(t,T)$. This is a world where the market price of risk is $-\sigma B(t,T)$. When we move to a world where the market price of risk is zero the drift of $F(0,T)$ increases to $\sigma^2 e^{-a(T-t)}B(t,T)$. Integrating this between $t = 0$ and $t = T$ we see that the forward rate grows by a total of

$$\frac{\sigma^2}{2a^2}(1 - e^{-aT})^2$$

between time 0 and time T in a world where the market price of risk is zero. The futures price has zero growth rate in this world. At time T the forward price equals the futures price. It follows that the futures price must exceed the forward price by

$$\frac{\sigma^2}{2a^2}(1 - e^{-aT})^2$$

at time zero.[1]

Define $G(0,t)$ as the instantaneous futures rate for maturity t so that

$$G(0,t) - F(0,t) = \frac{\sigma^2}{2a^2}(1 - e^{-at})^2$$

---

[1] To produce a result relating the futures rate for the period between times T_1 and T_2 to the forward rate for this period we can proceed as in Technical Note 1 on the author's web site. The drift of the forward rate is

$$\frac{\sigma^2 B(t,T_2)^2 - \sigma^2 B(t,T_1)^2}{2(T_2 - T_1)}$$

$$= \frac{\sigma^2}{2a^2(T_2 - T_1)}[e^{at}(-2e^{-aT_2} + 2e^{-aT_1}) + e^{2at}[e^{-2aT_2} - e^{-2aT_1}]$$

Integrating between time 0 and time T_1 we get

$$\frac{\sigma^2}{2a^2(T_2 - T_1)}[(e^{aT_1} - 1)(-2e^{-aT_2} + 2e^{-aT_1})/a + (e^{2aT_1} - 1)(e^{-2aT_2} - e^{-2aT_1})/(2a)]$$

$$= \frac{\sigma^2 B(T_1,T_2)}{4a^2(T_2 - T_1)}[4(1 - e^{-aT_1}) - (1 - e^{-2aT_1})(1 + e^{-a(T_2-T_1)})]$$

$$= \frac{B(T_1,T_2)}{T_2 - T_1}[B(T_1,T_2)(1 - e^{-2aT_1}) + 2aB(0,T_1)^2]\frac{\sigma^2}{4a}$$

This is the amount by which the futures rate exceeds the forward rate at time zero.

and

$$G_t(0,t) - F_t(0,t) = \frac{\sigma^2}{a}(1-e^{-at})e^{-at}$$

In the traditional risk-neutral world the expected value of r at time t is the futures rate, $G(0,t)$. This means that the expected growth in r at time t must be $G_t(0,t) - a[r - G(0,t)]$ so that $\theta(t) - ar = G_t(0,t) - a[r - G(0,t)]$. It follows that

$$\theta(t) = G_t(0,t) + aG(0,t)$$

$$= F_t(0,t) + aF(0,t) + \frac{\sigma^2}{a}(1-e^{-at})e^{-at} + \frac{\sigma^2}{2a}(1-e^{-at})^2$$

$$= F_t(0,t) + aF(0,t) + \frac{\sigma^2}{2a}(1-e^{-2at})$$

This proves equation (30.14).

Problem 30.15.

Suppose $a = 0.05$, $\sigma = 0.015$, and the term structure is flat at 10%. Construct a trinomial tree for the Hull–White model where there are two time steps, each one year in length.

The time step, Δt, is 1 so that $\Delta r = 0.015\sqrt{3} = 0.02598$. Also $j_{max} = 4$ showing that the branching method should change four steps from the center of the tree. With only three steps we never reach the point where the branching changes. The tree is shown in Figure S30.1.

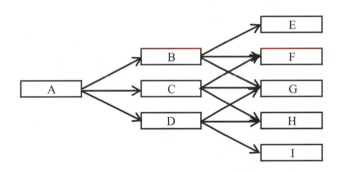

Node	A	B	C	D	E	F	G	H	I
r	10.00%	12.61%	10.01%	7.41%	15.24%	12.64%	10.04%	7.44%	4.84%
p_u	0.1667	0.1429	0.1667	0.1929	0.1217	0.1429	0.1667	0.1929	0.2217
p_m	0.6666	0.6642	0.6666	0.6642	0.6567	0.6642	0.6666	0.6642	0.6567
p_d	0.1667	0.1929	0.1667	0.1429	0.2217	0.1929	0.1667	0.1429	0.1217

Figure S30.1 Tree for Problem 30.15

Problem 30.16.

Calculate the price of a two-year zero-coupon bond from the tree in Figure 30.6.

A two-year zero-coupon bond pays off $100 at the ends of the final branches. At node B it is worth $100e^{-0.12\times1} = 88.69$. At node C it is worth $100e^{-0.10\times1} = 90.48$. At node D it is worth $100e^{-0.08\times1} = 92.31$. It follows that at node A the bond is worth

$$(88.69\times0.25 + 90.48\times0.5 + 92.31\times0.25)e^{-0.1\times1} = 81.88$$

or $81.88

Problem 30.17.
Calculate the price of a two-year zero-coupon bond from the tree in Figure 30.9 and verify that it agrees with the initial term structure.

A two-year zero-coupon bond pays off $100 at time two years. At node B it is worth $100e^{-0.0693\times1} = 93.30$. At node C it is worth $100e^{-0.0520\times1} = 94.93$. At node D it is worth $100e^{-0.0347\times1} = 96.59$. It follows that at node A the bond is worth

$$(93.30\times0.167 + 94.93\times0.666 + 96.59\times0.167)e^{-0.0382\times1} = 91.37$$

or $91.37. Because $91.37 = 100e^{-0.04512\times2}$, the price of the two-year bond agrees with the initial term structure.

Problem 30.18.
Calculate the price of an 18-month zero-coupon bond from the tree in Figure 30.10 and verify that it agrees with the initial term structure.

An 18-month zero-coupon bond pays off $100 at the final nodes of the tree. At node E it is worth $100e^{-0.088\times0.5} = 95.70$. At node F it is worth $100e^{-0.0648\times0.5} = 96.81$. At node G it is worth $100e^{-0.0477\times0.5} = 97.64$. At node H it is worth $100e^{-0.0351\times0.5} = 98.26$. At node I it is worth $100e^{0.0259\times0.5} = 98.71$. At node B it is worth

$$(0.118\times95.70 + 0.654\times96.81 + 0.228\times97.64)e^{-0.0564\times0.5} = 94.17$$

Similarly at nodes C and D it is worth 95.60 and 96.68. The value at node A is therefore

$$(0.167\times94.17 + 0.666\times95.60 + 0.167\times96.68)e^{-0.0343\times0.5} = 93.92$$

The 18-month zero rate is $0.08 - 0.05e^{-0.18\times1.5} = 0.0418$. This gives the price of the 18-month zero-coupon bond as $100e^{-0.0418\times1.5} = 93.92$ showing that the tree agrees with the initial term structure.

Problem 30.19.
What does the calibration of a one-factor term structure model involve?

The calibration of a one-factor interest rate model involves determining its volatility parameters so that it matches the market prices of actively traded interest rate options as closely as possible.

Problem 30.20.
Use the DerivaGem software to value 1×4, 2×3, 3×2, and 4×1 European swap options to receive fixed and pay floating. Assume that the one, two, three, four, and five year interest rates are 6%, 5.5%, 6%, 6.5%, and 7%, respectively. The payment frequency on the swap is semiannual and the fixed rate is 6% per annum with semiannual compounding. Use the Hull–White model with $a=3\%$ and $\sigma=1\%$. Calculate the volatility implied by Black's model for each option.

The option prices are 0.1302, 0.0814, 0.0580, and 0.0274. The implied Black volatilities are 14.28%, 13.64%, 13.24%, and 12.81%

Problem 30.21.
Prove equations (30.25), (30.26), and (30.27).

From equation (30.15)

$$P(t,t+\Delta t) = A(t,t+\Delta t)e^{-r(t)B(t,t+\Delta t)}$$

Also

$$P(t,t+\Delta t) = e^{-R(t)\Delta t}$$

so that

$$e^{-R(t)\Delta t} = A(t,t+\Delta t)e^{-r(t)B(t,t+\Delta t)}$$

or

$$e^{-r(t)B(t,T)} = \frac{e^{-R(t)B(t,T)\Delta t/B(t,t+\Delta t)}}{A(t,t+\Delta t)^{B(t,T)/B(t,t+\Delta t)}}$$

Hence equation (30.25) is true with

$$\hat{B}(t,T) = \frac{B(t,T)\Delta t}{B(t,t+\Delta t)}$$

and

$$\hat{A}(t,T) = \frac{A(t,T)}{A(t,t+\Delta t)^{B(t,T)/B(t,t+\Delta t)}}$$

or

$$\ln \hat{A}(t,T) = \ln A(t,T) - \frac{B(t,T)}{B(t,t+\Delta t)} \ln A(t,t+\Delta t)$$

Problem 30.22

(a) *What is the second partial derivative of P(t,T) with respect to r in the Vasicek and CIR models?*

(b) *In Section 30.2, $\hat{D}$ is presented as an alternative to the standard duration measure D. What is a similar alternative $\hat{C}$ to the convexity measure in Section 4.9?*

(c) *What is $\hat{C}$ for P(t,T)? How would you calculate $\hat{C}$ for a coupon-bearing bond?*

(d) *Give a Taylor Series expansion for $\Delta P(t,T)$ in terms of Δr and $(\Delta r)^2$ for Vasicek and CIR.*

(a) $\dfrac{\partial^2 P(t,T)}{\partial r^2} = B(t,T)^2 A(t,T)e^{-B(t,T)r} = B(t,T)^2 P(t,T)$

(b) A corresponding definition for $\hat{C}$ is

$$\frac{1}{Q}\frac{\partial^2 Q}{\partial r^2}$$

(c) When $Q=P(t,T)$, $\hat{C} = B(t,T)^2$. For a coupon-bearing bond $\hat{C}$ is a weighted average of the $\hat{C}$'s for the constituent zero-coupon bonds where weights are proportional to bond prices.

(d)

$$\Delta P(t,T) = \frac{\partial P(t,T)}{\partial r}\Delta r + \frac{1}{2}\frac{\partial^2 P(t,T)}{\partial r^2}\Delta r^2 + \dots$$

$$= -B(t,T)P(t,T)\Delta r + \frac{1}{2}B(t,T)^2 P(t,T)\Delta r^2 + \dots$$

Problem 30.23

Suppose that the short rate r is 4% and its real-world process is

$$dr = 0.1\,[0.05 - r]\,dt + 0.01\,dz$$

while the risk-neutral process is

$$dr = 0.1\,[0.11 - r]\,dt + 0.01\,dz$$

(a) What is the market price of interest rate risk?

(b) What is the expected return and volatility for a 5-year zero-coupon bond in the risk-neutral world?

(c) What is the expected return and volatility for a 5-year zero-coupon bond in the real world?

(a) The risk neutral process for r has a drift rate which is 0.006/r higher than the real world process. The volatility is 0.01/r. This means that the market price of interest rate risk is

−0.006/0.01 or −0.6.

(b) The expected return on the bond in the risk-neutral world is the risk free rate of 4%. The volatility is 0.01×B(0,5) where

$$B(0,5) = \frac{1 - e^{-0.1 \times 5}}{0.1} = 3.935$$

i.e., the volatility is 3.935%.

(c) In the real world the volatility of the bond is also 3.935%. The expected return is higher by 0.6×0.03935 or 2.361%. It is 6.361%.

CHAPTER 31
Interest Rate Derivatives: HJM and LMM

Problem 31.1.
Explain the difference between a Markov and a non-Markov model of the short rate.

In a Markov model the expected change and volatility of the short rate at time t depend only on the value of the short rate at time t. In a non-Markov model they depend on the history of the short rate prior to time t.

Problem 31.2.
Prove the relationship between the drift and volatility of the forward rate for the multifactor version of HJM in equation (31.6).

Equation (31.1) becomes

$$dP(t,T) = r(t)P(t,T)\,dt + \sum_k v_k(t,T,\Omega_t)P(t,T)\,dz_k(t)$$

so that

$$d\ln[P(t,T_1)] = \left[r(t) - \sum_k \frac{v_k(t,T_1,\Omega_t)^2}{2} \right]dt + \sum_k v_k(t,T_1,\Omega_t)\,dz_k(t)$$

and

$$d\ln[P(t,T_2)] = \left[r(t) - \sum_k \frac{v_k(t,T_2,\Omega_t)^2}{2} \right]dt + v_k(t,T_2,\Omega_t)\,dz_k(t)$$

From equation (31.2)

$$df(t,T_1,T_2) = \frac{\sum_k [v_k(t,T_2,\Omega_t)^2 - v_k(t,T_1,\Omega_t)^2]}{2(T_2 - T_1)}\,dt + \sum_k \frac{v_k(t,T_1,\Omega_t) - v_k(t,T_2,\Omega_t)}{T_2 - T_1}\,dz_k(t)$$

Putting $T_1 = T$ and $T_2 = T + \Delta t$ and taking limits as Δt tends to zero this becomes

$$dF(t,T) = \sum_k \left[v_k(t,T,\Omega_t)\frac{\partial v_k(t,T,\Omega_t)}{\partial T} \right]dt - \sum_k \left[\frac{\partial v_k(t,T,\Omega_t)}{\partial T} \right]dz_k(t)$$

Using $v_k(t,t,\Omega_t) = 0$

$$v_k(t,T,\Omega_t) = \int_t^T \frac{\partial v_k(t,\tau,\Omega_t)}{\partial \tau}\,d\tau$$

The result in equation (31.6) follows by substituting

$$s_k(t,T,\Omega_t) = \frac{\partial v_k(t,T,\Omega_t)}{\partial T}$$

Problem 31.3.
"When the forward rate volatility $s(t,T)$ in HJM is constant, the Ho–Lee model results."
Verify that this is true by showing that HJM gives a process for bond prices that is consistent with the Ho–Lee model in Chapter 30.

Using the notation in Section 31.1, when s is constant,
$$v_T(t,T) = s \qquad v_{TT}(t,T) = 0$$
Integrating $v_T(t,T)$

$$v(t,T) = sT + \alpha(t)$$
for some function α. Using the fact that $v(T,T) = 0$, we must have
$$v(t,T) = s(T-t)$$
Using the notation from Chapter 30, in Ho–Lee $P(t,T) = A(t,T)e^{-r(T-t)}$. The standard deviation of the short rate is constant. It follows from Itô's lemma that the standard deviation of the bond price is a constant times the bond price times $T-t$. The volatility of the bond price is therefore constant times $T-t$. This shows that Ho–Lee is consistent with a constant s.

Problem 31.4.

"When the forward rate volatility, $s(t,T)$ in HJM is $\sigma e^{-a(T-t)}$ the Hull–White model results." Verify that this is true by showing that HJM gives a process for bond prices that is consistent with the Hull–White model in Chapter 30.

Using the notation in Section 31.1, when $v_T(t,T) = s(t,T) = \sigma e^{-a(T-t)}$
$$v_{TT}(t,T) = -a\sigma e^{-a(T-t)}$$
Integrating $v_T(t,T)$
$$v(t,T) = -\frac{1}{a}\sigma e^{-a(T-t)} + \alpha(t)$$
for some function α. Using the fact that $v(T,T) = 0$, we must have
$$v(t,T) = \frac{\sigma}{a}[1 - e^{-a(T-t)}] = \sigma B(t,T)$$
Using the notation from Chapter 30, in Hull–White $P(t,T) = A(t,T)e^{-rB(t,T)}$. The standard deviation of the short rate is constant, σ. It follows from Itô's lemma that the standard deviation of the bond price is $\sigma P(t,T)B(t,T)$. The volatility of the bond price is therefore $\sigma B(t,T)$. This shows that Hull-White is consistent with $s(t,T) = \sigma e^{-a(T-t)}$.

Problem 31.5.
What is the advantage of LMM over HJM?

LMM is a similar model to HJM. It has the advantage over HJM that it involves forward rates that are readily observable. HJM involves instantaneous forward rates.

Problem 31.6.
Provide an intuitive explanation of why a ratchet cap increases in value as the number of factors increase.

A ratchet cap tends to provide relatively low payoffs if a high (low) interest rate at one reset date is followed by a high (low) interest rate at the next reset date. High payoffs occur when a low interest rate is followed by a high interest rate. As the number of factors increase, the correlation between successive forward rates declines and there is a greater chance that a low interest rate will be followed by a high interest rate.

Problem 31.7.
Show that equation (31.10) reduces to (31.4) as the δ_i tend to zero.

Equation (31.10) can be written

$$dF_k(t) = \zeta_k(t)F_k(t) \sum_{i=m(t)}^{k} \frac{\delta_i F_i(t)\zeta_i(t)}{1+\delta_i F_i(t)} dt + \zeta_k(t)F_k(t) dz$$

As δ_i tends to zero, $\zeta_i(t)F_i(t)$ becomes the standard deviation of the instantaneous t_i-maturity forward rate at time t. Using the notation of Section 31.1 this is $s(t,t_i,\Omega_t)$. As δ_i tends to zero

$$\sum_{i=m(t)}^{k} \frac{\delta_i F_i(t)\zeta_i(t)}{1+\delta_i F_i(t)}$$

tends to

$$\int_{\tau=t}^{t_k} s(t,\tau,\Omega_t) d\tau$$

Equation (31.10) therefore becomes

$$dF_k(t) = \left[s(t,t_k,\Omega_t) \int_{\tau=t}^{t_k} s(t,\tau,\Omega_t) d\tau \right] dt + s(t,t_k,\Omega_t) dz$$

This is the HJM result.

Problem 31.8.
Explain why a sticky cap is more expensive than a similar ratchet cap.

In a ratchet cap, the cap rate equals the previous reset rate, R, plus a spread. In the notation of the text it is $R_j + s$. In a sticky cap the cap rate equal the previous capped rate plus a spread. In the notation of the text it is $\min(R_j, K_j) + s$. The cap rate in a ratchet cap is always at least a great as that in a sticky cap. Since the value of a cap is a decreasing function of the cap rate, it follows that a sticky cap is more expensive.

Problem 31.9.
Explain why IOs and POs have opposite sensitivities to the rate of prepayments

When prepayments increase, the principal is received sooner. This increases the value of a PO. When prepayments increase, less interest is received. This decreases the value of an IO.

Problem 31.10.
"An option adjusted spread is analogous to the yield on a bond." Explain this statement.

A bond yield is the discount rate that causes the bond's price to equal the market price. The same discount rate is used for all maturities. An OAS is the parallel shift to the Treasury zero curve that causes the price of an instrument such as a mortgage-backed security to equal its market price.

Problem 31.11.
Prove equation (31.15).

When there are p factors equation (31.7) becomes

$$dF_k(t) = \sum_{q=1}^{p} \zeta_{k,q}(t)F_k(t) dz_q$$

Equation (31.8) becomes

$$dF_k(t) = \sum_{q=1}^{p} \zeta_{k,q}(t)[v_{m(t),q} - v_{k+1,q}]F_k(t)dt + \sum_{q=1}^{p} \zeta_{k,q}(t)(F_k(t)dz_q$$

Equation coefficients of dz_q in

$$\ln P(t,t_i) - \ln P(t,t_{i+1}) = \ln[1 + \delta_i F_i(t)]$$

Equation (31.9) therefore becomes

$$v_{i,q}(t) - v_{i+1,q}(t) = \frac{\delta_i F_i(t)\zeta_{i,q}}{1 + \delta_i F_i(t)}$$

Equation (31.15) follows.

Problem 31.12.
Prove the formula for the variance, $V(T)$, of the swap rate in equation (31.17).

From the equations in the text

$$s(t) = \frac{P(t,T_0) - P(t,T_N)}{\sum_{i=0}^{N-1} \tau_i P(t,T_{i+1})}$$

and

$$\frac{P(t,T_i)}{P(t,T_0)} = \prod_{j=0}^{i-1} \frac{1}{1 + \tau_j G_j(t)}$$

so that

$$s(t) = \frac{1 - \prod_{j=0}^{N-1} \frac{1}{1+\tau_j G_j(t)}}{\sum_{i=0}^{N-1} \tau_i \prod_{j=0}^{i} \frac{1}{1+\tau_j G_j(t)}}$$

(We employ the convention that empty sums equal zero and empty products equal one.)
Equivalently

$$s(t) = \frac{\prod_{j=0}^{N-1}[1 + \tau_j G_j(t)] - 1}{\sum_{i=0}^{N-1} \tau_i \prod_{j=i+1}^{N-1}[1 + \tau_j G_j(t)]}$$

or

$$\ln s(t) = \ln\left\{\prod_{j=0}^{N-1}[1 + \tau_j G_j(t)] - 1\right\} - \ln\left\{\sum_{i=0}^{N-1} \tau_i \prod_{j=i+1}^{N-1}[1 + \tau_j G_j(t)]\right\}$$

so that

$$\frac{1}{s(t)} \frac{\partial s(t)}{\partial G_k(t)} = \frac{\tau_k \gamma_k(t)}{1 + \tau_k G_k(t)}$$

where

$$\gamma_k(t) = \frac{\prod_{j=0}^{N-1}[1 + \tau_j G_j(t)]}{\prod_{j=0}^{N-1}[1 + \tau_j G_j(t)] - 1} - \frac{\sum_{i=0}^{k-1} \tau_i \prod_{j=i+1}^{N-1}[1 + \tau_j G_j(t)]}{\sum_{i=0}^{N-1} \tau_i \prod_{j=i+1}^{N-1}[1 + \tau_j G_j(t)]}$$

From Ito's lemma the q th component of the volatility of $s(t)$ is

$$\sum_{k=0}^{N-1} \frac{1}{s(t)} \frac{\partial s(t)}{\partial G_k(t)} \beta_{k,q}(t) G_k(t)$$

or

$$\sum_{k=0}^{N-1} \frac{\tau_k \beta_{k,q}(t) G_k(t) \gamma_k(t)}{1 + \tau_k G_k(t)}$$

242

The variance rate of $s(t)$ is therefore

$$V(t) = \sum_{q=1}^{P}\left[\sum_{k=0}^{N-1}\frac{\tau_k\beta_{k,q}(t)G_k(t)\gamma_k(t)}{1+\tau_k G_k(t)}\right]^2$$

Problem 31.13.
Prove equation (31.19).

$$1+\tau_j G_j(t) = \prod_{m=1}^{M}[1+\tau_{j,m}G_{j,m}(t)]$$

so that

$$\ln[1+\tau_j G_j(t)] = \sum_{m=1}^{M}\ln[1+\tau_{j,m}G_{j,m}(t)]$$

Equating coefficients of dz_q

$$\frac{\tau_j\beta_{j,q}(t)G_j(t)}{1+\tau_j G_j(t)} = \sum_{m=1}^{M}\frac{\tau_{j,m}\beta_{j,m,q}(t)G_{j,m}(t)}{1+\tau_{j,m}G_{j,m}(t)}$$

If we assume that $G_{j,m}(t) = G_{j,m}(0)$ for the purposes of calculating the swap volatility we see from equation (31.17) that the volatility becomes

$$\sqrt{\frac{1}{T_0}\int_{t=0}^{T_0}\sum_{q=1}^{P}\left[\sum_{k=n}^{N-1}\sum_{m=1}^{M}\frac{\tau_{k,m}\beta_{k,m,q}(t)G_{k,m}(0)\gamma_k(0)}{1+\tau_{k,m}G_{k,m}(0)}\right]^2 dt}$$

This is equation (31.19).

CHAPTER 32
Swaps Revisited

Problem 32.1.
Calculate all the fixed cash flows and their exact timing for the swap in Business Snapshot 32.1. Assume that the day count conventions are applied using target payment dates rather than actual payment dates.

Results are as follows

Target payment date	Day of week	Actual payment date	Days from previous to current target pmt dates	Fixed Payment ($)
Jul 11, 2010	Sunday	Jul 12, 2010	181	2,975,342
Jan 11, 2011	Tuesday	Jan 11, 2011	184	3,024,658
Jul 11, 2011	Monday	Jul 11, 2011	181	2,975,342
Jan 11, 2012	Wednesday	Jan 11, 2012	184	3,024,658
Jul 11, 2012	Wednesday	Jul 11, 2012	182	2,991,781
Jan 11, 2013	Friday	Jan 11, 2013	184	3,024,658
Jul 11, 2013	Thursday	Jul 11, 2013	181	2,975,342
Jan 11, 2014	Saturday	Jan 13, 2014	184	3,024,658
Jul 11, 2014	Friday	Jul 11, 2014	181	2,975,342
Jan 11, 2015	Sunday	Jan 12, 2015	184	3,024,658

The fixed rate day count convention is Actual/365. There are 181 days between January 11, 2010 and July 11, 2010. This means that the fixed payments on July 11, 2010 is

$$\frac{181}{365} \times 0.06 \times 100,000,000 = \$2,975,342$$

Other fixed payments are calculated similarly.

Problem 32.2.
Suppose that a swap specifies that a fixed rate is exchanged for twice the LIBOR rate. Can the swap be valued using the "assume forward rates are realized" rule?

Yes. The swap is the same as one on twice the principal where half the fixed rate is exchanged for the LIBOR rate.

Problem 32.3.
What is the value of a two-year fixed-for-floating compounding swap where the principal is $100 million and payments are made semiannually? Fixed interest is received and floating is paid. The fixed rate is 8% and it is compounded at 8.3% (both semiannually compounded). The floating rate is LIBOR plus 10 basis points and it is compounded at LIBOR plus 20 basis points. The LIBOR zero curve is flat at 8% with semiannual compounding.

The final fixed payment is in millions of dollars:
$$[(4 \times 1.0415 + 4) \times 1.0415 + 4] \times 1.0415 + 4 = 17.0238$$
The final floating payment assuming forward rates are realized is

$$[(4.05 \times 1.041 + 4.05) \times 1.041 + 4.05] \times 1.041 + 4.05 = 17.2238$$

The value of the swap is therefore $-0.2000 / (1.04^4) = -0.1710$ or $-\$171,000$.

Problem 32.4.

What is the value of a five-year swap where LIBOR is paid in the usual way and in return LIBOR compounded at LIBOR is received on the other side? The principal on both sides is $100 million. Payment dates on the pay side and compounding dates on the receive side are every six months and the yield curve is flat at 5% with semiannual compounding.

The value is zero. The receive side is the same as the pay side with the cash flows compounded forward at LIBOR. Compounding cash flows forward at LIBOR does not change their value.

Problem 32.5.

Explain carefully why a bank might choose to discount cash flows on a currency swap at a rate slightly different from LIBOR.

In theory, a new floating-for-floating swap should involve exchanging LIBOR in one currency for LIBOR in another currency (with no spreads added). In practice, macroeconomic effects give rise to spreads. Financial institutions often adjust the discount rates they use to allow for this. Suppose that USD LIBOR is always exchanged Swiss franc LIBOR plus 15 basis points. Financial institutions would discount USD cash flows at USD LIBOR and Swiss franc cash flows at LIBOR plus 15 basis points. This would ensure that the floating-for-floating swap is valued consistently with the market.

Problem 32.6.

Calculate the total convexity/timing adjustment in Example 32.3 of Section 32.4 if all cap volatilities are 18% instead of 20% and volatilities for all options on five-year swaps are 13% instead of 15%. What should the five year swap rate in three years' time be assumed for the purpose of valuing the swap? What is the value of the swap?

In this case, $y_i = 0.05$, $\sigma_{y,i} = 0.13$, $\tau_i = 0.5$, $F_i = 0.05$, $\sigma_{F,i} = 0.18$, and $\rho_i = 0.7$ for all i. It is still true that $G_i'(y_i) = -437.603$ and $G_i''(y_i) = 2261.23$. Equation (32.2) gives the total convexity/timing adjustment as $0.0000892t_i$ or 0.892 basis points per year until the swap rate is observed. The swap rate in three years should be assumed to be 5.0268%. The value of the swap is $119,069.

Problem 32.7.

Explain why a plain vanilla interest rate swap and the compounding swap in Section 32.2 can be valued using the "assume forward rates are realized" rule, but a LIBOR-in-arrears swap in Section 32.4 cannot.

In a plain vanilla swap we can enter into a series of FRAs to exchange the floating cash flows for their values if the "assume forward rates are realized rule" is used. In the case of a compounding swap Section 32.2 shows that we are able to enter into a series of FRAs that exchange the final floating rate cash flow for its value when the "assume forward rates are realized rule" is used. There is no way of entering into FRAs so that the floating-rate cash flows in a LIBOR-in-arrears swap are exchanged for their values when the "assume forward rates are realized rule" is used.

Problem 32.8.
In the accrual swap discussed in the text, the fixed side accrues only when the floating reference rate lies below a certain level. Discuss how the analysis can be extended to cope with a situation where the fixed side accrues only when the floating reference rate is above one level and below another.

Suppose that the fixed rate accrues only when the floating reference rate is below R_X and above R_Y where $R_Y < R_X$. In this case the swap is a regular swap plus two series of binary options, one for each day of the life of the swap. Using the notation in the text, the risk-neutral probability that LIBOR will be above R_X on day i is $N(d_2)$ where

$$d_2 = \frac{\ln(F_i / R_X) - \sigma_i^2 t_i^2 / 2}{\sigma_i \sqrt{t_i}}$$

The probability that it will be below R_Y where $R_Y < R_X$ is $N(-d'_2)$ where

$$d'_2 = \frac{\ln(F_i / R_Y) - \sigma_i^2 t_i^2 / 2}{\sigma_i \sqrt{t_i}}$$

From the viewpoint of the party paying fixed, the swap is a regular swap plus binary options. The binary options corresponding to day i have a total value of

$$\frac{QL}{n_2} P(0, s_i)[N(d_2) + N(-d'_2)]$$

(This ignores the small timing adjustment mentioned in Section 32.6.)

CHAPTER 33
Energy and Commodity Derivatives

Problem 33.1.
What is meant by HDD and CDD?

A day's HDD is $\max(0, 65 - A)$ and a day's CDD is $\max(0, A - 65)$ where A is the average of the highest and lowest temperature during the day at a specified weather station, measured in degrees Fahrenheit.

Problem 33.2.
How is a typical natural gas forward contract structured?

It is an agreement by one side to deliver a specified amount of gas at a roughly uniform rate during a month to a particular hub for a specified price.

Problem 33.3.
Distinguish between the historical data and the risk-neutral approach to valuing a derivative. Under what circumstances do they give the same answer?

The historical data approach to valuing an option involves calculating the expected payoff using historical data and discounting the payoff at the risk-free rate. The risk-neutral approach involves calculating the expected payoff in a risk-neutral world and discounting at the risk-free rate. The two approaches give the same answer when percentage changes in the underlying market variables have zero correlation with stock market returns. (In these circumstances all risks can be diversified away.)

Problem 33.4.
Suppose that each day during July the minimum temperature is $68°$ Fahrenheit and the maximum temperature is $82°$ Fahrenheit. What is the payoff from a call option on the cumulative CDD during July with a strike of 250 and a payment rate of $5,000 per degree day?

The average temperature each day is $75°$. The CDD each day is therefore 10 and the cumulative CDD for the month is $10 \times 31 = 310$. The payoff from the call option is therefore $(310 - 250) \times 5,000 = \$300,000$.

Problem 33.5.
Why is the price of electricity more volatile than that of other energy sources?

Unlike most commodities electricity cannot be stored easily. If the demand for electricity exceeds the supply, as it sometimes does during the air conditioning season, the price of electricity in a deregulated environment will skyrocket. When supply and demand become matched again the price will return to former levels.

Problem 33.6.
Why is the historical data approach appropriate for pricing a weather derivatives contract

and a CAT bond?

There is no systematic risk (i.e., risk that is priced by the market) in weather derivatives and CAT bonds.

Problem 33.7.
"HDD and CDD can be regarded as payoffs from options on temperature." Explain this statement.

HDD is $\max(65-A,0)$ where A is the average of the maximum and minimum temperature during the day. This is the payoff from a put option on A with a strike price of 65. CDD is $\max(A-65,0)$. This is the payoff from call option on A with a strike price of 65.

Problem 33.8.
Suppose that you have 50 years of temperature data at your disposal. Explain carefully the analyses you would carry out to value a forward contract on the cumulative CDD for a particular month.

It would be useful to calculate the cumulative CDD for July of each year of the last 50 years. A linear regression relationship
$$CDD = a + bt + e$$
could then be estimated where a and b are constants, t is the time in years measured from the start of the 50 years, and e is the error. This relationship allows for linear trends in temperature through time. The expected CDD for next year (year 51) is then $a+51b$. This could be used as an estimate of the forward CDD.

Problem 33.9.
Would you expect the volatility of the one-year forward price of oil to be greater than or less than the volatility of the spot price? Explain your answer.

The volatility of the one-year forward price will be less than the volatility of the spot price. This is because, when the spot price changes by a certain amount, mean reversion will cause the forward price will change by a lesser amount.

Problem 33.10.
What are the characteristics of an energy source where the price has a very high volatility and a very high rate of mean reversion? Give an example of such an energy source.

The price of the energy source will show big changes, but will be pulled back to its long-run average level fast. Electricity is an example of an energy source with these characteristics.

Problem 33.11.
How can an energy producer use derivative markets to hedge risks?

The energy producer faces quantity risks and price risks. It can use weather derivatives to hedge the quantity risks and energy derivatives to hedge against the price risks.

Problem 33.12.
Explain how a 5×8 option contract for May 2009 on electricity with daily exercise works.

Explain how a 5×8 option contract for May 2009 on electricity with monthly exercise works. Which is worth more?

A 5×8 contract for May, 2009 is a contract to provide electricity for five days per week during the off-peak period (11PM to 7AM). When daily exercise is specified, the holder of the option is able to choose each weekday whether he or she will buy electricity at the strike price at the agreed rate. When there is monthly exercise, he or she chooses once at the beginning of the month whether electricity is to be bought at the strike price at the agreed rate for the whole month. The option with daily exercise is worth more.

Problem 33.13.
Explain how CAT bonds work.

CAT bonds (catastrophe bonds) are an alternative to reinsurance for an insurance company that has taken on a certain catastrophic risk (e.g., the risk of a hurricane or an earthquake) and wants to get rid of it. CAT bonds are issued by the insurance company. They provide a higher rate of interest than government bonds. However, the bondholders agree to forego interest, and possibly principal, to meet any claims against the insurance company that are within a prespecified range.

Problem 33.14.
Consider two bonds that have the same coupon, time to maturity and price. One is a B-rated corporate bond. The other is a CAT bond. An analysis based on historical data shows that the expected losses on the two bonds in each year of their life is the same. Which bond would you advise a portfolio manager to buy and why?

The CAT bond has very little systematic risk. Whether a particular type of catastrophe occurs is independent of the return on the market. The risks in the CAT bond are likely to be largely "diversified away" by the other investments in the portfolio. A B-rated bond does have systematic risk that cannot be diversified away. It is likely therefore that the CAT bond is a better addition to the portfolio.

CHAPTER 34
Real Options

Problem 34.1.

Explain the difference between the net present value approach and the risk-neutral valuation approach for valuing a new capital investment opportunity. What are the advantages of the risk-neutral valuation approach for valuing real options?

In the net present value approach, cash flows are estimated in the real world and discounted at a risk-adjusted discount rate. In the risk-neutral valuation approach, cash flows are estimated in the risk-neutral world and discounted at the risk-free interest rate. The risk-neutral valuation approach is arguably more appropriate for valuing real options because it is very difficult to determine the appropriate risk-adjusted discount rate when options are valued.

Problem 34.2.

The market price of risk for copper is 0.5, the volatility of copper prices is 20% per annum, the spot price is 80 cents per pound, and the six-month futures price is 75 cents per pound. What is the expected percentage growth rate in copper prices over the next six months?

In a risk-neutral world the expected price of copper in six months is 75 cents. This corresponds to an expected growth rate of $2\ln(75/80) = -12.9\%$ per annum. The decrease in the growth rate when we move from the real world to the risk-neutral world is the volatility of copper times its market price of risk. This is $0.2 \times 0.5 = 0.1$ or 10% per annum. It follows that the expected growth rate of the price of copper in the real world is -2.9%.

Problem 34.3.

Consider a commodity with constant volatility σ and an expected growth rate that is a function solely of time. Show that, in the traditional risk-neutral world,

$$\ln S_T \approx \varphi\left[\ln F(T) - \frac{\sigma^2 T}{2}, \sigma^2 T\right]$$

where S_T is the value of the commodity at time T, $F(t)$ is the futures price at time 0 for a contract maturing at time t, and $\varphi(m,v)$ is a normal distribution with mean m and variance v.

In this case

$$\frac{dS}{S} = \mu(t)\,dt + \sigma\,dz$$

or

$$d\ln S = [\mu(t) - \sigma^2/2]\,dt + \sigma\,dz$$

so that $\ln S_T$ is normal with mean

$$\ln S_0 + \int_{t=0}^{T} \mu(t)dt - \sigma^2 T/2$$

and standard deviation $\sigma\sqrt{T}$. Section 33.4 shows that

$$\mu(t) = \frac{\partial}{\partial t}[\ln F(t)]$$

so that

$$\int_{t=0}^{T} \mu(t)dt = \ln F(T) - \ln F(0)$$

Since $F(0) = S_0$ the result follows.

Problem 34.4.

Derive a relationship between the convenience yield of a commodity and its market price of risk.

We explained the concept of a convenience yield for a commodity in Chapter 5. It is a measure of the benefits realized from ownership of the physical commodity that are not realized by the holders of a futures contract. If y is the convenience yield and u is the storage cost, equation (5.17) shows that the commodity behaves like an investment asset that provides a return equal to $y - u$. In a risk-neutral world its growth is, therefore,

$$r - (y - u) = r - y + u$$

The convenience yield of a commodity can be related to its market price of risk. From Section 34.2, the expected growth of the commodity price in a risk-neutral world is $m - \lambda s$, where m is its expected growth in the real world, s its volatility, and λ is its market price of risk. It follows that

$$m - \lambda s = r - y + u$$

or

$$y = r + u - m + \lambda s$$

Problem 34.5.

The correlation between a company's gross revenue and the market index is 0.2. The excess return of the market over the risk-free rate is 6% and the volatility of the market index is 18%. What is the market price of risk for the company's revenue?

In equation (34.2) $\rho = 0.2$, $\mu_m - r = 0.06$, and $\sigma_m = 0.18$. It follows that the market price of risk lambda is

$$\frac{0.2 \times 0.06}{0.18} = 0.067$$

Problem 34.6.

A company can buy an option for the delivery of one million units of a commodity in three years at $25 per unit. The three year futures price is $24. The risk-free interest rate is 5% per annum with continuous compounding and the volatility of the futures price is 20% per annum. How much is the option worth?

The option can be valued using Black's model. In this case $F_0 = 24$, $K = 25$, $r = 0.05$, $\sigma = 0.2$, and $T = 3$. The value of an option to purchase one unit at $25 is

$$e^{-rT}[F_0 N(d_1) - KN(d_2)]$$

where

$$d_1 = \frac{\ln(F_0 / K) + \sigma^2 T / 2}{\sigma\sqrt{T}}$$

$$d_2 = \frac{\ln(F_0 / K) - \sigma^2 T / 2}{\sigma\sqrt{T}}$$

This is 2.489. The value of the option to purchase one million units is therefore $2,489,000.

Problem 34.7.
A driver entering into a car lease agreement can obtain the right to buy the car in four years for $10,000. The current value of the car is $30,000. The value of the car, S, is expected to follow the process

$$dS = \mu S\, dt + \sigma S\, dz$$

where $\mu = -0.25$, $\sigma = 0.15$, and dz is a Wiener process. The market price of risk for the car price is estimated to be -0.1. What is the value of the option? Assume that the risk-free rate for all maturities is 6%.

The expected growth rate of the car price in a risk-neutral world is
$-0.25 - (-0.1 \times 0.15) = -0.235$ The expected value of the car in a risk-neutral world in four years, $\hat{E}(S_T)$, is therefore $30,000e^{-0.235 \times 4} = \$11,719$. Using the result in the appendix to Chapter 14 the value of the option is

$$e^{-rT}[\hat{E}(S_T)N(d_1) - KN(d_2)]$$

where

$$d_1 = \frac{\ln(\hat{E}(S_T) / K) + \sigma^2 T / 2}{\sigma\sqrt{T}}$$

$$d_2 = \frac{\ln(\hat{E}(S_T) / K) - \sigma^2 T / 2}{\sigma\sqrt{T}}$$

$r = 0.06$, $\sigma = 0.15$, $T = 4$, and $K = 10,000$. It is $1,832.